Beckett® Price Guide to Hot Wheels™

Beckett Media
4635 McEwen Rd.
Dallas, TX 75244
972-991-6657

www.Beckett.com/HotWheels

Go to www.hotwheels.com/cars to track your Hot Wheels cars online.

CONTENTS

4 40th Anniversary Timeline

11 Real Life Hot Wheels Cars

12 The Making of Hot Wheels Cars

14 Hot Wheels Collecting Tips and Guidelines

16 Hot Wheels Collector Clubs

18 Exclusive Interview with Alec Tam, director of Mattel's Hot Wheels design team

21 Pictorial Price Guide 2006-2008

246 Hot Wheels Checklist and Price Guide

256 Hot Wheels Hot List

SPECIAL THANKS TO: Mattel's Hot Wheels staff and Rob Graves of southtexasdiecast.com for providing a lot of images and information for this book.

PUBLISHED BY BECKETT MEDIA LP

Chief Executive Officer Peter Gudmundsson
Founder & Advisor Dr. James Beckett III
Chief Operating Officer Margaret Steele
Vice President Sales & Marketing Mike Obert
Associate Publisher Tracy Hackler

EDITORIAL AND CREATIVE

Editorial Director Doug Kale
Assistant Editor Rebecca Bundy
Art Director Cathy Hutzler
Sports Data Manager Dan Hitt
Production Manager Peter Adauto
Price Guide Editor Keith Hower
Editorial Staff Kevin Haake, David Lee, Al Muir
Price Guide Staff Matt Brumley, Brian Fleischer, Grant Sandground, Tim Trout
Art Staff Bill Bridgeforth, Eric Knagg
Production Staff Gean Paul Figari, Daniel Moscoso

SALES & MARKETING

Director of Sports Marketing Pepper Hastings
Director of Gaming Marketing Jenifer Grellhesl
Gaming Advertising Sales Todd Westover
Sports Advertising Sales Ted Barker, Brandon Cacek
Advertising Coordinator Patty Burrell
Dealer Sales Staff Kris Capps, Sam Mood, Brett Robertson
Corporate Sales Crissy Mulligan
Subscriptions Manager Bob Richardson
Product Sales Sonya Lewis

FINANCE

Chief Financial Officer Jennifer LePage
Accounting Mitchell Dyson (Controller), Susan Denniston, Theresa Joe, Bettie Junkin, Loretta Gibbs, Sherry Su
Apprise Enthusiast Media Corporate Controller Mark Medlock
Human Resources Jane Ann Layton (Sr. Manager), Mary Kerr

TECHNOLOGY GROUP

IT Director Shane Sedate
Senior Software Developer Reggie Samuel
Software Developers Mike Cabassol, Steve Baggett
Software Architect Jeremy Hinkle
System Administrator Steve Hawkins
Network/Desktop Support Brandy Johnston

WEB COMMERCE AND SERVICES GROUP

Web Commerce Senior Manager Shawn Schietroma
Web Commerce Staff Traci Kaplan, Bill Sutherland, Jack Doyle, Dave Sliepka, Andrew Tolentino, Brandon Caballero, Danielle Ramsey
Web Development Manager Brad Thornhill
Web Development Staff Ryan Marks
Beckett Grading Services Senior Manager Mark Anderson
Beckett Grading Services Staff Jeromy Murray (Operations Manager), Scott Kirklen (Grader Manager), David Poole, Joe Clemons, Brian Nelson, Bryan Hornbeck, Maria Horner, Eddie Brandon, Steve Tyndall, Steve Dalton, Andy Broome, J.J. Arrendondo, Gabe Rangel, Rosanna Gonzalez, Matt McCliment, Roberto Ramirez, Luis Mellado, Paul Moscoso, David Porras, Aram Munoz, Kevin Bajraszewski, Aaron Gibson, Alfonso Bellatin

LOGISTICS AND DISTRIBUTION

Albert Chavez (Manager), Uno Kevric, Heather Feeny, Carlos Moreno, Anatoliy Strakh, Tim Yoder

AN APPRISE MEDIA COMPANY

Chief Executive Officer Charles G. McCurdy
Senior Vice President Michael Behringer

BECKETT® and STATBASE® are registered trademarks of Beckett Media LP Copyright 2008. Printed in the USA.

HOT WHEELS and associated trademark and trade dress are owned by, and used under license from, Mattel, Inc. © 2008 Mattel, Inc. All Rights Reserved. Mattel, Inc. makes no representation as to the authenticity of the materials contained herein. All opinions are those of the author and not of Mattel, Inc.

The current values in this book should be used only as a guide. They are not intended to set prices, which vary from one section of the country to another. Auction prices as well as dealer prices vary greatly and are affected by condition as well as demand. Neither the authors nor the publisher assumes responsibility for any losses that might be incurred as a result of consulting this guide.

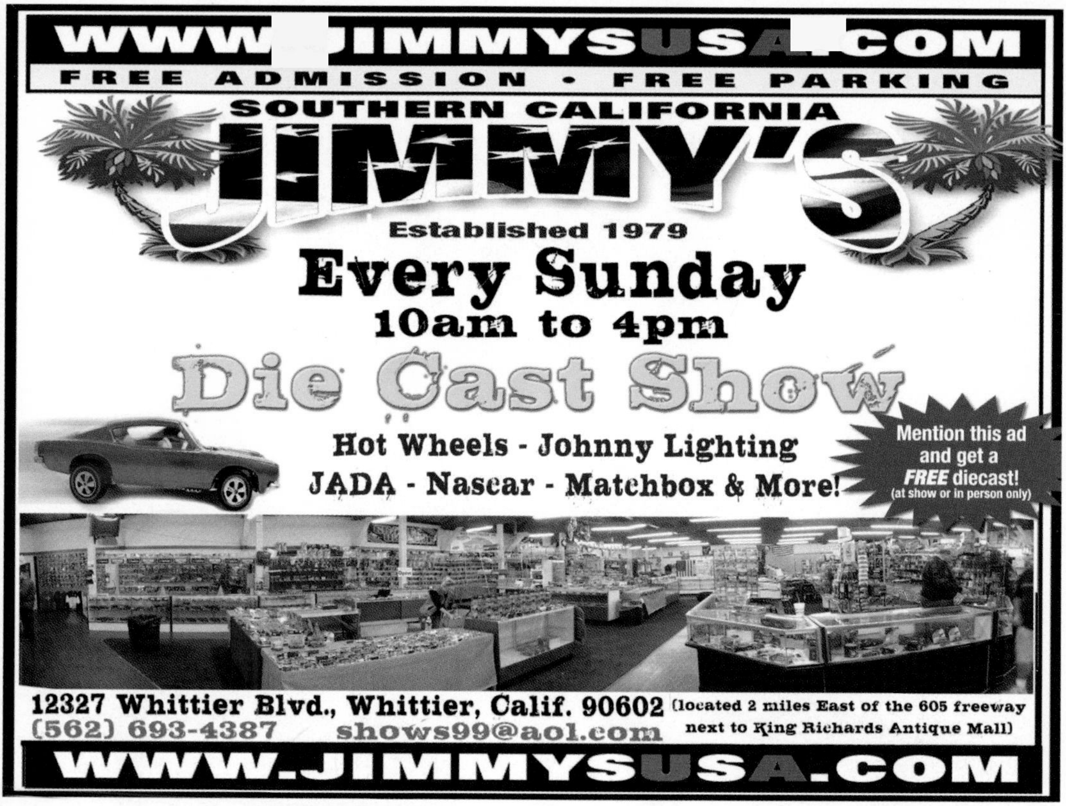

WWW.JIMMYSUSA.COM

FREE ADMISSION • FREE PARKING

SOUTHERN CALIFORNIA

JIMMY'S

Established 1979

Every Sunday

10am to 4pm

Die Cast Show

Hot Wheels - Johnny Lighting

JADA - Nascar - Matchbox & More!

Mention this ad and get a *FREE* diecast! (at show or in person only)

12327 Whittier Blvd., Whittier, Calif. 90602 (located 2 miles East of the 605 freeway next to King Richards Antique Mall)

(562) 693-4387 shows99@aol.com

WWW.JIMMYSUSA.COM

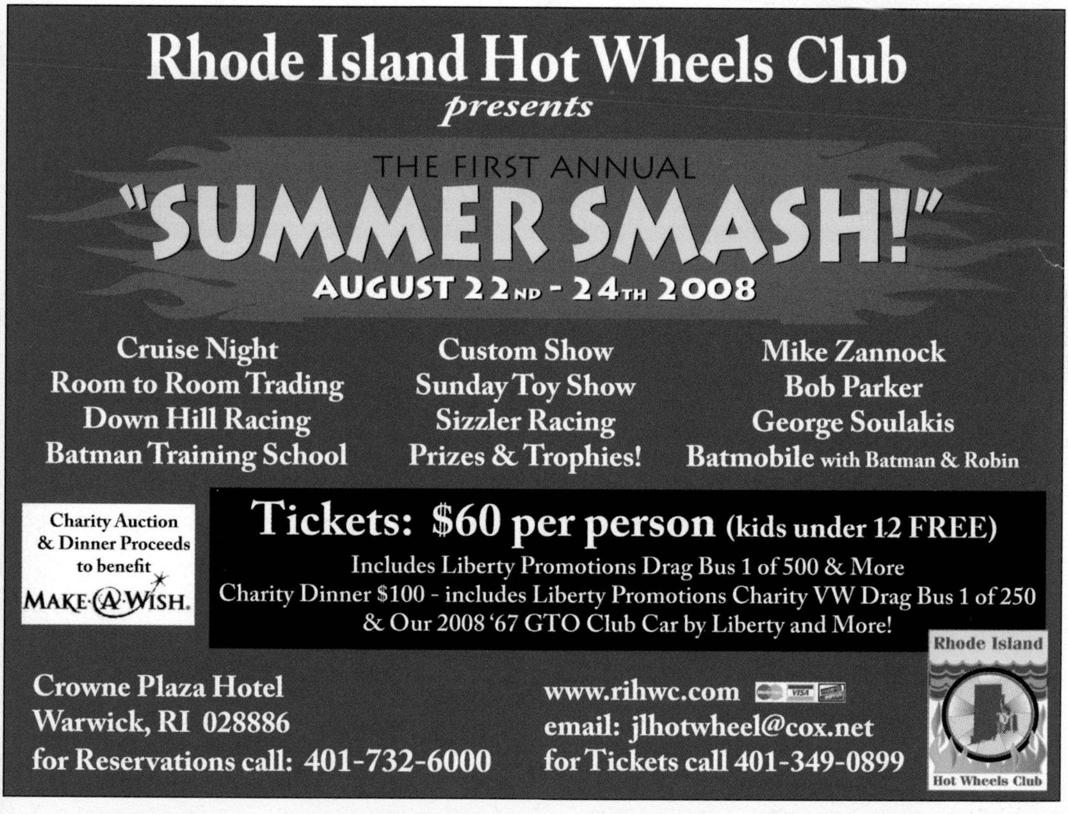

Rhode Island Hot Wheels Club

presents

THE FIRST ANNUAL

"SUMMER SMASH!"

AUGUST 22ND - 24TH 2008

Cruise Night
Room to Room Trading
Down Hill Racing
Batman Training School

Custom Show
Sunday Toy Show
Sizzler Racing
Prizes & Trophies!

Mike Zannock
Bob Parker
George Soulakis
Batmobile with Batman & Robin

Charity Auction & Dinner Proceeds to benefit MAKE-A-WISH.

Tickets: $60 per person (kids under 12 FREE)

Includes Liberty Promotions Drag Bus 1 of 500 & More

Charity Dinner $100 - includes Liberty Promotions Charity VW Drag Bus 1 of 250 & Our 2008 '67 GTO Club Car by Liberty and More!

Crowne Plaza Hotel
Warwick, RI 028886
for Reservations call: 401-732-6000

www.rihwc.com
email: jlhotwheel@cox.net
for Tickets call 401-349-0899

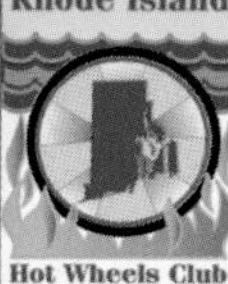

40th ANNIVERSARY TIMELINE

It's been 40 years since the first Hot Wheels cars ran off the assembly line and landed on store shelves. Here's a quick reference guide to some of the hottest cars and changes over the years.

1968

This was the first year of Mattel's Hot Wheels die-cast car series. Only 16 different vehicles were released in 1968.

FAN FAVORITES> **Beatnik Bandit, Custom Barracuda, Custom Camaro, Custom Corvette and Custom Firebird.**

1969

Due to high demand, Mattel increased their new Hot Wheels line by an additional 24 cars in 1969.

FAN FAVORITES> **Classic '31 Ford Woody, Classic '57 T-Bird, Twin Mill and Volkswagen Beach Bomb.**

1970

Mattel released 33 new models that included a special mail-away Collector's Club Car and work trucks called "Heavyweights."

FAN FAVORITES> **Cement Mixer, King Kuda, Red Baron, Snake & Mongoose and Whip Creamer.**

1971

After the success of the 1970 series, Mattel decided to add several new "Heavyweights" and hot rods called "Spoilers" to the 1971 line.

FAN FAVORITES> **Bye-Focal, Grass Hopper, Mutt Mobile and S'Cool Bus.**

*Cars pictured are from the 40th anniversary set.

40TH ANNIVERSARY TIMELINE

1972

In 1972, sales on Hot Wheels cars began to slow down, so Mattel only issued seven new vehicles.

FAN FAVORITES > Funny Money, Rear Engine, Snake & Mongoose and Side Kick.

1973

Mattel switched from Spectraflame paints to enamel paints for their Hot Wheels line.

FAN FAVORITES > Sweet 16, Superfine Turbine and Double Header.

1974

This was the year that Mattel introduced their line of cars called Flying Colors. These cars had wild colors and decorations.

FAN FAVORITES > Heavy Chevy, Rodger Dodger, Sir Rodney Roadster and Volkswagen Bug.

1975

The Flying Colors cars were a big success in 1974, so Mattel decided to add 23 new vehicles to the line.

FAN FAVORITES > American Victory, Large Charge, Mustang Stocker and Ramblin' Wrecker.

1976

The 1976 Hot Wheels line introduced a line of shiny silver cars called Super Chromes. The Corvette Stingray was the most popular.

FAN FAVORITES > Corvette Stingray, Lowdown and Poison Pinto.

1977

Mattel decided to package all of their '77 cars with either redline tires or the basic black wall tires.

FAN FAVORITES > '57 Chevy and the GMC Motor Home.

40TH ANNIVERSARY TIMELINE

1978

All vehicles in the '78 line were released with black wall tires. The Hot Bird was popular with collectors.

FAN FAVORITES> '57 T-Bird, Baja Breaker, Hot Bird and Science Friction.

1979

Several new van and truck models were introduced in 1979. The Greased Gremlin was a hot one.

FAN FAVORITES> Captain America car, Spider-Man van, and Greased Gremlin.

1980

The 1980 line included classic cars, construction vehicles, delivery trucks and sports cars.

FAN FAVORITES> 3-Window '34, Split Window '63 Corvette and the Turbo Mustang.

1981

The invasion of vans and trucks into the Hot Wheels line continued with eight new designs. One of the hottest cars was the Dixie Challenger.

FAN FAVORITES> '37 Bugatti, Bronco 4-Wheeler and Dixie Challenger.

1982

Mattel reissued 28 vehicles and introduced 23 new ones to us in 1982. The Camaro Z-28 was a fast one on the tracks.

FAN FAVORITES> '55 Chevy, Camaro Z-28, Firebird Funny Car, P-928 Porsche and the Sheriff Patrol.

1983

The 1983 line included 96 models including 20 new vehicles. Collectors love the '40 Ford 2-Door.

FAN FAVORITES> '67 Camaro, Classic Cobra, '40 Ford 2-Door, '80s Corvette and the '80s Firebird.

40TH ANNIVERSARY TIMELINE

1984

Mattel introduced the popular Ultra Hots cars with cool new wheels such as the Flame Runner, Predator and Sol-Aire CX4.

FAN FAVORITES > '65 Mustang Convertible, Baja Bug, Blown Camaro Z-28 and the Good Humor Truck.

1985

The Pontiac Fiero 2M4 was a big hit with Hot Wheels collectors in '85. Mattel also released army tanks, jeeps, cannon and gunner vehicles this year.

FAN FAVORITES > Fat Fendered '40, Pontiac Fiero 2M4, Nissan 300ZX and Thunderstreak.

1986

Mattel unleashed a new subset series of Hot Wheels cars this year called Speed Demons.

FAN FAVORITES > Cargoyle, Double Demon, Eevil Weevil, Fangster, Turboa and Vampyra.

1987

There were three new Speed Demons models added to the '87 line: Phantomachine, Sharkruiser and Zombot.

FAN FAVORITES > Ferrari Testarossa and the Monster Vette.

1988

The final two Speed Demons models were added in 1988. They were Rodzilla and Ratmobile. The Talbot Lago was a fan favorite.

FAN FAVORITES > Lamborghini Countach, Radar Ranger and Talbot Lago.

1989

Collectors went crazy for trucks and buses in 1989. The VW Bug was also popular.

FAN FAVORITES > '32 Ford Delivery, Custom Corvette, Delivery Truck, School Bus and VW Bug.

40TH ANNIVERSARY TIMELINE

1990

Mattel introduced a new series in 1990 that was an instant hit—California Customs. The cars in this series had bright colors and wild designs.

FAN FAVORITES > **Corvette Funny Car, Firebird and Purple Passion.**

1991

This was a great year for sleek-looking car designs. The Limozeen was a big hit.

FAN FAVORITES > **'59 Caddy, Ferrari 250, Lamborghini Diablo, Limozeen and Street Beast.**

1992

Mattel released a series called Gleam Team that was metallic and shiny and collectors loved them. The '56 Flashsider was also popular.

FAN FAVORITES > **Aeroflash, Corvette Stingray, '56 Flashsider and the Hummer.**

1993

This was the 25th anniversary year of Hot Wheels cars and Mattel celebrated by re-releasing eight vehicles from the first few years of the brand.

FAN FAVORITES > **Red Baron, Silhouette, Splittin' Image, Twin Mill, Olds 442 and Wienermobile.**

1994

The 25th Anniversary Collection was such a hit that Mattel decided to continue the craze by issuing a similar series called The Vintage Collection.

FAN FAVORITES > **Mutt Mobile, S'Cool Bus, Snake, Whip Creamer, Rigor Motor and Splittin' Image II.**

1995

Mattel introduced Treasure Hunt cars (TH) and began using "First Editions" (FE) for new models. There were 12 different THs and 12 different FEs.

FAN FAVORITES > **'67 Camaro, VW Bug, Dodge Ram 1500 and '58 Corvette Coupe.**

40TH ANNIVERSARY TIMELINE

1996

This was the second year for TH and FE Models. The fan favorite Volkswagon Drag Bus was quickly removed from the mainline.

FAN FAVORITES > '57 Chevy, Dodge Viper, 1996 Mustang GT and VW Bus.

1997

This was the third year of the Treasure Hunt cars. However, 2007 First Editions, which were a little easier to find, were driving a lot of the sales.

FAN FAVORITES > 1970 Plymouth Barracuda, '97 Corvette, Scorchin' Scooter and Way 2 Fast.

1998

A 30-car series celebrating the 30th anniversary of Hot Wheels cars was released. Mattel decid-ed to unleash 40 new FE models.

FAN FAVORITES > Go Kart, Hot Seat, '63 T-Bird, '68 Mustang, Dairy Delivery and Mustang Cobra.

1999

Many different sports cars and classic cars were released in '99. The '70 Chevelle SS was one of the best sellers.

FAN FAVORITES > '70 Chevelle SS, '38 Phantom Corsair, Ferrari F355 Berlinetta and Ford GT-40.

2000

Mattel rolled in the new millennium with 12 new Treasure Hunts, 36 new models and 250 other cars.

FAN FAVORITES > '65 Vette, '67 Dodge Charger, Blast Lane, Deora II and Pro Stock Firebird.

2001

Mattel brought back some wackiness to the Hot Wheels line in 2001 with vehicles like Fright Bike, Hyper Mite, Mo' Scoot and Outsider.

FAN FAVORITES > '71 Plymouth GTX, Evil Twin, Honda Civic Si and Surfin' School Bus.

40TH ANNIVERSARY TIMELINE

2002

New models continued to be a driving force behind the sales of Hot Wheels cars.

FAN FAVORITES> 2001 Mini Cooper, '68 Cougar, Corvette SR-2 and Volkswagen New Beetle Cup.

2003

Mattel released 42 2003 First Editions, 12 Treasure Hunts, as well as over 100 mainline vehicles.

FAN FAVORITES> Twang Thang, Lamborghini Diablo, 8 Crate, 1968 Boss Hoss and Corvette Stingray.

2004

For the 10th anniversary of the 1995 First Editions cars, Mattel unleashed a whopping 101 brand new FEs in 2004.

FAN FAVORITES> '69 Dodge Charger, Mustang Funny Car and 'Tooned '69 Camaro.

2005

The amount of new models released dropped to 60 in 2005. The 1969 Pontiac Firebird was very popular.

FAN FAVORITES> 1969 Pontiac Firebird, 2005 Ford Mustang GT and 1971 Dodge Charger.

2006

Mattel released 223 different models: 38 2006 First Editions, 12 Treasure Hunts, five new Red Line (red striped wheels) Series cars and five new Mystery cars.

FAN FAVORITES> '70 Plymouth Superbird, '69 Corvette, '69 Camaro and '67 Mustang.

2007

Mattel dropped the use of "First Editions" in favor of "New Models" and released 36 new vehicles.

FAN FAVORITES> '66 Nova, '69 Ford Mustang and 1966 TV Series Batmobile.

REAL LIFE HOT WHEELS CARS

Can you imagine seeing one of these cool cars driving down the road? Which one is your favorite?

TWIN MILL

The Twin Mill was the first life-size car created based on a Hot Wheels design. Conceived in 1968 by Ira Gilford, the twin supercharged big-block engines became the vehicle's most recognizable feature and contribute to its high-performance appearance. A full-sized Twin Mill was commissioned for the 30th anniversary of Hot Wheels cars in 1998, and unveiled in 2001 at SEMA. The twin Chevrolet motors, supplied by GM Performance Products, are not just for show—this fully operational racer produces upwards of 1400 horsepower. The Twin Mill was repainted for the 2007 SEMA Show in PPG's Hot Wheels Spectraflame Anti-freeze Green paint.

DEORA II

The original Deora was part of the first Hot Wheels line in 1968. In 1964, Chrysler commissioned Mike and Larry Alexander to customize their new economy pickup, the Dodge A-100. Based on automotive designer Harry Bentley Bradley's illustration, the Alexander brothers created a low, cab-forward design with a front-opening cab; giving it a very sleek, futuristic appearance. The 1968 Hot Wheels Deora became a huge hit and an automotive legend. In 2000, Hot Wheels designer Nathan Proch created the Deora II as homage to the groundbreaking and original spirit of Hot Wheels cars. In 2003, in preparation for the 35th anniversary of Hot Wheels cars, the Deora II was built and the 1:64-scale, die-cast Deora II has been a staple in the Hot Wheels line ever since.

THE MAKING OF A HOT WHEELS CAR

Ever wondered how Hot Wheels cars are made? What happens between the initial concepts to the final product? Here you will find the major steps involved in making these very popular cars.

2

1. CONCEPT

The designers make recommendations on different cars to produce. These could be real automobiles or cars that are developed by the designers themselves. The design staff reviews all of the submissions and decides which concepts will be produced.

2. DESIGN

Once the concepts are approved, the designers go to work. For each concept, the designer will produce many drawings of how the vehicle should appear. They will calculate final dimensions, determine how the car will be assembled and design the different parts needed. If a real car is being reproduced, the designer will take many measurements of the full size car to make sure all the dimensions are correct.

3. MODEL OR PATTERN

From these drawings a large size model (about 10-12 inches long) is produced. The model represents all of the parts that will be used to make the final product. These parts include the body, windshield, interior, wheels and the base or chassis. These models are important because they allow the designer to see how all of the parts will fit together. The model also represents how the car will be produced and assembled in the factory.

In the past couple of years, there has been a shift from producing large models to making digital 3-D models on computers. A rapid plastic prototype can be made from the digital 3-D models to verify that all of the parts can be assembled as specified by the designer.

3

4. LICENSE APPROVAL

If the design is based on a real car, the model is sent to the design or trademark owner (Ford, GM, Chrysler, Volkswagen, Ferrari, etc.) for license approval. Permission must be received from the trademark owner before producing the car.

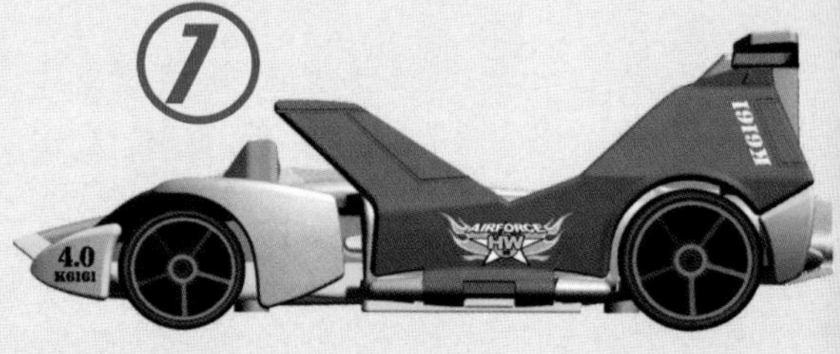

5. CASTING MOLDS (TOOLING)

After the designer has approved the final model, the casting molds are produced. Casting molds are used to make the final body parts that will be used to make the Hot Wheels cars. Some of the bodies are made with a metal alloy called ZAMAC (Zinc, Aluminum, Magnesium and Copper). Other bodies are made with plastic. The alloy or plastic is melted and forced into the molds under high pressure to form the body. The body is then removed from the mold and buffed to remove any sharp edges.

6. PROTOTYPE

Before Hot Wheels cars goes into mass production, the first versions produced (called "first shots") are assembled to make a few complete cars. These prototypes are usually not painted. The prototype cars are sent back to the designer to make sure that all the parts are correct and that they all properly fit together to form the final product.

7. GRAPHIC DESIGN

Most cars have some sort of decoration or graphics to represent a theme or style. Sometimes the graphics can be very minor (such as headlights and taillights) or they are more elaborate (stripes, flames and objects). Graphic designers lay out these designs based on the dimensions of the final prototype.

8. FINAL ENGINEERING PROTOTYPE

The factory will make a few additional prototypes based on the approved E-sheets. These prototypes are called FEP's (Final Engineering Pilot). They have all the paint, decoration and parts specified on the E-sheets (blueprints). The design staff will evaluate and inspect FEP's to verify that the cars are correctly produced. After this approval, normal production can begin.

9. FINAL PRODUCTION

After the molds and final designs are all approved, the cars are ready for production. The bodies are produced, painted and graphics are applied. The finished cars are then inspected, sorted, packaged, packed into boxes and shipped to the different stores that sell Hot Wheels cars.

HOT WHEELS COLLECTING
TIPS & GUIDELINES

Collecting Hot Wheels Cars is a hobby that is enjoyed by people all over the world. These cars have been a favorite toy of kids and adults since 1968 and continue to be very popular today.

Because Hot Wheels cars are found in almost every store selling toys, starting a collection is easy. How, what and where to collect are questions that are asked by many new collectors. Here are some tips and guidelines that may help answer these questions.

KEEPING CARS IN OR OUT OF THE PACKAGE

Cars that are kept in their original packages are always more collectible and their value is usually much higher than with cars that are opened and played with. The most desired cars by collectors usually have perfect packaging (no bent corners or other defects). Many collectors store their packaged cars in clear cases that are specially designed to protect and hold Hot Wheels cars. Mattel even introduced its own line of Kar Keepers to help ccollectors protect their cars.

Opening Hot Wheels car packages decreases their value, but increases their play value. They're much easier to display and store. It is much more fun to be able to play with and race cars on a track set than looking at them through a package. There are many different types of cases available to neatly store loose cars together.

COLLECTING BY SERIES OR COLLECTOR NUMBERS

Since 1995, Hot Wheels cars have been released in different series, such as first editions or new models, Treasure Hunts, and segments, each year. These are easy to identify and are clearly labeled on the packaging. The balance of the released cars each year are called regular issue or open stock.

2006 086

The new models are Hot Wheels designs that have appeared for the very first time. These are also known as first editions.

Segment Series include cars that are grouped by special themes.

The names of the segments, and whether there are open stock, depend on the year. In 2008, nearly all cars were in one of the segments: New Models, Treasure Hunts, Track Stars, Mystery Cars, Web Trading Cars, and Teams (which were 12 teams of 4, all with different themes).

Treasure Hunt cars are randomly packed in case assortments and are highly desired by collectors. There are 12 different cars released in this segment each year.

Regular issues are cars that aren't part of any segment or theme. They usually only have a collector number and car name on the packaging.

Every released car has a collector number, which makes it easy to organize them in numerical order.

COLLECTING SIMILAR STYLES, DESIGNS OR COLORS

Many people collect only certain styles or models of cars. They may have a favorite color they like or a special car they dream of owning one day. This type of collection is more personal and is easier to collect.

VARIATIONS

Sometimes a car with the same collector number or segment will be released with a different body color, window color, interior color, wheels or graphic design. The result of these changes can turn out to be a very limited release and are highly sought after by collectors.

WHERE TO FIND HOT WHEELS CARS

Newer releases can all be found at most retail stores that carry toys. These stores usually have a great selection of cars to choose from and also sell related gift sets, track sets and play sets.

Previously released cars are harder to find at retail stores. Collectors usually look for older cars at garage/yard sales, estate sales and at local Hot Wheels clubs. Flea Markets, Toy Shows and online auction sites are also good places to find older releases.

HOT WHEELS CLUBS

These clubs usually have monthly meetings and are very family oriented. Many clubs are usually very helpful to new collectors by promoting the hobby, relaying the latest information on car availability, and organizing Hot Wheels related activities. This may include downhill races, buying/selling/trading and Hot Wheels customizing. Go to the next page to find a club near you.

IDENTIFYING THE SEGMENTS

Here's a helpful guide to identifying the different segments of Hot Wheels cars.

2008 New Models

First time ever in the Hot Wheels line (look for the yellow stripe)

Treasure Hunt

Grab them if you see them, because these treasures are hard to find (look for the green stripe)

Track Cars

Our top track performers (look for the orange stripe)

Mystery

Life is like a Mystery car...since the blister is black, you never know what you're gonna get. (look for the black stripe)

Code Cars

Each car has its own code. Enter it online and see what you'll find! (look for the red stripe)

Web Trading Cars

Go online, trade these cars, and play interactive games (look for the red stripe)

Teams

With 12 teams of four cars, you can pick your favorites and collect 'em all! (look for the purple stripe)

All Stars

Some of the all-time favorites (look for the blue stripe)

TREASURE HUNTS TIPS

For stores that restock Hot Wheels cars overnight, chances of finding a Treasure Hunt are best when they open for business the next day.

HOT WHEELS COLLECTOR CLUBS

Join one today in your local area

Birmingham, AL
Heart of Dixie Hotwheelers
Paul Douglas / mpdouglas@charter.net

Huntsville, AL
Rocket City Hotwheelers
Joe Davis / joed@charter.net

Jasper, AL
Outlaw Hot Wheels
Ted / ted_m_lynn@msn.com

Little Rock, AR
Rock City Redliners
Shawn Neel /
rockcityredliners@yahoo.com

Phoenix, AZ
Arizona Outlaws Hot Wheels Collectors Club
www.azoutlaws.net
Wayne Henderson / azoutlaws@cox.net

Wheels of Fire Hot Wheels Club
Ken Adams / H.W.Teched@cox.net

Yuma, AZ
Hot Wheels of Yuma
Jeff Hitchens / AZHitch03@aol.com
Romero39@juno.com

Albany, CA
Bay Area Diecast Association
SorensenProperties@yahoo.com

Bakersfield, CA
MOHWC
Mike Scales / mscales@sbcglobal.net

Eureka, CA
Redwood Coast Diecast Club
Andrew Howard / moparkidd@sbcglobal.net

Laguna Niguel, CA
So-Cal Originals
www.socaloriginals.com
Mike Hutton / mike@socaloriginals.com

Riverside, CA
Hot Rod Hot Wheelers of the Inland Empire
Richard Whitmark /
nwhitmark@surfside.net

Riverside, CA
Jurupa Mountain Hot Wheels
Chelle Smith / HotWheelzGrl@aol.com

San Jose, CA
Northern California Hot Wheels Club
Luciano Torres /
norcalhotwheels@sbcglobal.net

Colorado Springs, CO
Pikes Peak Hot Wheelers
Bryan / BAPonting@msn.com

Denver, CO
Rocky Mountain Hot Wheelers
www.rmhwc.org
Peter Kistler / info@rmhwc.org

Loveland, CO
Colorado Diecast Collectors
Lance Comings /
coloradodiecast@aol.com

Middletown, CT
Southern New England Hot Wheelers
WWW.SNEHW.COM
Al / Tatumahn@aol.com

Windsor Locks, CT
CT. Valley Die-cast (C.V.D)
www.cvdcollectors.bravehost.com
Ken / cwik111@yahoo.com

Crestview, Fl
Hub City Car Club
Kevin Smith / sandy054@centurytel.net

Jacksonville, FL
First Coast Hot Wheels Collectors
James Hudgins /
james@firstcoasthotwheels.com

Lehigh, FL
Hot Wheel Collectors of Southwest Florida
www.swflorida-hwc.com

Tallahassee, FL
Tallahassee Hot Wheels Club
James Graves / gfieldj@aol.com

Tampa Bay, FL
Tampa Bay Hot Wheels Club
Al / kunardallan@yahoo.com

Atlanta, GA
Peachstate Hot Wheels
www.peachstatehotwheels.com
Travis / tagkavr@aol.com

Des Moines, IA
All Iowa Hot Wheels Collectors Club
Steve Dippold / steve67GTO@msn.com

Fort Dodge, IA
Fort Dodge Area Hot Wheels Collectors
Calvin Stewart / stewfam@lvcta.com

Hayden, ID
Northwest Die-cast Collectors Club
Rick Fristoe / nwdiecastclub@aol.com

Chicago, IL
Windy City Hot Wheelers
www.windycityhotwheelers.com
Jay Milkeris /
xxtunemanxx@hotmail.com

Peoria, IL
Central Illinois Hot Wheels Club
centralillinoishotwheelsclub@
insightbb.com

Indianapolis, IN
Indy Hot Wheels Club
www.indyhotwheelsclub.com
Dave Koch / littlemkk@yahoo.com

Muncie, IN
East Central Indiana Hot Wheels Club
www.geocities.com/ecihwc
Brian/April Hanaway /
ecihwc@yahoo.com

South Bend, IN
Michiana Hot Wheelers
Jim Baldwin /
jandjbaldwin1@verizon.net

Kansas City, KS
MO-KAN Hotwheelers
Kevin Zwart / kzcars@yahoo.com

Benton, KY
Bluegrass Hot Wheels Club
ptrob@vci.net

Louisville, KY
Derby City Hot Wheelers
erupped.tripod.com/derbycityhotwheelers
bigloucat@bellsouth.net

Braintree, MA
Boston Area Toy Collectors Club
www.bostontoyclub.com

Southboro, MA
East Coast Real Riders
Joe Small / fgxl500@aol.com

Baltimore, MD
Chesapeake Bay Hot Wheels Club
Joel Buckner /
cowboy20000@msn.com

Baltimore, MD
The Charm City Collector's Club - C4
Roy Friend Jr. /
c4hotwheels@c4hotwheels.tk

Bangor, ME
Eastern Maine Diecast Association
Roger Priest / Rpriest@maine.edu

Detroit, MI
Motor City Hot Wheelers
www.motorcityhotwheelers.com
Sheri Abbey / lca@tir.com

Fraser, MI
Fraytown Redliners
Dave Griff / gobluegriff@yahoo.com

Kansas City, MO
MO-KAN Hotwheelers
Kevin Zwart / kzcars@yahoo.com

St. Louis, MO
Gateway Hot Wheelers Club
www.gatewayhotwheelers.com
Robert Wicker / ghwcrobert@aol.com

Greensboro, NC
East Coast Hot Wheels Club
Rick Putek / rputek@charter.net

Plaistow, NH
Northern New England Hot Wheelers
Phil Davis / phillipdavis@yahoo.com

Ridgewood, NJ
New Jersey Diecast Collector's Club (NJDCC)
Ken Packowski / cgmgd@allstate.com

Albuquerque, NM
Roadrunners Collector Club
Curtis Moseley /
cnmhotwheels@cs.com

Columbus, OH
Central Ohio Hot Wheels Club
www.centralohiohotwheels.com
Patrick Hardina / teddytiggr@aol.com

Dayton, OH
Exclusively Hot Wheels Club
Roger Chappel /
r.chappel@insightbb.com

Marysville, OH
Hot Wheels Collector Club of Marysville
Jame Story /
Thestory6583@sbcglobal.net

Shelby, OH
Mid-Ohio Hot Wheelers Club
John Bloom / jbloom@neo.rr.com

Tulsa, OK
Klub Kool Stuff
www.kriskoolstuff.com
Kris / Darryl

Tulsa, OK
T-Town Wheelers
Robert Priebe /
coolwheels@valornet.com

Salem, OR
Mid-Valley Hotwheelers Club
Larry Webb / webb6@hotmail.com

Allentown, PA
Pennsylvania Hot Wheels Association
www.hotwheelsshack.proboards33.com
djyr2003@gmail.com

Cranberry, PA
Steel City Diecast Club
Rick Sobek /
rjlsobek@connecttime.net

Cranston, RI
Rhode Island Hot Wheels Club
Jim Lombardi / JLHotwheel@cox.net

Anderson, SC
Palmetto State Hot Wheels Club
Jim Pietrowski /
redryder31@charter.net

Darlington, SC
East Coast Hot Wheels Club
www.echwc.com
Jason Patterson /
crewchief4344@juno.com

Saskatoon, SK, CAN
Prairiefire Hot Wheels Club
John Turanich /
prairiefirehwc@hotmail.com

Knoxville, TN
East Tennessee Hot Wheelers
Tim Brantley / timsseadoo@aol.com

Memphis, TN
Hot Wheels Collectors of Memphis
Greg / hwcmemphis@hotmail.com

Austin, TX
Bat City Hot Wheels Collectors
www.batcityhwc.com
Bob Ratliff / batcityhwc@austin.rr.com

Dallas/Ft Worth, TX
North Texas Diecast Collectors Club
www.northtexasdiecast.com
Tommy / northtexasdiecast@yahoo.com

Houston, TX
Space City Hot Wheels Collectors Club
www.spacecityhw.com
Chuck Gronemeyer /
chuck@spacecityhw.com

San Angelo, TX
San Angelo Diecast Collectors Club
Leonard Manis / ljm72@yahoo.com

San Antonio, TX
South Texas Diecast Collectors
www.southtexasdiecast.com

Salt Lake City, UT
Salt Flat Hot Wheelers
Randy Muir / flyingmur@msn.com

Roanoke, VA
Star City Hot Wheels
www.starcityhotwheels.com
Tim Whitlock /
starcityhotwheels@cox.net

Roanoke/Lynchburg, VA
East Coast Hot Wheels Club
www.echwc.com
Carl Crawford / crayfish3609@aol.com

Winchester, VA
Winchester/Shenandoah Valley Hot Wheels Club
Dan Hammond / hwdan2@earthlink.net

Republic, WA
Hot Wheels Collectors Club of Washington
Richard Guilliot / (509) 775-8806 /
hotwheelsclub@hotmail.com

Milwaukee, WI
Milwaukee Hot Wheels Club
Rob Johnston / GTR-Rob@sbcglobal.net

Oshkosh, Wi
Fox Cities Diecast
Fred Dunlop /
foxcitiesdiecast@hotmail.com

Bridgeport, WV
Mountaineer Hot Wheels Club
Scott Owen / sameowen@msn.com

EXCLUSIVE INTERVIEW

A Q & A with Alec Tam, director of Mattel's Hot Wheels design team

BY DOUG KALE

Recently, I got the rare chance to interview Alec Tam, a director of Mattel's Hot Wheels design team. Alec's dad, Paul Tam, was also a designer for the Hot Wheels brand back in the 1970s. Designing Hot Wheels cars must be one of the coolest jobs in the world. So, let's find out what Alec had to say about his job and the world of Hot Wheels cars.

Did you play with cars when you were very young? Can you tell us about your favorite childhood car?

Yes. Since my dad was a Hot Wheels designer, he always had tons of wild Hot Wheels cars around—some were prototypes that he was working on. The ones I enjoyed the most were battery powered cars called Sizzlers that would race on a gigantic, wide track with banked turns—like stock car racing.

When did you start thinking about a career in car design or designing in general?

My dad would always bring drawings, prototypes and renderings home. He was also constantly sketching concepts of wild cars and toys, so I thought that was fun. He also showed me the technical side of designing and drawing things at a very early age. My mom was also a designer, so I guess I had it in my genes! Seriously, I was pretty good at it and enjoyed the challenges of problem solving that is inherent in designing cars and toys.

You became a Hot Wheels designer back in 2000. Tell us what the first car you designed was and what it was like to see your creation on the shelves?

The first Hot Wheels car I designed was called Monoposto. As the name implies, it was a single seat roadster. I remember being at the local retailer and seeing my car on shelf, that was cool. Then I thought about how my car might inspire a child to become a designer or a car enthusiast him or herself one day; that realization was very rewarding.

A few years ago you had taken one of your father's most memorable car designs, Whip Creamer, updated the design and released it as Whip Creamer II. What were some of your thoughts when you were planning the redesign of that car?

I was focused mostly on updating the aesthetics. The concept of the car itself was very much a fantasy when he designed it—a turbine-powered, ultra-low profile speed car, and it still is today. So I kept the original concept and just reskinned it in today's ideas of what makes a cool looking car. My goal was to make this still futuristic and valid concept palatable for today's kids.

Whip Creamer II

What type of things, past or present, influence the types of car designs you come up with for the Hot Wheels brand?

As a designer, I have to be open to everything; you never know where an idea may come from. In general, I make sure I'm observant of the latest trends in car culture and pop culture. As Hot Wheels, we have a long history of creating custom cars, so car trends are at the top of my list. I also read a lot of magazines, books, technical articles, newspapers and of course the web. It's all just a way to kick start your mind.

Are you a Hot Wheels collector? If so, which one is your all-time favorite?

I collect, but in comparison to the size of the collections of some of our most enthusiastic collectors, I don't even consider myself a true collector. My love is for cool designs and cars I have a connection to. I'll collect on that criteria. I don't actually have one favorite car; they're all good for different reasons and I appreciate them from that perspective.

Do you think your designs have influenced some auto makers such as GM, Ford or Chrysler?

I know we have. We have a new line, called Hot Wheels Designer's Challenge, where we invited auto manufacturers to design their version of what a Hot Wheels car was to them. These were essentially real concept cars straight from the car company's studios designed just for Hot Wheels. Most of the designers were either collectors or were inspired by Hot Wheels as children to become real car designers. I couldn't point to any one particular car, but I would say we probably have influenced much of the thinking behind many of the cars and trends you see today.

Can you tell us more about the Hot Wheels Designer's Challenge?

We invited six of the world's premier car companies—GM, Dodge, Ford, Mitsubishi, Honda and Lotus—to design what they thought a Hot Wheels inspired car from their design studios might look like. The challenge was to see if they could infuse the Hot Wheels values of speed, power, performance and attitude into what their own brands stood for. As an example, Mitsubishi created a fantastic car that would look right at home at a major auto show, except it had two huge engines sticking out of the front and back! Concepts like this would probably be deemed too wild for a real car, but are perfect for a Hot Wheels car.

After a design is approved, how long does it take before the car hits the store shelves?

I can't be specific, but it's less than a year.

What type of car do you currently drive?

The current car that I'm working on is a 1965 Mustang Fastback. It's got a powerful, loud motor, rides like a truck and always needs work, but I love it! My mom had a coupe version and it was really my very first car memory.

What can Hot Wheels collectors expect to see in future releases of Hot Wheels products?

Everything! We pride ourselves on having something for everyone especially cars that people have fond memories of, or have an emotional connection to like muscle cars, hot rods and classics. We also strive to have the latest, hot performance cars that are available for sale today.

Thank you for a terrific interview Alec!

BECKETT HOT WHEELS PRICE GUIDE

HOW TO GRADE YOUR HOT WHEELS CARS COLLECTION

ONLY A GUIDE Beckett listings are to be used only as a guide. The prices do not represent an offer to buy or sell on the part of any party.

HOW PRODUCTS ARE LISTED All Hot Wheels cars listed in this guide are 1:64 scale. Wal-Mart, Kmart and Toys R Us have each had their share of exclusive Hot Wheels cars. We've noted those in the Price Guide listings.

Here's a sample of the guide:

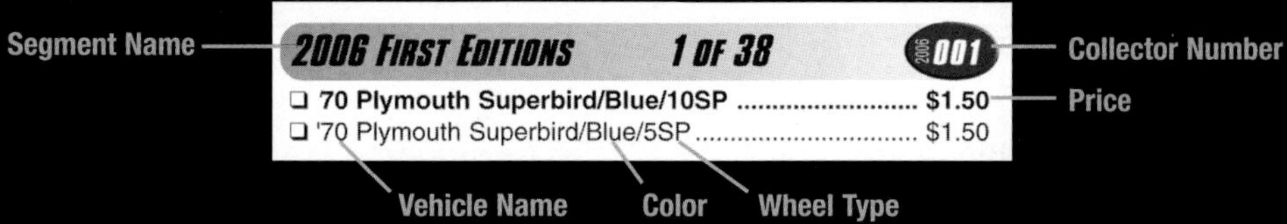

CONDITION GUIDE

Most Hot Wheels products are sold in their original packaging. Due to variations and descriptions, packaging is sometimes as important as the die-cast vehicle itself. Prices listed are for unblemished die-cast products in their original, undamaged packaging.

Here are some guidelines to determine conditions:

Mint (MT)
A vehicle and package that has no blemishes is considered Mint. The item looks like it just rolled off the manufacturing line. Mint Hot Wheels cars are valued at 125% of this guide.

Near Mint – Mint (NmMT)
This vehicle has a very tiny flaw along the edge of the packaging or a price sticker residue. NmMT Hot Wheels cars are valued at 100% of this guide.

Near Mint (NRMT)
This is a vehicle with one very minor flaw. Any one of the following would lower a Mint piece to NRMT: decals on the vehicle being slightly smudged, barely noticeable scratches on the packaging, a small bend in the packaging. NRMT Hot Wheels cars are valued at 75-90% of this guide.

Excellent (EX)
This is a vehicle with noticeable defects or wear. Any of the following would be characteristics of an EX die-cast piece: wrinkled decals, paint smudges, packaging with easily noticeable scratches or wear. EX die-casts are valued at 50-75% of this guide.

Good (G)
This is a vehicle with major defects or wear. All of the following would lower a vehicle to G: Faded decals, a loose wheel, scratches on the die-cast, packaging with several creases. G die-casts are valued at 25-50% of this guide.

Poor (P)
This is a vehicle that has been well-used or abused. A vehicle in this condition usually has been taken out of the packaging and been played with. Characteristics of P are: scratched off decals, dents in the die-cast, scratches all over the die-cast, unattractive and mutilated boxes. P die-casts are valued at 5-25% of this guide.

Vehicles Without Packaging (Loose)
Die-casts without original packaging and in Mint condition are valued at 40-50% of this guide.

WHEEL IDENTIFICATION GUIDE

Here's the complete list for all wheel variations. Each wheel is assigned a code (an abbreviation) for use in the following pages in our pictorial price guide.

 **10SP** 10 Spoke Wheel	 **10SPBLING** Bling 10 Spoke Wheel	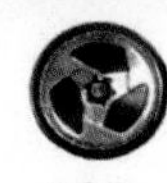 **3SP** 3 Spoke	 **5DOT** 5 Dot (5DOT) or 5 Hole (5HOLE)
 **5SP** 5 Spoke	**5SPBLING** Bling 5 Spoke Wheel	 **6SPBLING** Bling 6 Spoke Wheel	**7SP** 7 Spoke
 **BFG5SP** BF Goodrich 5 Spoke	 **BFGRR** BF Goodrich Real Riders	 **BlackGY5SP** Black 5 Spoke w/ 'Goodyear'	 **BlackGY7SP** Black 7 Spoke w/ 'Goodyear'
 **BLING** Bling 'Spinner Type' Wheel	 **BW** Basic Wheels or Black Walls	 **CM6** Co-Molded Wheel 6-Spoke	 **CoMo** Co-Molded Wheel
 **Corgi** Corgi Wheel Style 1	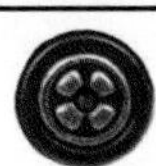 **Corgi** Corgi Wheel Style 2	 **CT** Construction Tires	 **FTE** Faster Than Ever
 **GHO** Gold Hot Ones	 **GY5SP** 5 Spoke w/ 'Goodyear'	 **GY7SP** 7 Spoke w/ 'Goodyear'	 **GYBW** Basic Wheels w/ 'Goodyear'
 **GYRR** Real Rider w/ 'Goodyear'	 **HH** Hot Hub	 **HO** Hot Ones	 **LIW** Lime Wheels
 **MGW** Micro Gear Wheels	 **Micro5SP** Micro 5 Spoke Wheel	 **OH5SP** Open Hole 5 Spoke	 **OR5SP** Off Road 5 Spoke

ORCT
Off Road Construction Tires
ORMC
Off-Road Motorcycle
ORRR
Off Road Real Riders (Grey or White Hubs)
ORSB
Off Road Sawblade or Directional
PC5
5 Spoke Pro Circuit
PC6
6 Spoke Pro-Circuit
PCOM
Power Command
POW
Progressive Oval
PR5
Named after Phil Riehlman
RLA
Red Line or Red Stripe 1968-1977
RLB
Red Line or Red Stripe 1973-1977
RLC
Red Line 2002-Present
RL5SP
Red Line 5 Spoke
RL7SP
7 Spoke w/Red Line
RLRR
Red Line Real Riders
RR
Real Riders (Grey or White Hubs)
RR
Real Riders without 'Goodyear'
RR5SP
5 Spoke Mag Style Real Riders
RR6SP
6 Spoke Real Riders
RRBNG
BNG Real Rider
RRMAG
Mag Style Real Riders
RRPrf
Prefered Series Real Riders
SB
Sawblade or Directional
ScPR5
Screamin' PR5 Wheel
SCW
Screamin' Wheels
SK5
Skinny Wheel
SS5SP
Street Show 5 Spoke
SSO5SP
Street Show Open 5 Spoke
TW
Turbo Wheels
UH
Ultra Hots
WLRR
White Line Real Riders
WSP
Wire Spoke (WSP) or Lace Wheels (LW)
WW
Basic White Wall
WWRR
White Wall Real Riders
Y5
'Y' 5 Spoke Wheel
*Listings in the price guide will have the color added to the wheel description. For example: GoldSP or Blue5Dot.

2006 HOT WHEELS PRICE GUIDE

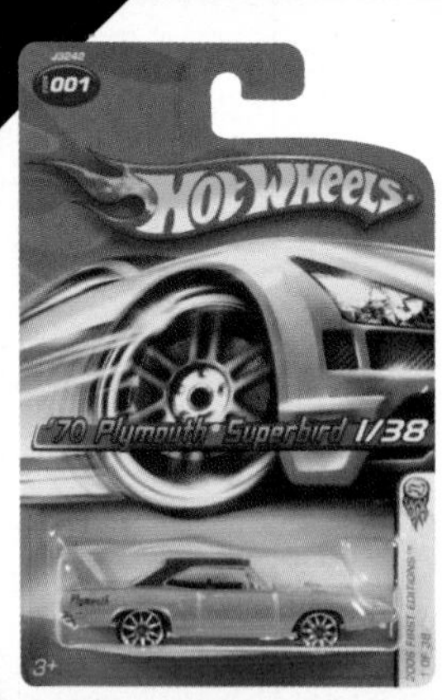

2006 FIRST EDITIONS 1 OF 38 2006 001

❑ **'70 Plymouth Superbird/Blue/10SP $1.50**
❑ '70 Plymouth Superbird/Blue/5SP $1.50

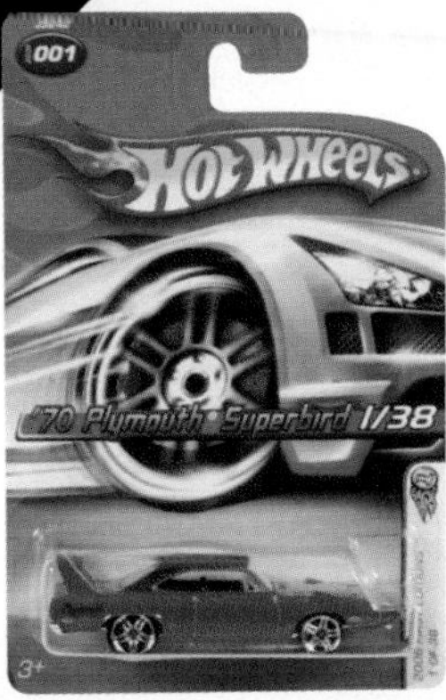

2006 FIRST EDITIONS 1 OF 38

- ❑ '70 Plymouth Superbird/Copper/10SP $30.00
- ❑ **'70 Plymouth Superbird/Copper/PR5 .... $1.50**

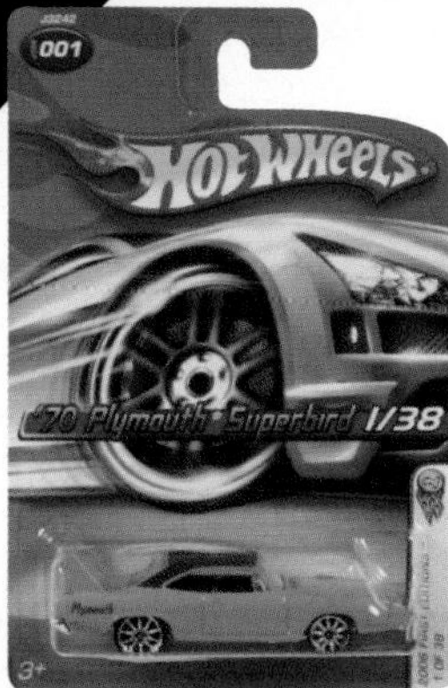

2006 FIRST EDITIONS 1 OF 38

- ❑ '70 Plymouth Superbird/Green/10SP $1.50
- ❑ **'70 Plymouth Superbird/Green/5SP $1.50**
- ❑ '70 Plymouth Superbird/Green/FTE $4.00

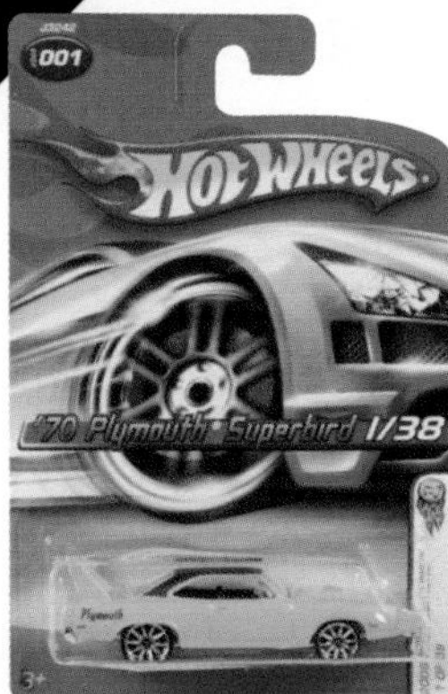

2006 FIRST EDITIONS 1 OF 38

- ❑ **'70 Plymouth Superbird/Yellow/10SP $1.50**
- ❑ '70 Plymouth Superbird/Yellow/5SP $25.00
- ❑ '70 Plymouth Superbird/Yellow/FTE $25.00

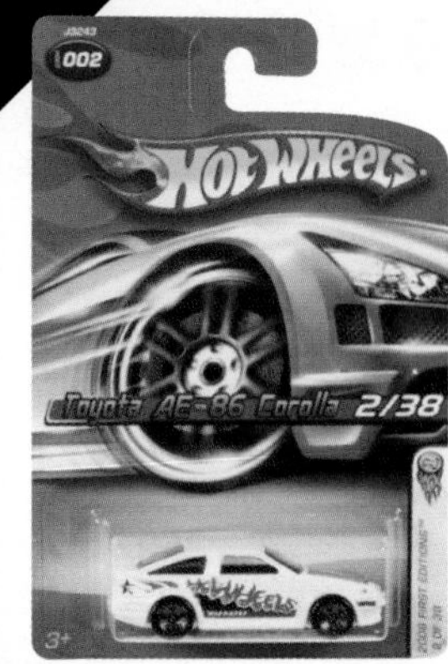

2006 First Editions 2 of 38

2006 002

- ❑ Toyota AE-86 Corolla/Flat Grey/FTE $40.00
- ❑ Toyota AE-86 Corolla/Flat Grey/Red5SP $30.00
- ❑ Toyota AE-86 Corolla/White/FTE $4.00
- ❑ Toyota AE-86 Corolla/White/Red3SP $40.00
- **❑ Toyota AE-86 Corolla/White/Red5SP $1.50**

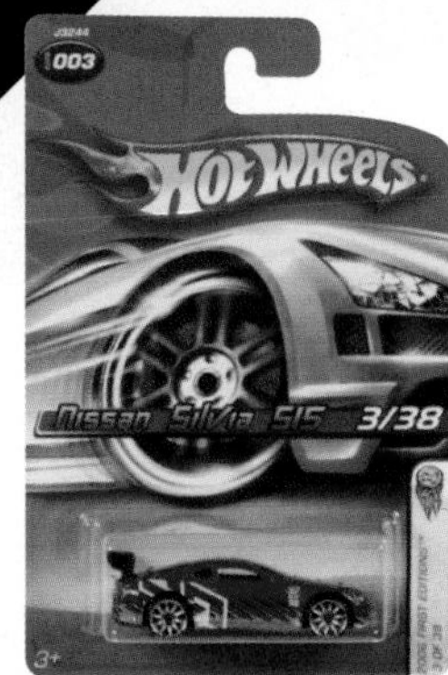

2006 First Editions 3 of 38

2006 003

- **❑ Nissan Silvia S15/M Dark Red/10SP $1.50**
- ❑ Nissan Silvia S15/M Dark Red/FTE $3.00

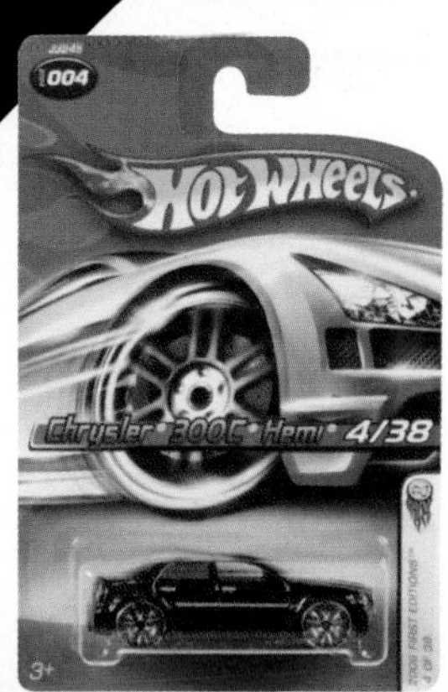

2006 First Editions 4 of 38

2006 004

- ❑ Chrysler 300C Hemi/Black/Bling $1.50

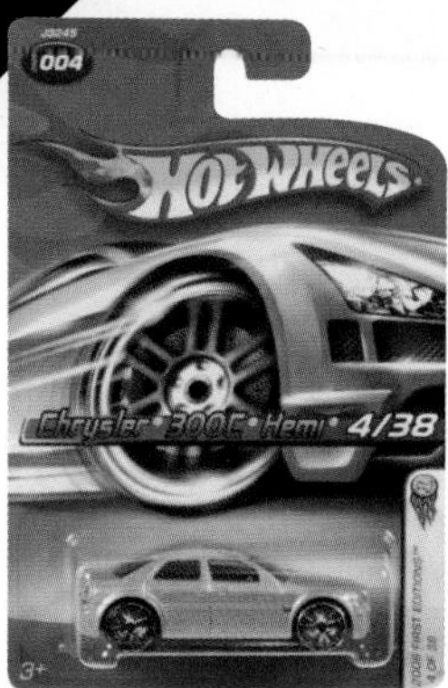

2006 First Editions 4 of 38

- ❑ **Chrysler 300C Hemi/M Silver/Bling $1.50**
- ❑ Chrysler 300C Hemi/M Silver/FTE $3.00

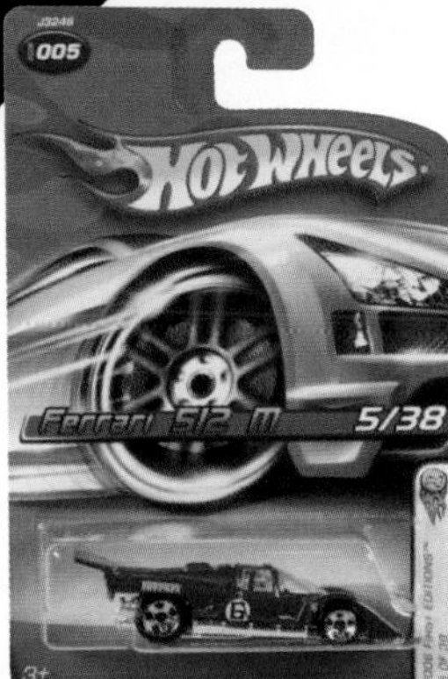

2006 First Editions 5 of 38

- ❑ Ferrari 512 M/Blue/FTE lg. 6.. $4.00
- ❑ Ferrari 512 M/Blue/FTE sm. 6...................................... $8.00
- ❑ **Ferrari 512 M/Blue/Gold5SP lg. 6............................ $1.50**
- ❑ Ferrari 512 M/Blue/Gold5SP sm. 6 .... $3.00

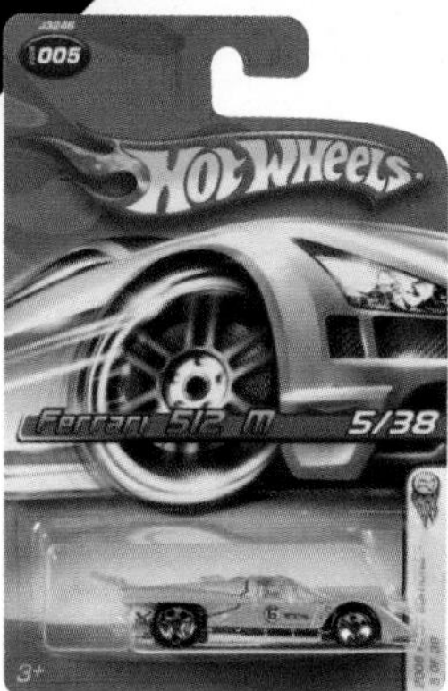

2006 First Editions 5 of 38

- ❑ **Ferrari 512 M/Grey/Gold5SP lg. 6 .... $1.50**
- ❑ Ferrari 512 M/Grey/Gold5SP sm. 6.............................. $1.50

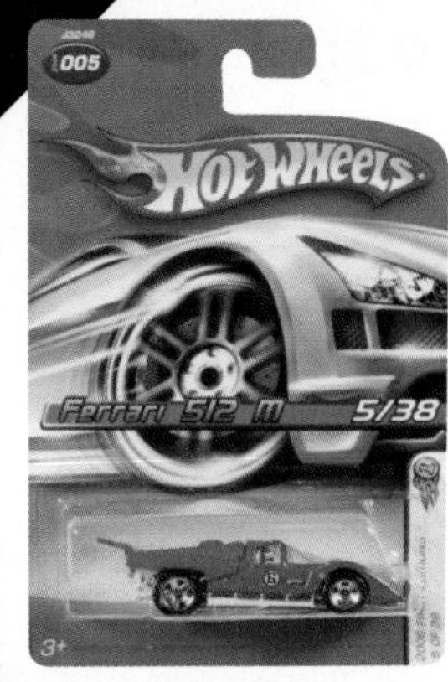

2006 First Editions 5 of 38

2006 005

- ❑ **Ferrari 512 M/Red/Gold5SP lg. 6 .... $3.00**
- ❑ Ferrari 512 M/Red/Gold5SP sm. 6 .... $1.50

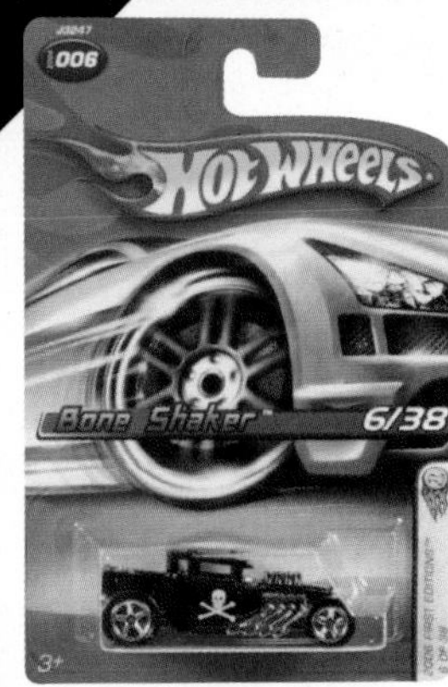

2006 First Editions 6 of 38

2006 006

- ❑ **Bone Shaker/Black/5SP $3.00**
- ❑ Bone Shaker/Black/FTE $15.00
- ❑ Bone Shaker/Black/RL5SP $80.00

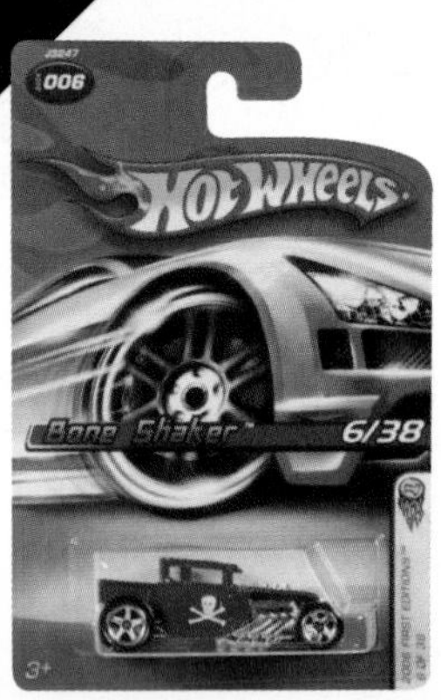

2006 First Editions 6 of 38

2006 006

- ❑ Bone Shaker/Dark Red/5SP $3.00

2006 First Editions 6 of 38 2006 006

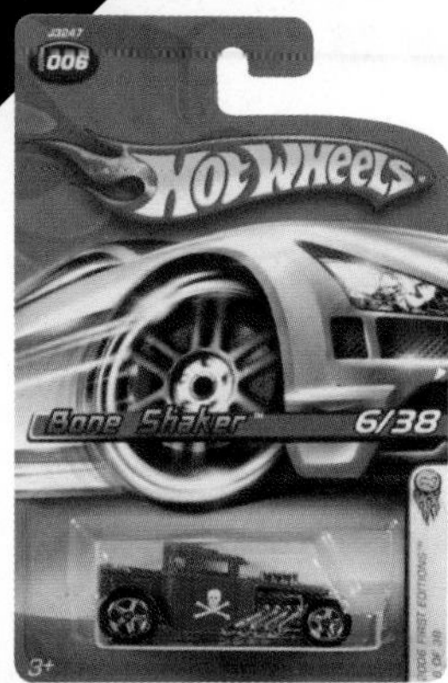

- ❑ **Bone Shaker/Flat Brown/Gold5SP $3.00**
- ❑ Bone Shaker/Flat Brown/Gold5SP no country base $4.00
- ❑ Bone Shaker/Flat Brown/GoldPR5 .... $4.00

2006 First Editions 7 of 38 2006 007

- ❑ '69 Corvette/Dark Red/PR5.. $1.50

2006 First Editions 7 of 38 2006 007

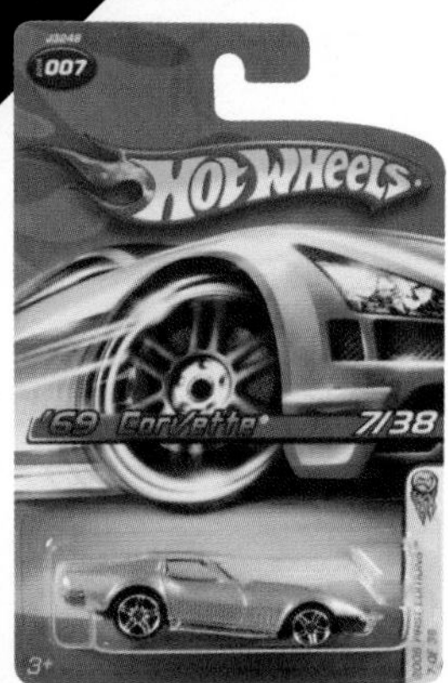

- ❑ **'69 Corvette/M Gold/PR5.. $1.50**
- ❑ '69 Corvette/Pearl White/OH5SP (Kmart) $3.00
- ❑ '69 Corvette/Pearl White/PR5 (Kmart) $40.00

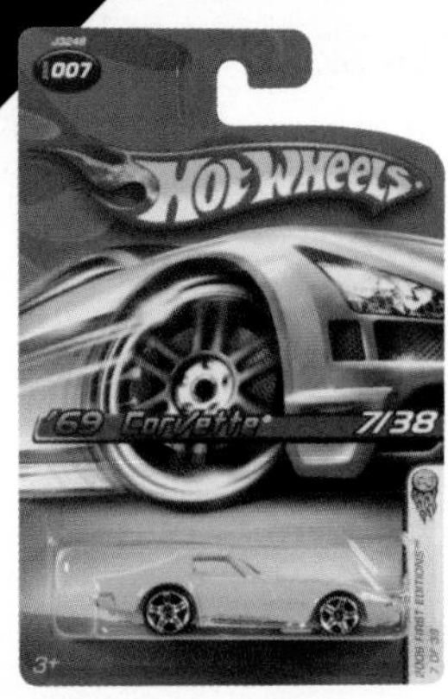

2006 FIRST EDITIONS 7 OF 38 2006 007

❑ '69 Corvette/Yellow/FTE $3.00
❑ **'69 Corvette/Yellow/PR5 .... $1.50**

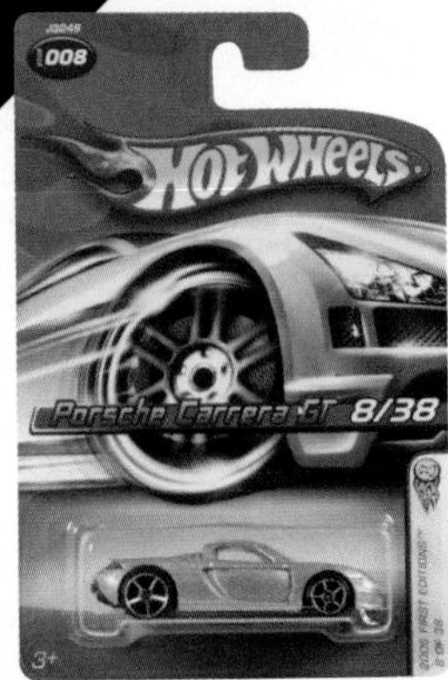

2006 FIRST EDITIONS 8 OF 38 2006 008

❑ Porsche Carrera GT/Silver/FTE $3.00
❑ **Porsche Carrera GT/Silver/OH5SP $1.50**

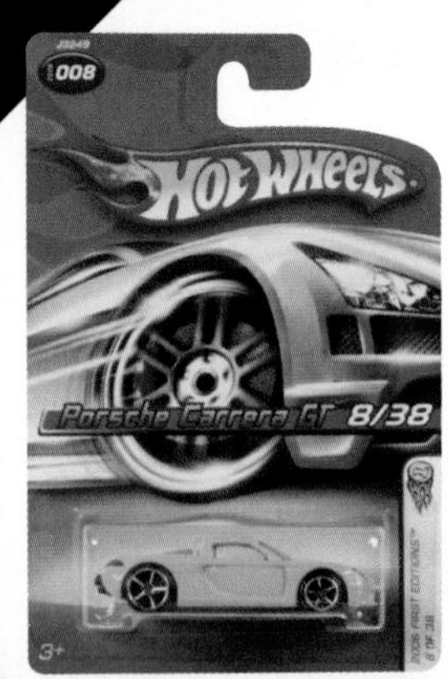

2006 FIRST EDITIONS 8 OF 38 2006 008

❑ **Porsche Carrera GT/Yellow/OH5SP $1.50**
❑ Porsche Carrera GT/Yellow/OH5SP
w/o back window.. $10.00

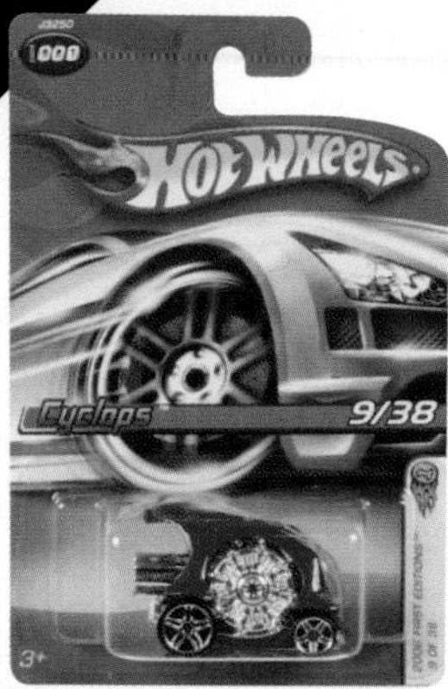

2006 First Editions 9 of 38 2006 009

- ❑ Cyclops/Dark Red/PR5 w/black Tampos...................... $4.00
- **❑ Cyclops/Dark Red/PR5 w/blue Tampos $1.50**

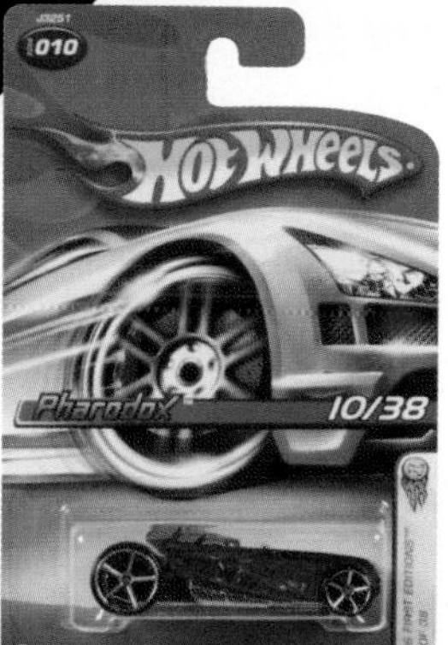

2006 First Editions 10 of 38 2006 010

- **❑ Pharodox/Clear Blue/FTE $3.00**
- ❑ Pharodox/Clear Blue/GoldOH5SP $1.50

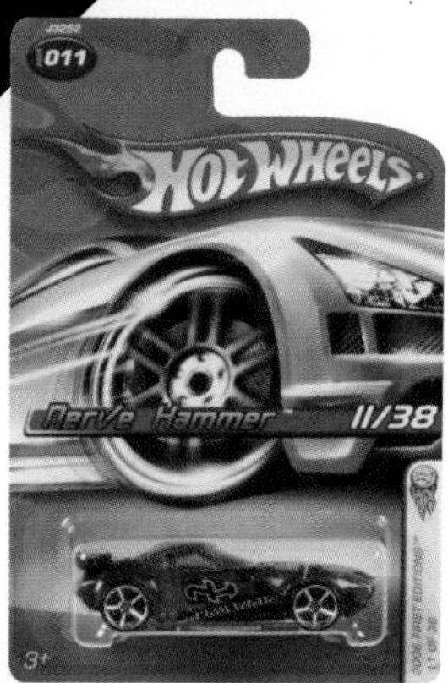

2006 First Editions 11 of 38 2006 011

- ❑ Nerve Hammer/Clear Red/FTE.................................... $3.00
- ❑ Nerve Hammer/Clear Red/OH5SP $1.50
- **❑ Nerve Hammer/Clear Red/OH5SP clear windows .. $1.50**

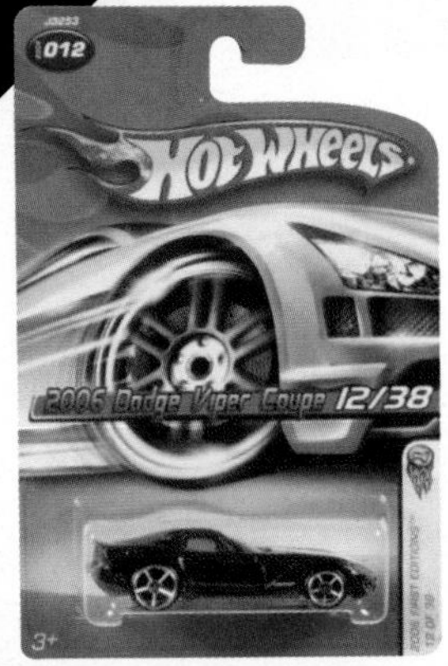

2006 FIRST EDITIONS 12 OF 38

❑ 2006 Dodge Viper Coupe/M Black/OH5SP................. $1.50

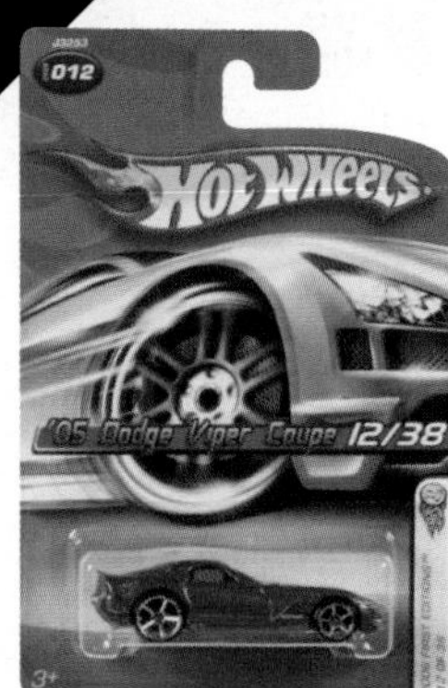

2006 FIRST EDITIONS 12 OF 38

❑ 2006 Dodge Viper Coupe/M Blue/FTE $4.00
❑ 2006 Dodge Viper Coupe/M Blue/OH5SP $1.50

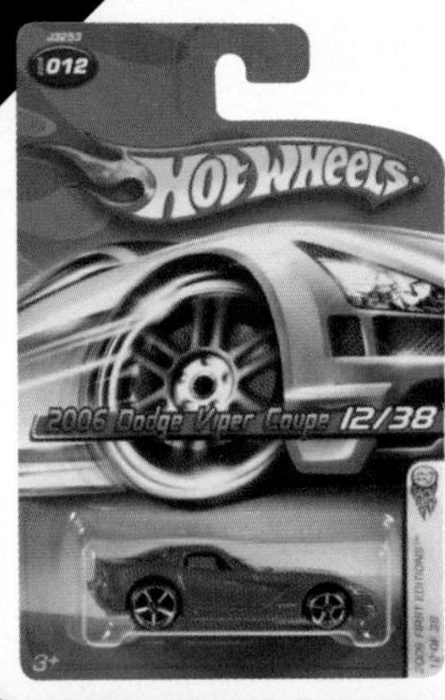

2006 FIRST EDITIONS 12 OF 38

❑ 2006 Dodge Viper Coupe/M Orange/OH5SP $1.50

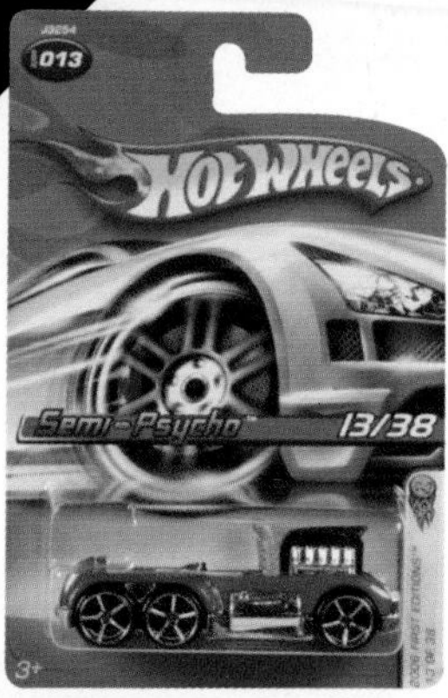

2006 First Editions 13 of 38

❑ Semi-Psycho/M Orange/OH5SP $1.50

2006 First Editions 14 of 38

❑ Chrysler Firepower Concept/M Dark Blue/10SP.......... $1.50

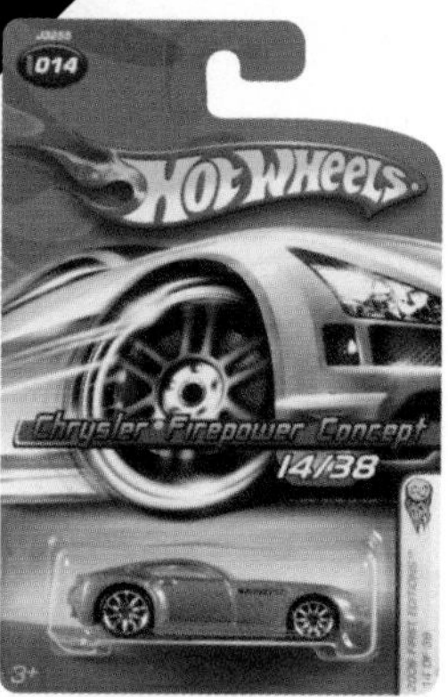

2006 First Editions 14 of 38

❑ **Chrysler Firepower Concept/M Lt.Blue/10SP $1.50**
❑ Chrysler Firepower Concept/M Lt.Blue/FTE $4.00

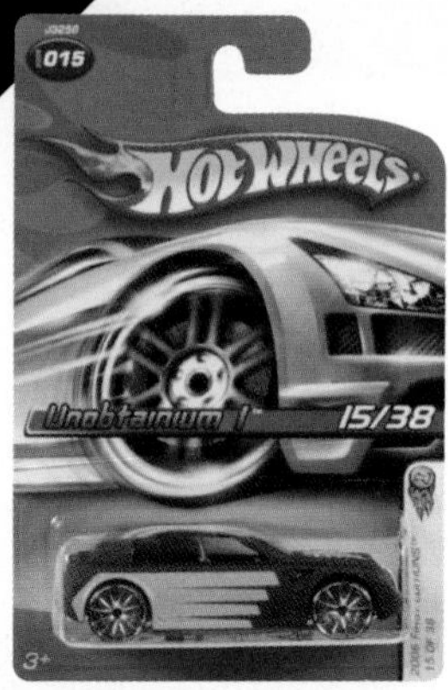

2006 First Editions 15 of 38

❑ Unobtainium 1/Flat Black/BLING $1.50

❑ **Unobtainium 1/Flat Black/BLING clear windows $3.00**

2006 First Editions 15 of 38

❑ Unobtainium 1/Pearl Pink/BLING $1.50

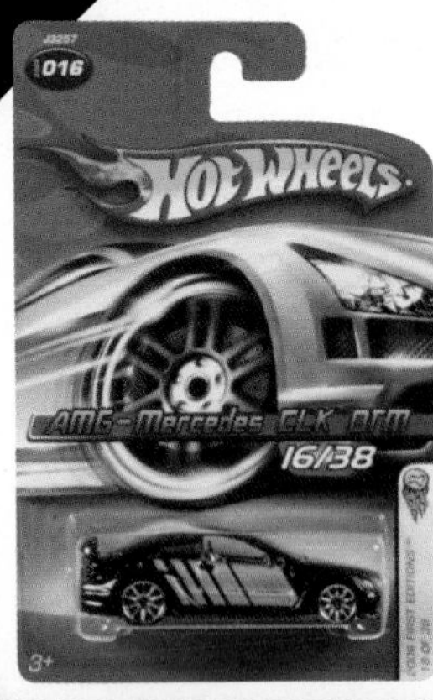

2006 First Editions 16 of 38

❑ AMG-Mercedes-Benz CLK DTM/Black/10SP $1.50

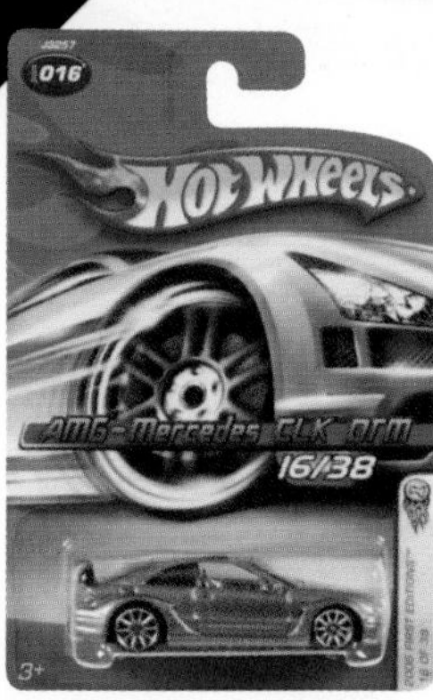

2006 First Editions 16 of 38 2006 016

- ❑ AMG-Mercedes-Benz CLK DTM/M Silver/10SP $1.50
- ❑ **AMG-Mercedes-Benz CLK DTM/M Silver/10SP w/o Tampos $1.50**
- ❑ AMG-Mercedes-Benz CLK DTM/M Silver/FTE $4.00

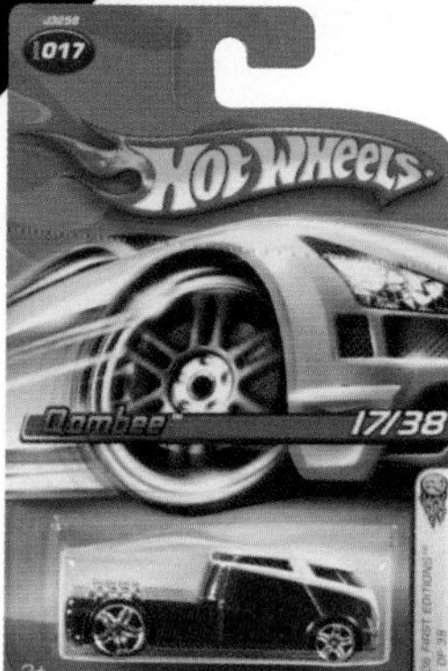

2006 First Editions 17 of 38 2006 017

- ❑ Qombee/M Blue & White/PR5...................................... $1.50

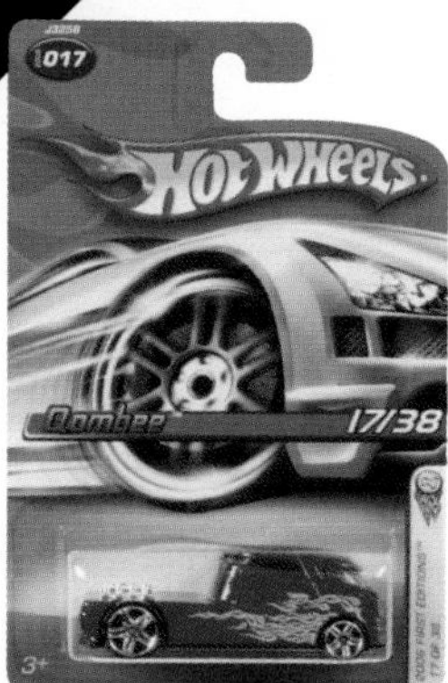

2006 First Editions 17 of 38 2006 017

- ❑ Qombee/M Dark Red/PR5 .... $1.50

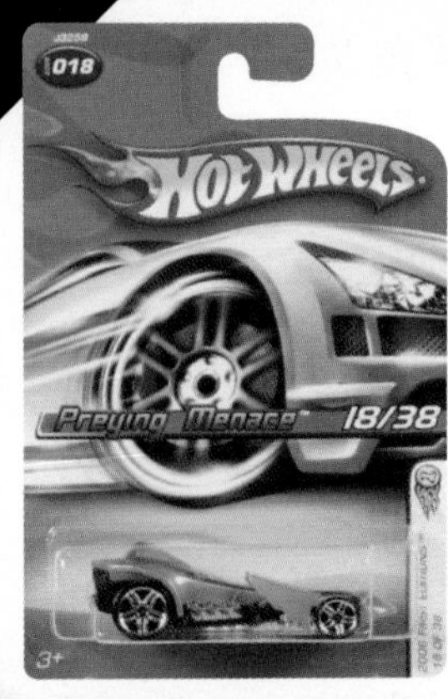

2006 First Editions 18 of 38 2006 018

- ❑ Preying Menace/Green/FTE $4.00
- ❑ Preying Menace/Green/OH5SP $10.00
- ❑ **Preying Menace/Green/PR5 .... $1.50**

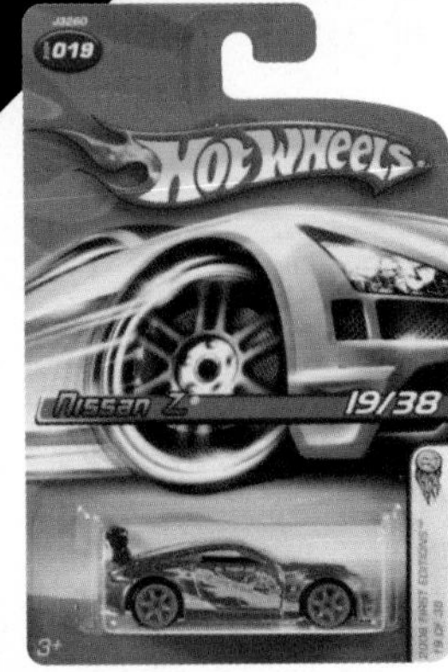

2006 First Editions 19 of 38 2006 019

- ❑ Nissan Z/Blue/OrangeCM6 .... $1.50

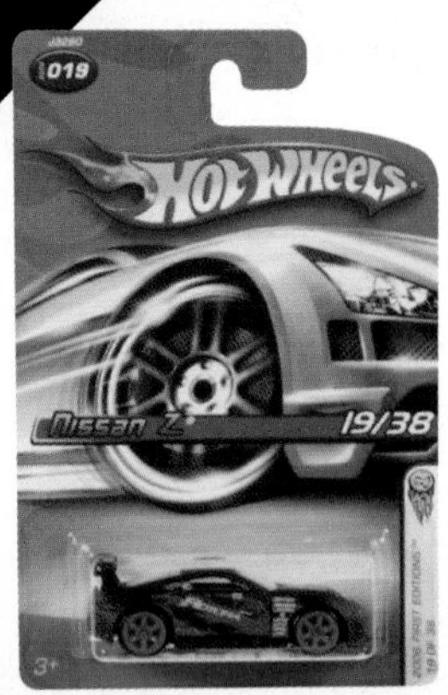

2006 First Editions 19 of 38 2006 019

- ❑ Nissan Z/Flat Black/RedCM6 .... $1.50

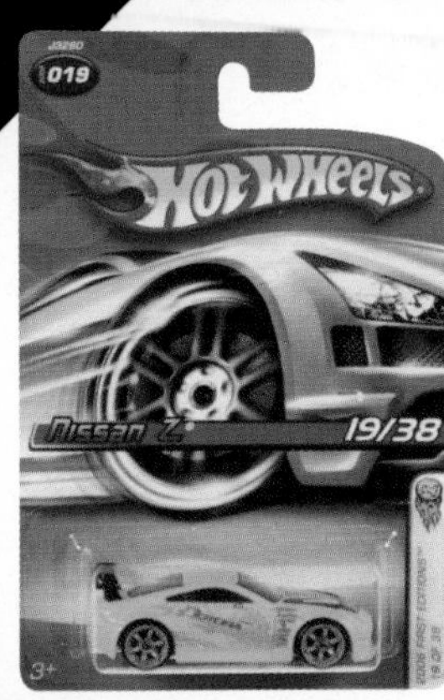

2006 First Editions 19 of 38

2006 019

- ❑ Nissan Z/M Yellow/ChromeCM6 .... $30.00
- ❑ **Nissan Z/M Yellow/CM6 .... $1.50**
- ❑ Nissan Z/M Yellow/FTE $4.00

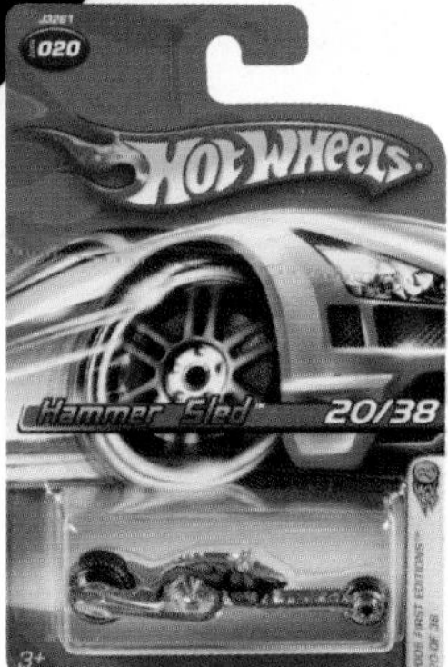

2006 First Editions 20 of 38

2006 020

- ❑ Hammer Sled/M Gold/GoldMC5 .... $1.50

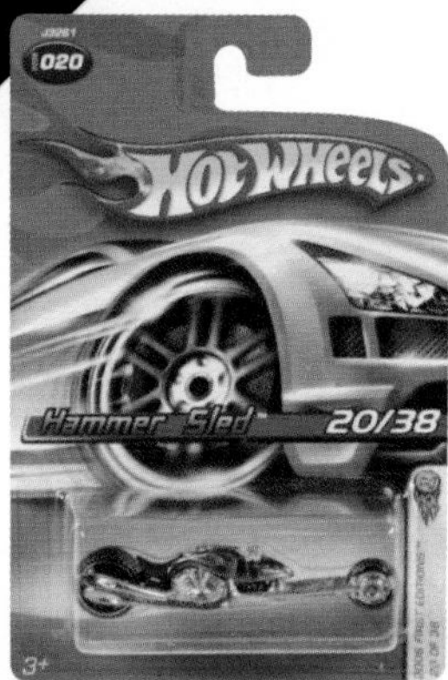

2006 First Editions 20 of 38

2006 020

- ❑ Hammer Sled/M Purple/MC3 .... $5.00
- ❑ **Hammer Sled/M Purple/MC5 .... $1.50**

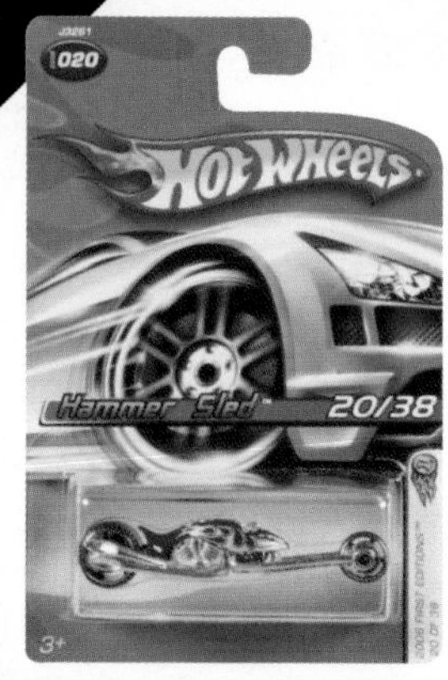

2006 First Editions 20 of 38

- ❑ Hammer Sled/Red/MC5 .... $1.50

2006 First Editions 21 of 38

2006 021

- ❑ **'69 Camaro/M Black/5SP $1.50**
- ❑ '69 Camaro/M Black/FTE $4.00
- ❑ '69 Camaro/M Black/PR5 .... $3.00

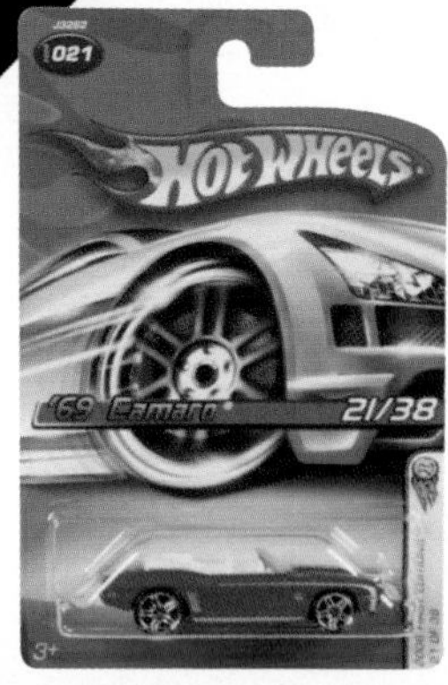

2006 First Editions 21 of 38

- ❑ '69 Camaro/M Orange/PR5 black base $3.00
- ❑ **'69 Camaro/M Orange/PR5 chrome base $1.50**

2006 First Editions 21 of 38 2006 021

- ❑ **'69 Camaro/M Purple/5SP $1.50**
- ❑ '69 Camaro/M Red/PR5 .... $4.00

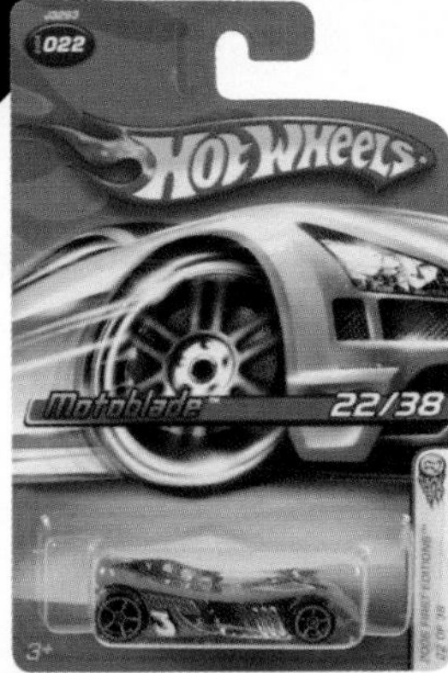

2006 First Editions 22 of 38 2006 022

- ❑ Motoblade/Clear Orange/OrangeOH5SP $1.50

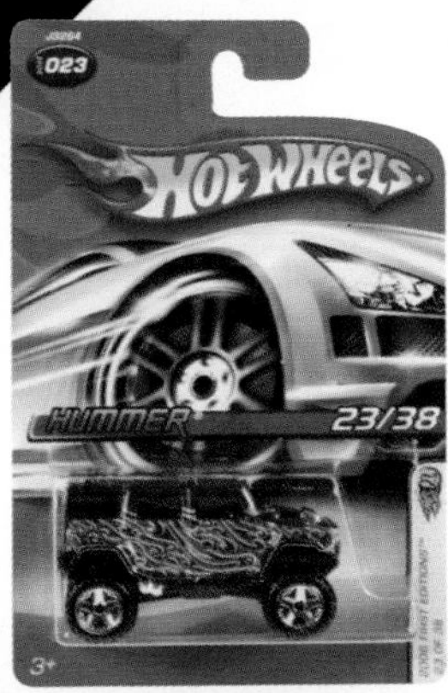

2006 First Editions 23 of 38 2006 023

- ❑ **Hummer/Dark Blue/OR5SP red on window $6.00**
- ❑ Hummer/Dark Blue/OR5SP white on window $1.50

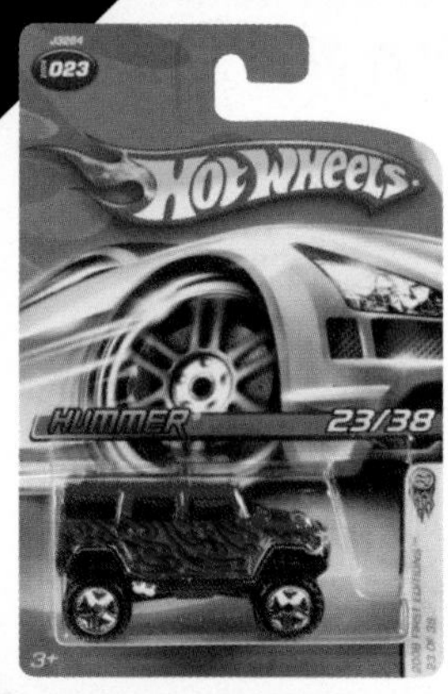

2006 First Editions 23 of 38

❑ Hummer/Dark Red/OR5SP $1.50

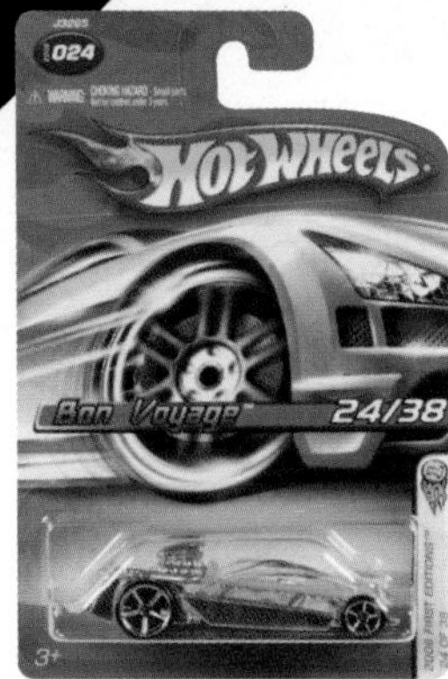

2006 First Editions 24 of 38

2006 024

❑ Bon Voyage/Lt. Brown/FTE.. $4.00
❑ Bon Voyage/Lt. Brown/OH5SP $1.50
❑ Bon Voyage/Lt. Brown/OH5SP red wood $1.50

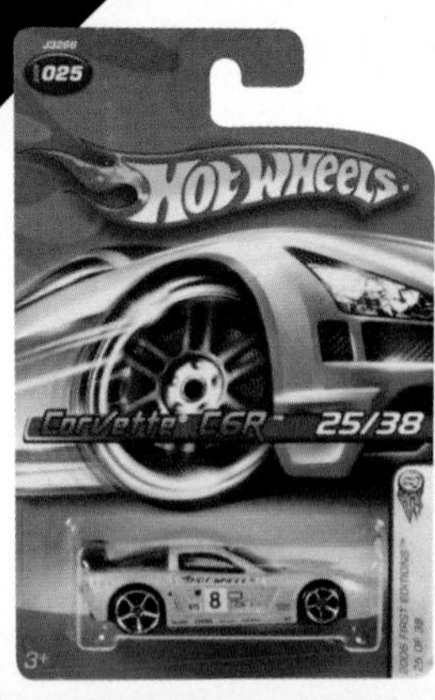

2006 First Editions 25 of 38

❑ Corvette C6R/Silver/10SP... $12.00
❑ Corvette C6R/Silver/OH5SP $1.50
❑ Corvette C6R/Silver/Y5 .... $6.00

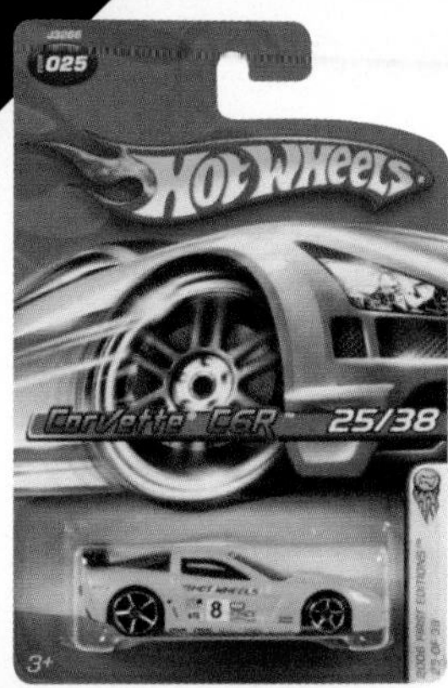

2006 FIRST EDITIONS 25 OF 38 2006 025

- ❑ Corvette C6R/Yellow/FTE $4.00
- ❑ **Corvette C6R/Yellow/OH5SP $1.50**

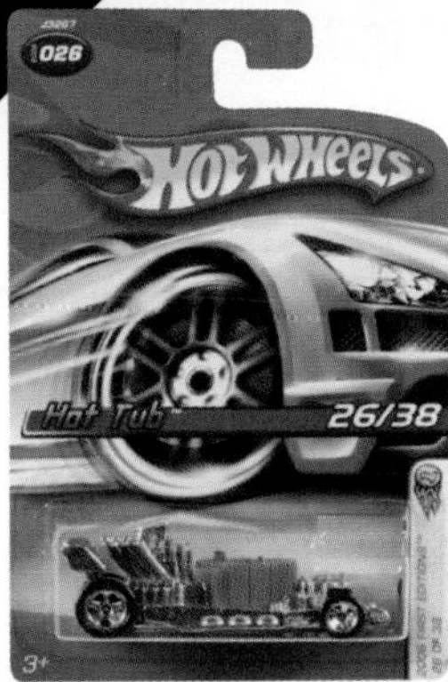

2006 FIRST EDITIONS 26 OF 38 2006 026

- ❑ **Hot Tub/Brown/5SP $1.50**
- ❑ Hot Tub/Brown/FTE.. $4.00

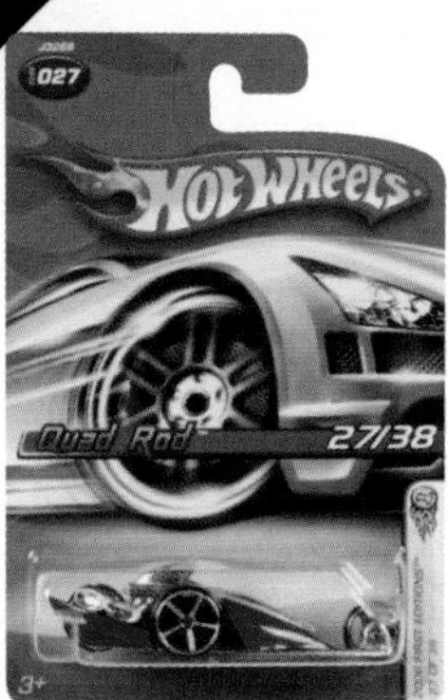

2006 FIRST EDITIONS 27 OF 38 2006 027

- ❑ Quad Rod/Dark Red/OH5SP $1.50

2006 First Editions 28 of 38

❑ Honda Civic Si/Dark Red/OH5SP $1.50

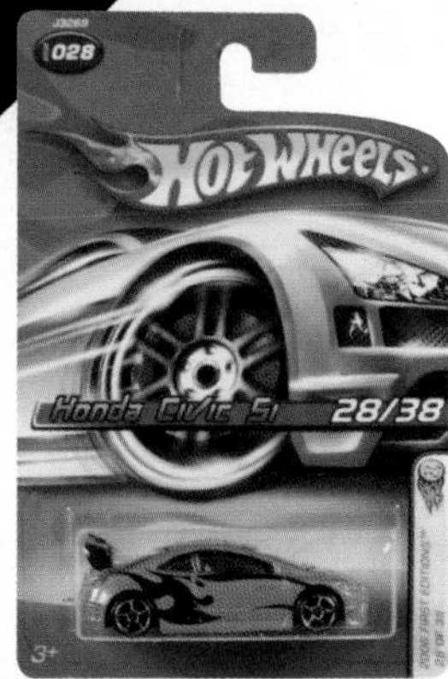

2006 First Editions 28 of 38

2006 028

❑ Honda Civic Si/M Gold/GoldO5SP Civic on front $6.00
❑ Honda Civic Si/M Gold/GoldO5SP Civic on rear $1.50

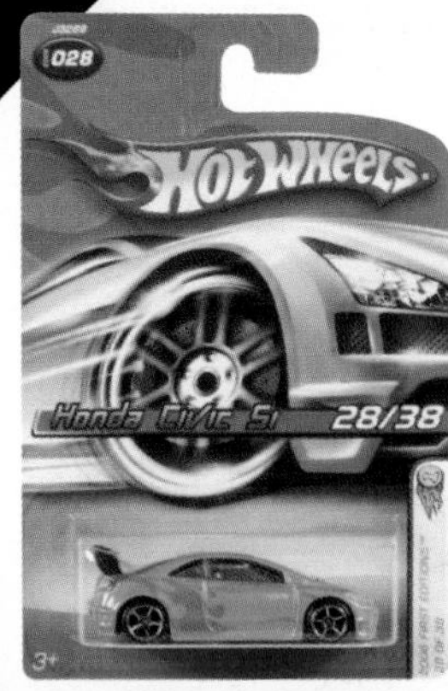

2006 First Editions 28 of 38

❑ Honda Civic Si/M Green/FTE $4.00
❑ Honda Civic Si/M Green/O5SP (Sema Edition) $25.00
❑ Honda Civic Si/M Green/OH5SP $1.50

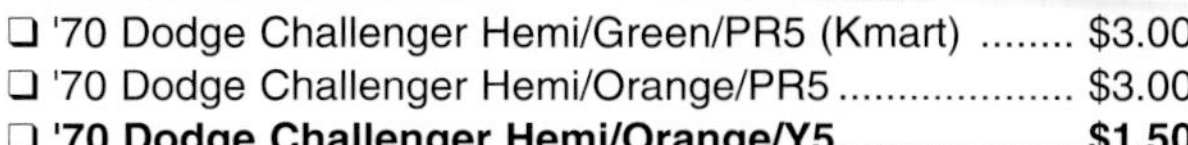

2006 First Editions 29 of 38

2006 029

- ❑ '70 Dodge Challenger Hemi/Green/PR5 (Kmart) $3.00
- ❑ '70 Dodge Challenger Hemi/Orange/PR5 .... $3.00
- **❑ '70 Dodge Challenger Hemi/Orange/Y5.................... $1.50**

2006 First Editions 29 of 38

2006 029

- ❑ '70 Dodge Challenger Hemi/Purple/FTE...................... $4.00
- **❑ '70 Dodge Challenger Hemi/Purple/PR5 .... $1.50**

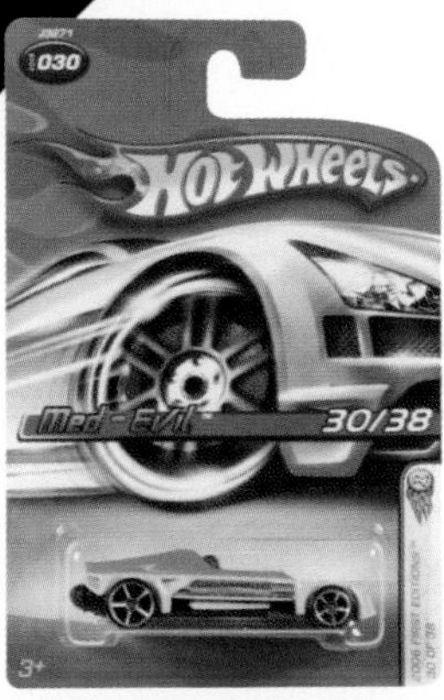

2006 First Editions 30 of 38

2006 030

- ❑ Med-Evil/Lt. Blue & Orange/FTE................................. $4.00
- **❑ Med-Evil/Lt. Blue & Orange/OH5SP.......................... $1.50**
- ❑ Med-Evil/Lt. Blue/FTE $12.00
- ❑ Med-Evil/Lt. Blue/OrangeOH5SP $1.50

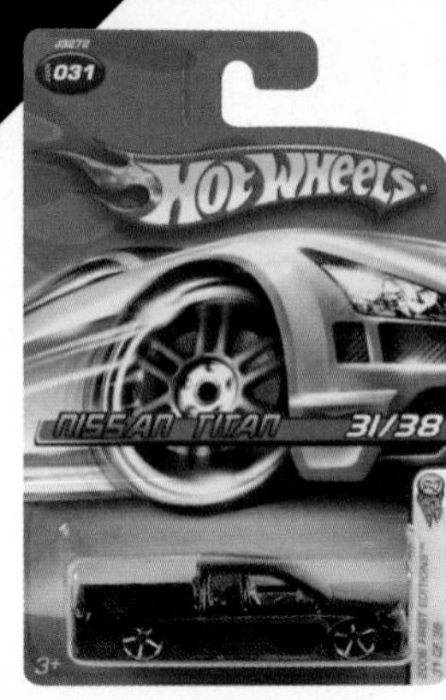

2006 First Editions 31 of 38

2006 031

- ❑ Nissan Titan/Black/5DOT $3.00
- ❑ Nissan Titan/Black/OH5SP $6.00
- ❑ **Nissan Titan/Black/Y5 .... $1.50**

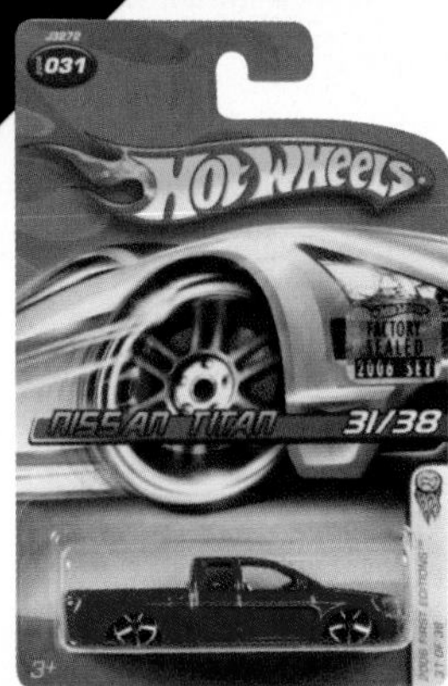

2006 First Editions 31 of 38

2006 031

- ❑ **Nissan Titan/Dark Red/OH5SP $1.50**
- ❑ Nissan Titan/Dark Red/OH5SP KMC $10.00
- ❑ Nissan Titan/Dark Red/Y5.. $3.00

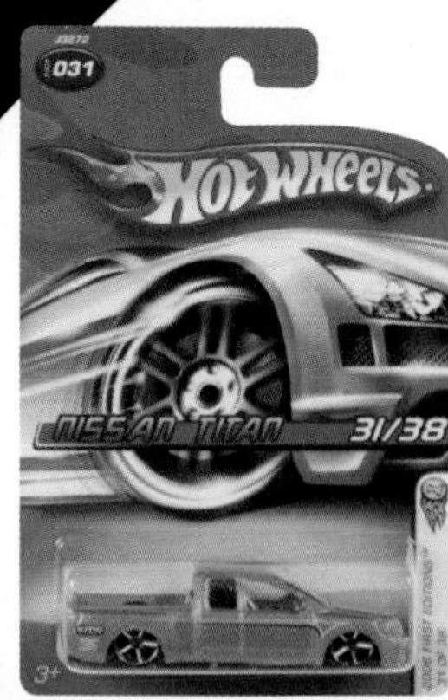

2006 First Editions 31 of 38

2006 031

- ❑ Nissan Titan/Grey/FTE $4.00
- ❑ **Nissan Titan/Grey/O5SP $1.50**
- ❑ Nissan Titan/Grey/PR5 .... $25.00

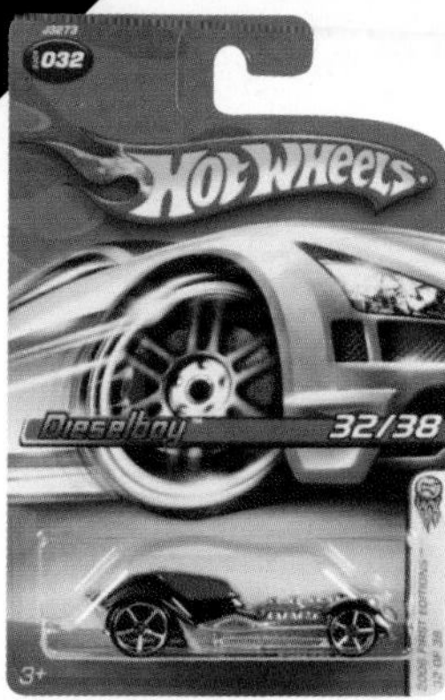

2008 FIRST EDITIONS 32 OF 38

2006 032

❑ **Dieselboy/Black/OH5SP $1.50**
❑ Dieselboy/Black/OH5SP black DIESELBOY................ $3.00
❑ Dieselboy/Black/RedOH5SP $6.00

2006 FIRST EDITIONS 33 OF 38

2006 033

❑ Ferrari F430 Spider/Black/PR5 black Interior $20.00
❑ **Ferrari F430 Spider/Black/PR5 tan Interior.............. $1.50**

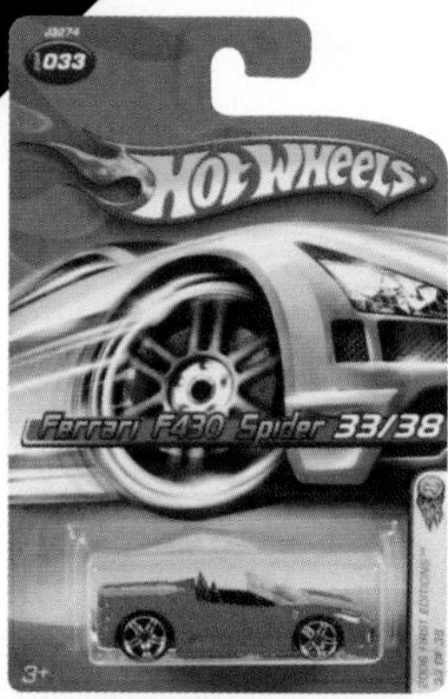

2006 FIRST EDITIONS 33 OF 38

2006 033

❑ Ferrari F430 Spider/Red/FTE $4.00
❑ **Ferrari F430 Spider/Red/PR5 .... $1.50**

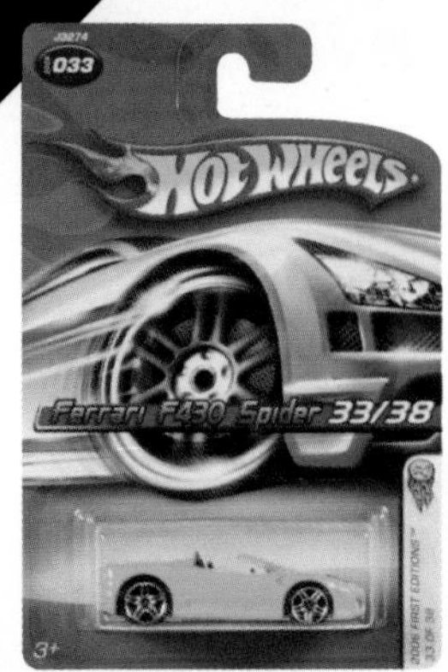

2006 FIRST EDITIONS 33 OF 38

❑ Ferrari F430 Spider/Yellow/PR5 .... $1.50

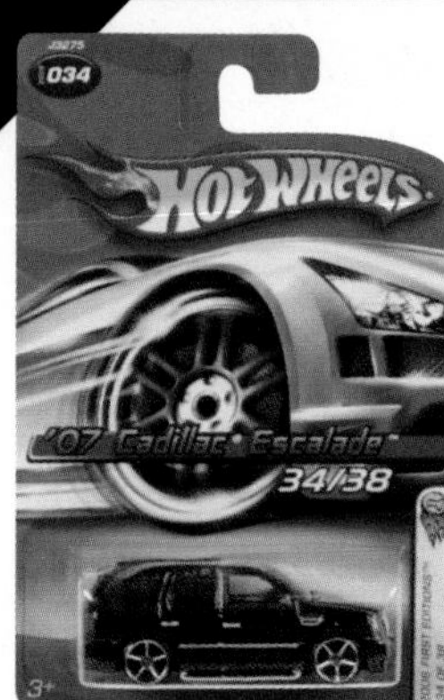

2006 FIRST EDITIONS 34 OF 38

❑ '07 Cadillac Escalade/Black/FTE $4.00
❑ **'07 Cadillac Escalade/Black/OH5SP $1.50**
❑ '07 Cadillac Escalade/Black/Y5.................................... $1.50

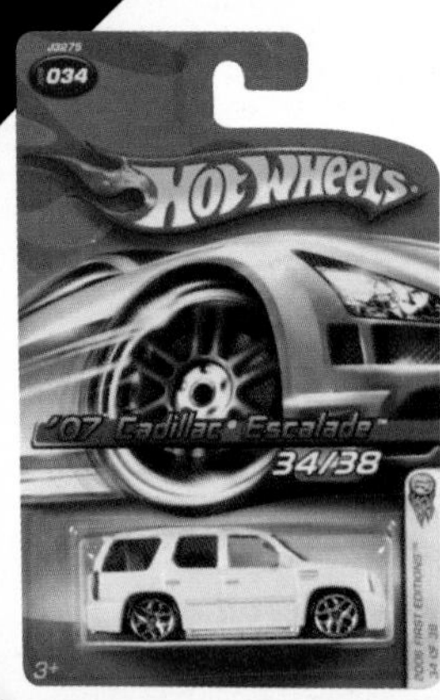

2006 FIRST EDITIONS 34 OF 38

❑ '07 Cadillac Escalade/Pearl White/5DOT $1.50
❑ **'07 Cadillac Escalade/Pearl White/Y5 .... $1.50**

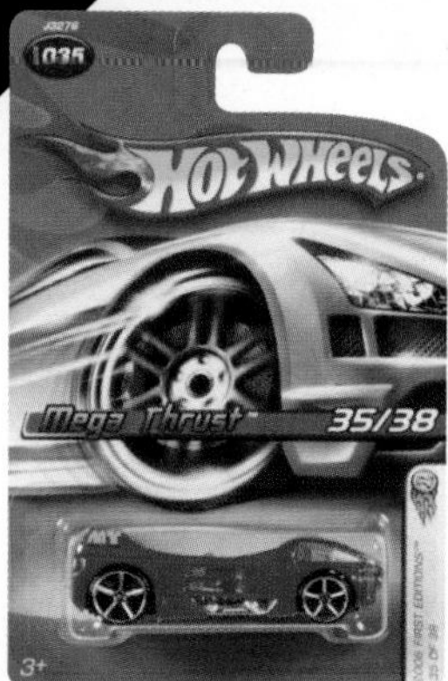

2006 First Editions 35 of 38 2006 035

- ❑ Mega Thrust/M Orange/FTE $4.00
- **❑ Mega Thrust/M Orange/OH5SP $1.50**

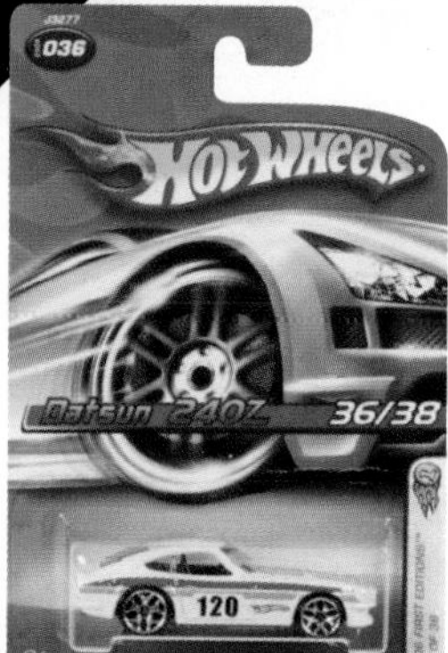

2006 First Editions 36 of 38 2006 036

- ❑ Datsun 240Z/M Grey/10SP (Kmart) $3.00
- ❑ Datsun 240Z/Pearl White/10SP $40.00
- ❑ Datsun 240Z/Pearl White/FTE $25.00
- **❑ Datsun 240Z/Pearl White/Y5 .... $1.50**

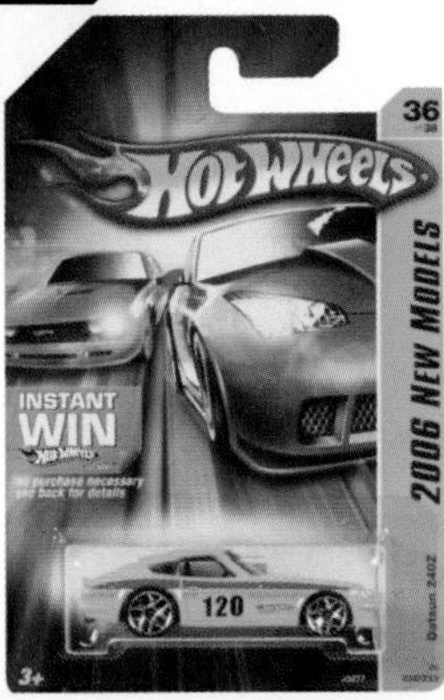

2006 First Editions 36 of 38 2006 036

- ❑ Datsun 240Z/Yellow/10SP.. $1.50
- **❑ Datsun 240Z/Yellow/Y5 .... $1.50**

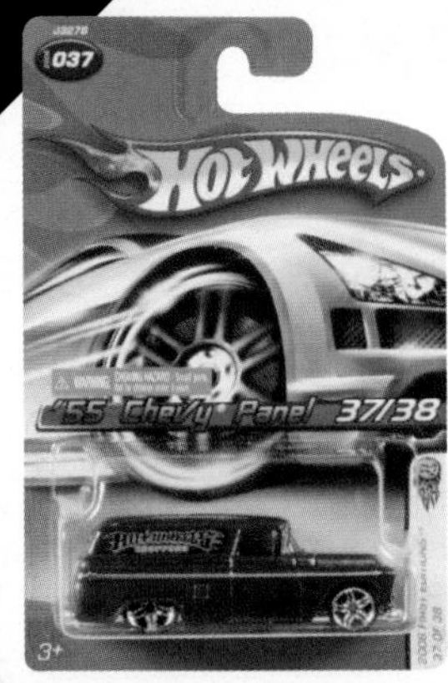

2006 FIRST EDITIONS 37 OF 38

- ❑ **'55 Chevy Panel/M Dark Blue/PR5 .... $25.00**
- ❑ '55 Chevy Panel/M Dark Blue/PR5 black grill $40.00

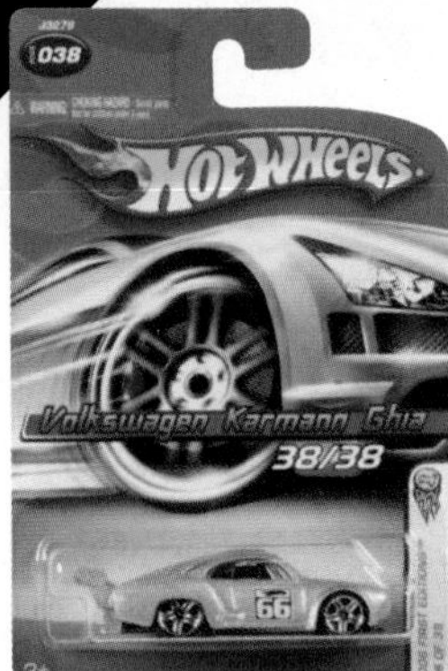

2006 FIRST EDITIONS 38 OF 38

- ❑ Volkswagen Karmann Ghia/M Grey/PR5 .... $12.00

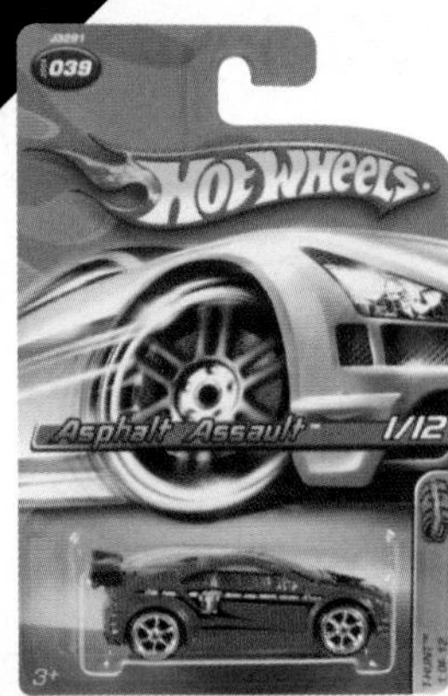

TREASURE HUNT 1 OF 12

- ❑ Asphalt Assault/Red/Bling6SP black base $30.00
- ❑ **Asphalt Assault/Red/Bling6SP chrome base $15.00**

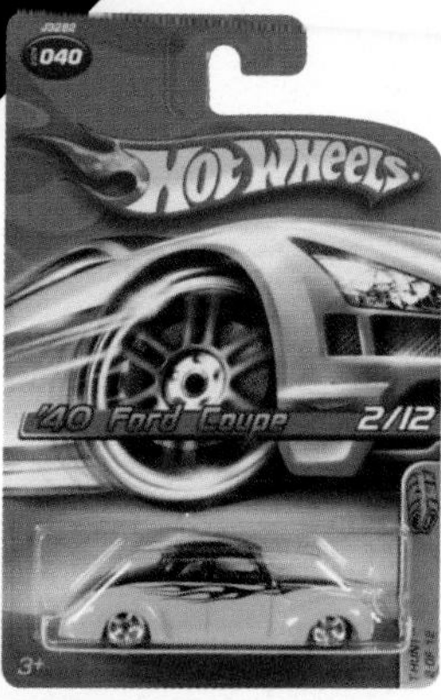

TREASURE HUNT 2 OF 12

2006 040

❑ '40 Ford Coupe/Black & Yellow/RR5SP $25.00

TREASURE HUNT 3 OF 12

2006 041

❑ Sooo Fast/Spectraflame Copper/RLRR5SP $30.00

TREASURE HUNT 4 OF 12

2006 042

❑ Custom '59 Cadillac/Blue/WWRRBNG black interior.... $200.00

❑ Custom '59 Cadillac/Blue/WWRRBNG white interior $20.00

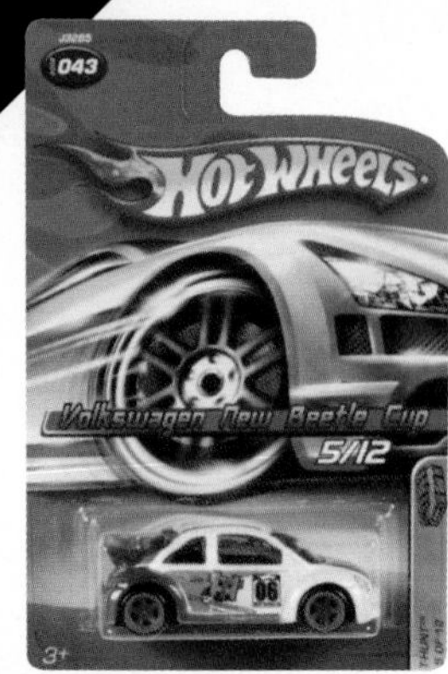

TREASURE HUNT 5 OF 12

❑ Volkswagen New Beetle Cup/Pearl White & Blue/OrangeRR5SP $25.00

TREASURE HUNT 6 OF 12

2006 044

❑ '67 Mustang/Pearl White/RR5SP $25.00

TREASURE HUNT 7 OF 12

2006 045

❑ 1969 Dodge Charger/Orange/RR $30.00

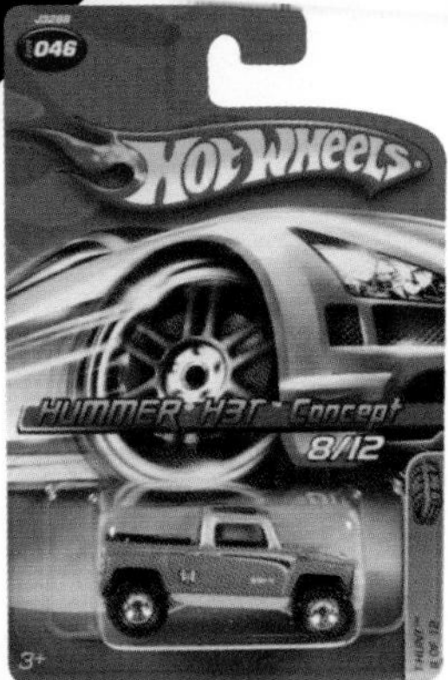

Treasure Hunt 8 of 12

❑ Hummer H3T/Gold & Silver/ORRR $10.00

Treasure Hunt 9 of 12

2006 047

❑ CUL8R/Spectraflame Green/CM6 .... $15.00

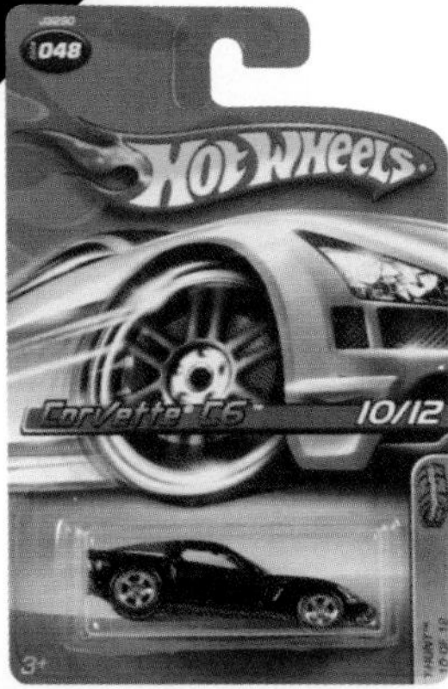

Treasure Hunt 10 of 12

❑ C6 Corvette/Black/GoldRR5SP $20.00

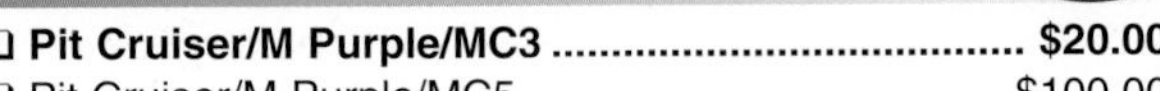

Treasure Hunt 11 of 12

2006 049

- ❑ **Pit Cruiser/M Purple/MC3 .... $20.00**
- ❑ Pit Cruiser/M Purple/MC5 .... $100.00

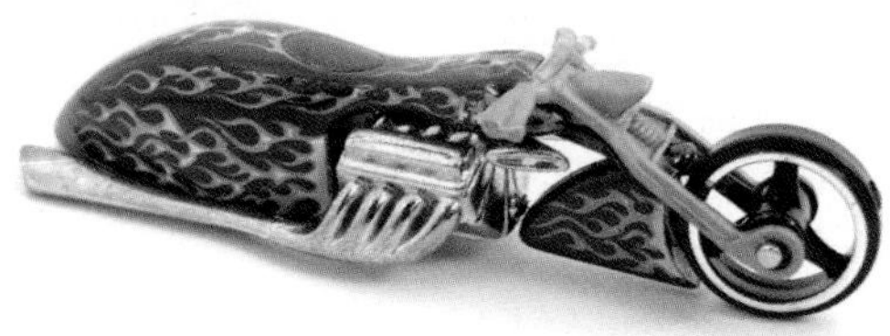

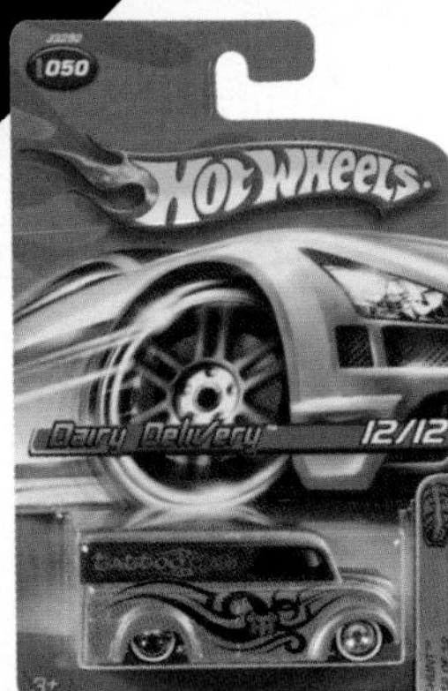

Treasure Hunt 12 of 12

2006 050

- ❑ Dairy Delivery/M Olive Green/GoldWLRR $40.00

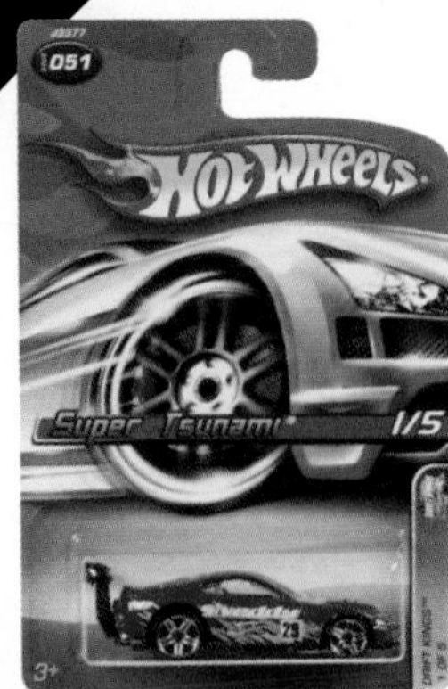

Drift Kings 1 of 5

2006 051

- ❑ Super Tsunami/Dark Red/GoldPR5.............................. $1.50

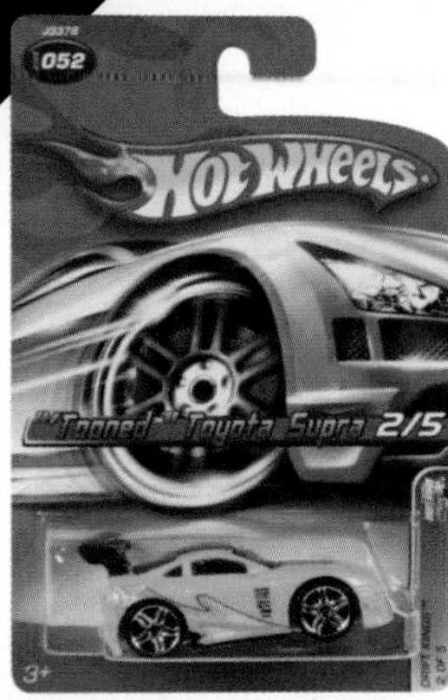

DRIFT KINGS 2 OF 5

- ❑ **'Tooned Toyota Supra/M Yellow/PR5 black hood $1.50**
- ❑ 'Tooned Toyota Supra/M Yellow/PR5 black roof $1.50

DRIFT KINGS 3 OF 5

- ❑ 24/Seven/Green/PR5 .... $1.50

DRIFT KINGS 3 OF 5

- ❑ 24/Seven/Red/PR5 .... $1.50

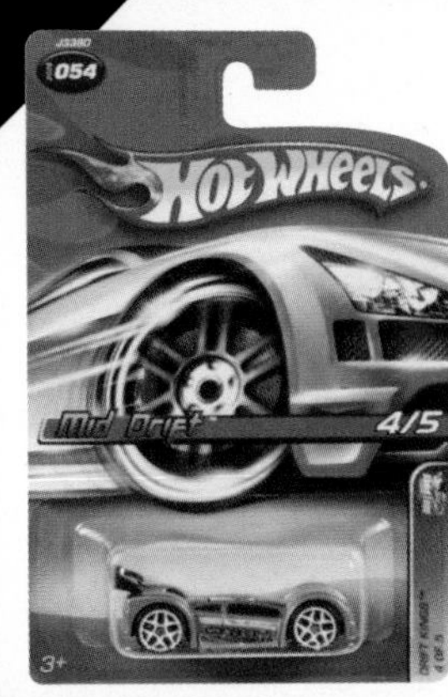

Drift Kings 4 of 5 — 2006 054

- ❑ Mid Drift/M Blue/10SP $40.00
- ❑ Mid Drift/M Blue/White10SP $40.00
- ❑ **Mid Drift/M Blue/WhiteY5 .... $1.50**

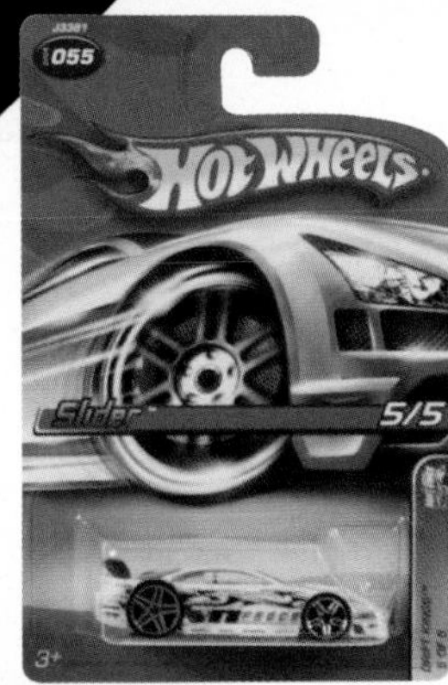

Drift Kings 5 of 5 — 2006 055

- ❑ Slider/Pearl White/OrangePR5 .... $1.50

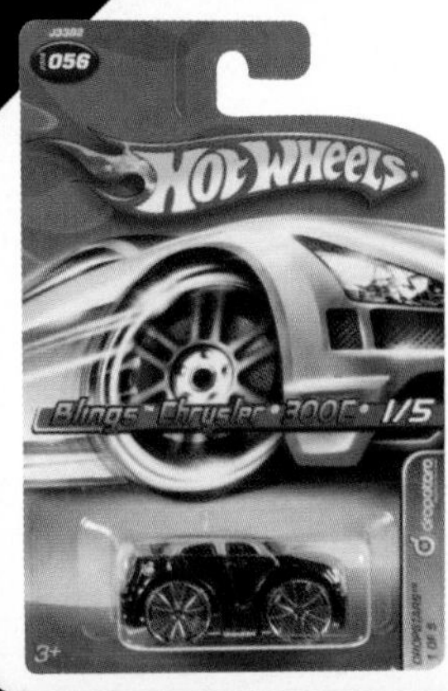

Dropstars 1 of 5 — 2006 056

- ❑ **Chrysler 300C/M Blue & Champagne/BLING $1.50**
- ❑ Chrysler 300C/M Blue & Champagne/FTE (Toys R Us Starter) $12.00

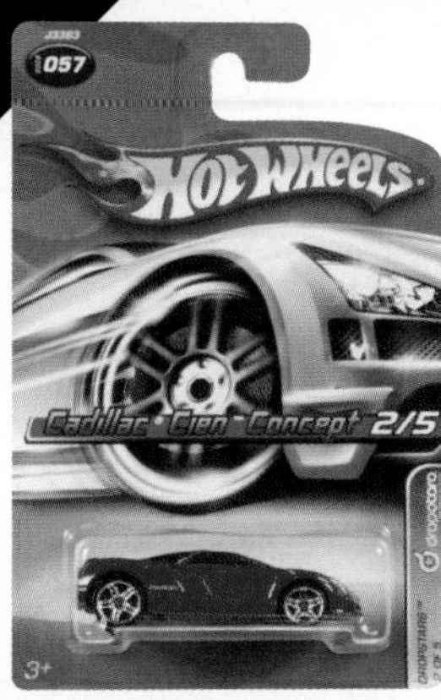

DROPSTARS 2 OF 5

2006 057

- ❑ Cadillac Cien/Dark M Red/FTE $4.00
- ❑ Cadillac Cien/Dark M Red/OH5SP $12.00
- **❑ Cadillac Cien/Dark M Red/PR5 .... $1.50**

DROPSTARS 3 OF 5

2006 058

- ❑ Mercedes-Benz G500/M Orange & Black/BLING $1.50

DROPSTARS 4 OF 5

2006 059

- ❑ 1964 Impala/Grey & Black/WSP $1.50

DROPSTARS 4 OF 5

❑ 1964 Impala/M Orange & Black/10SP $1.50

DROPSTARS 5 OF 5

❑ Nissan Skyline/M Dark Blue/10SP $25.00
❑ Nissan Skyline/M Dark Blue/O5SP $1.50

DROPSTARS 5 OF 5

❑ Nissan Skyline/M Grey/OH5SP.................................... $1.50

DROPSTARS 5 OF 5

❑ Nissan Skyline/M Teal/O5SP.. $1.50

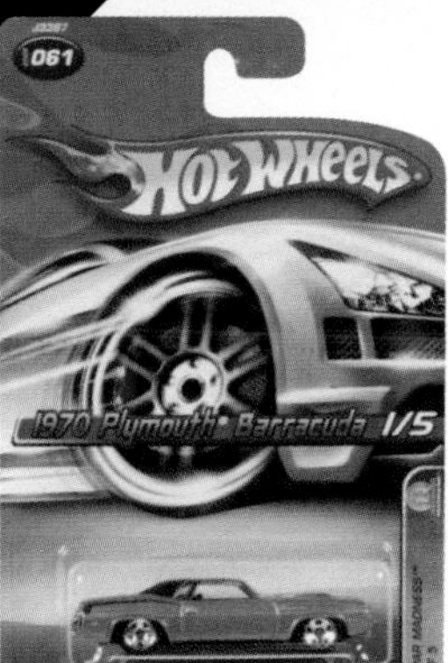

MOPAR MADNESS 1 OF 5

❑ 1970 Plymouth Barracuda/M Blue/5SP........................ $1.50

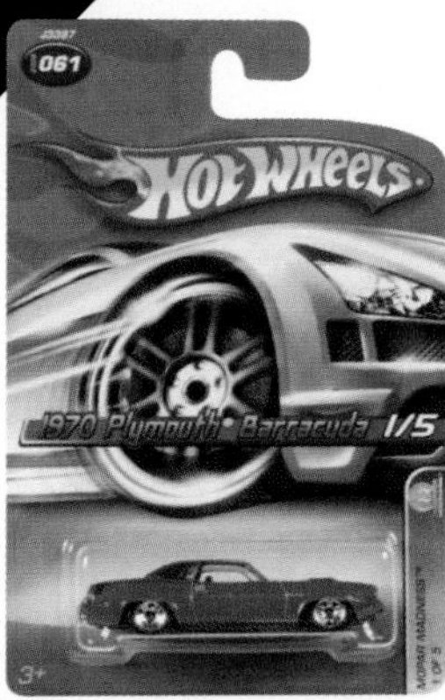

MOPAR MADNESS 1 OF 5

❑ 1970 Plymouth Barracuda/M Dark Orange/5SP $1.50
❑ 1970 Plymouth Barracuda/Pearl Yellow/5SP (Kmart) .. $1.50
❑ 1970 Plymouth Barracuda/Pearl Yellow/7SP (Kmart) $80.00

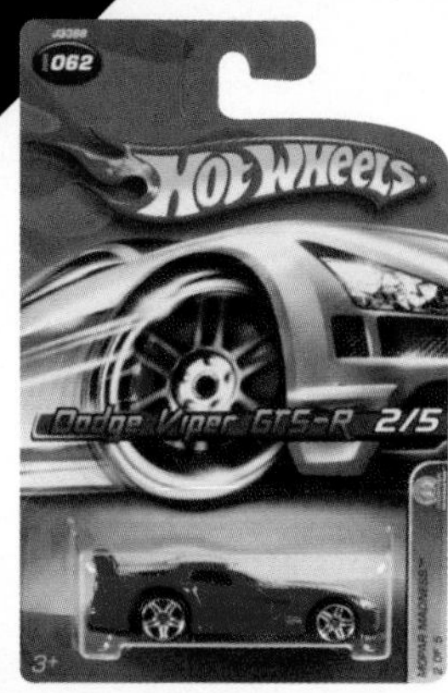

Mopar Madness 2 of 5

❑ Dodge Viper GTS-R/Dark Red/PR5 .... $1.50

Mopar Madness 2 of 5

❑ Dodge Viper GTS-R/M Black/PR5 .... $1.50

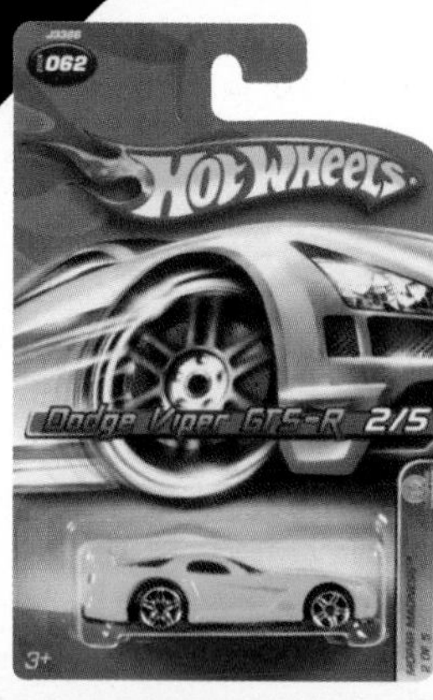

Mopar Madness 2 of 5

❑ Dodge Viper GTS-R/M Yellow/PR5 red interior $10.00

❑ **Dodge Viper GTS-R/M Yellow/PR5 yellow interior .. $1.50**

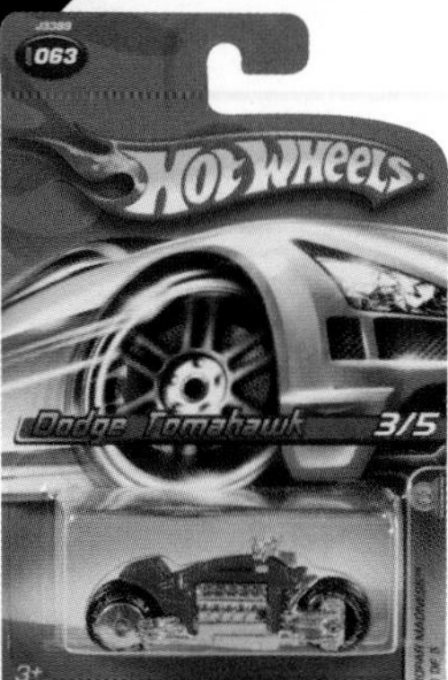

Mopar Madness 3 of 5

2006 063

❑ Dodge Tomahawk/Red/TMHK $1.50

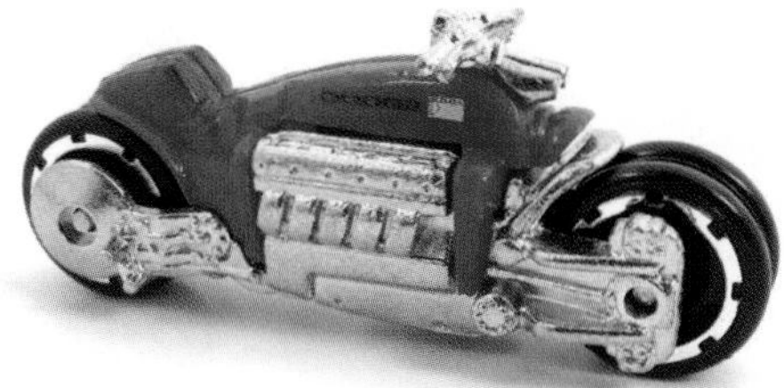

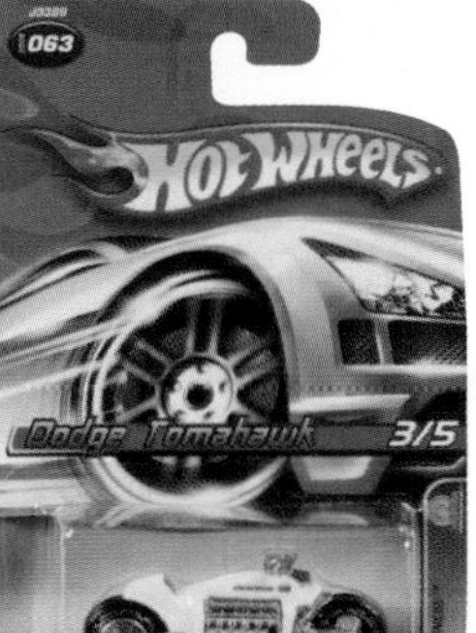

Mopar Madness 3 of 5

2006 063

❑ Dodge Tomahawk/White/TMHK $1.50

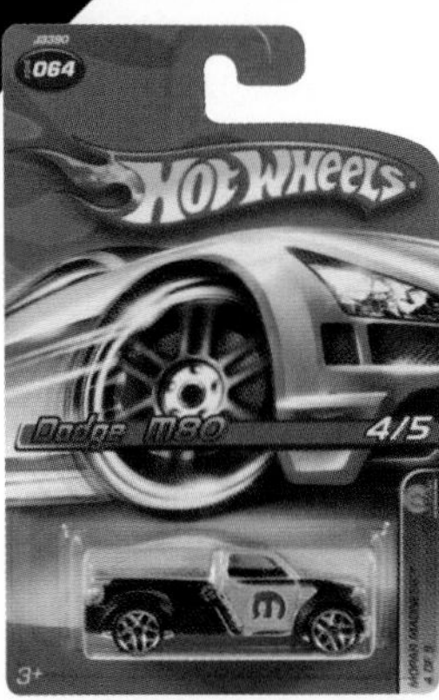

Mopar Madness 4 of 5

2006 064

❑ Dodge M80/M Silver/FTE $4.00
❑ **Dodge M80/M Silver/Y5 .... $1.50**

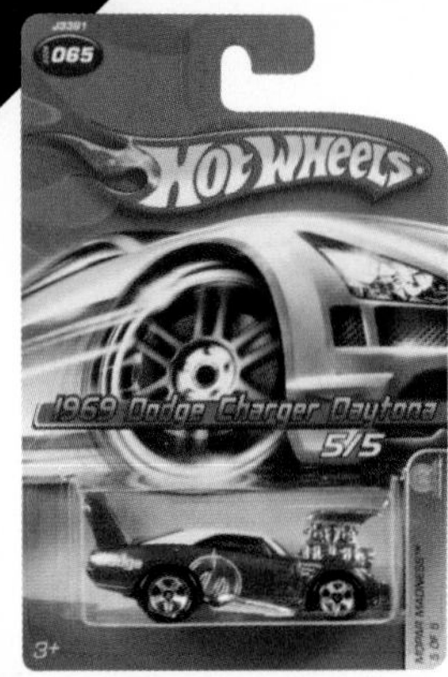

Mopar Madness 5 of 5

- ❑ 1969 Dodge Charger Daytona/Dark Blue/5SP $1.50

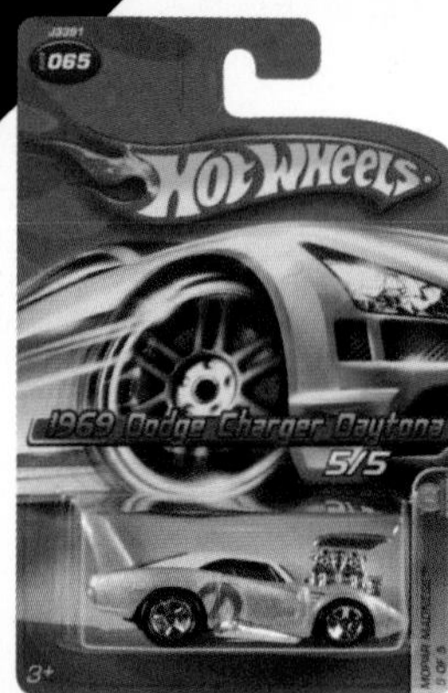

Mopar Madness 5 of 5

- ❑ 1969 Dodge Charger Daytona/Lt. Blue/5SP $1.50

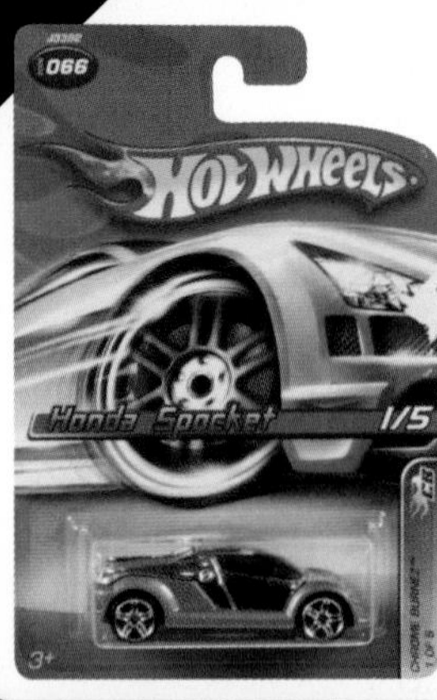

Chrome Burnerz 1 of 5

- ❑ Honda Spocket/Chrome/FTE $4.00
- ❑ **Honda Spocket/Chrome/PR5 .... $1.50**

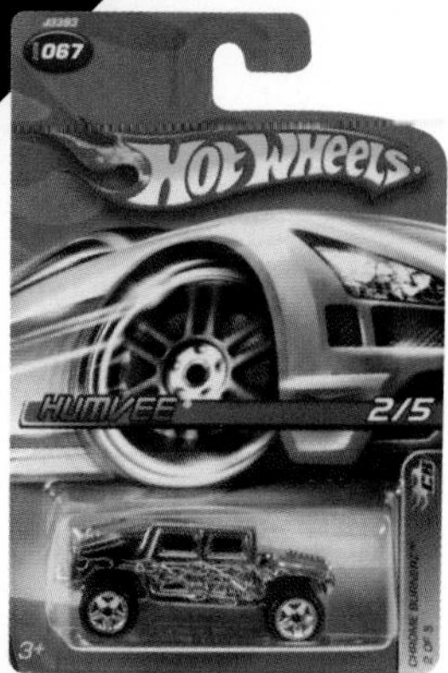

Chrome Burnerz 2 of 5

❑ Humvee/Chrome/OR5SP black & white flames $1.50

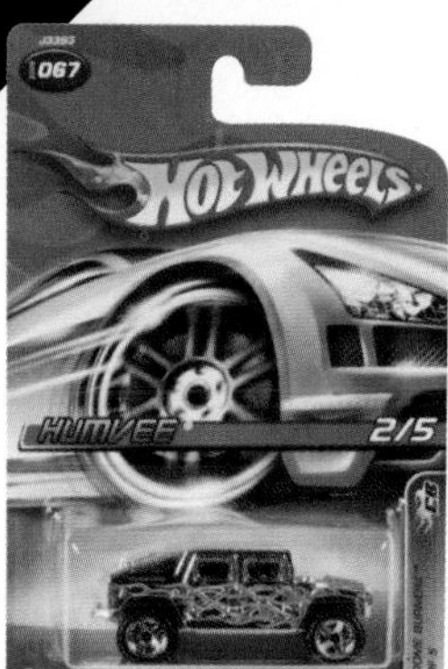

Chrome Burnerz 2 of 5

❑ Humvee/Chrome/OR5SP green & yellow flames $1.50

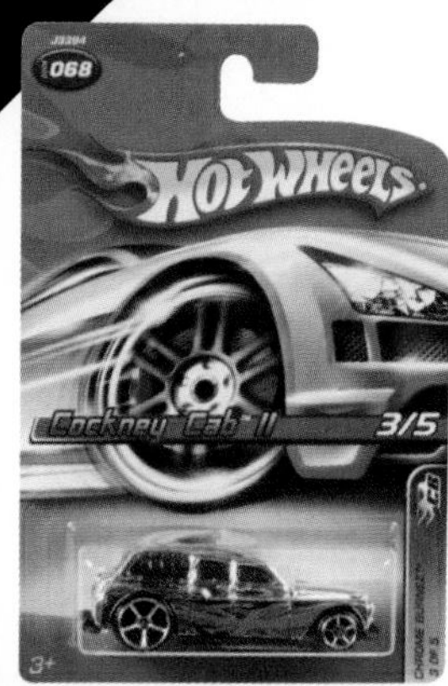

Chrome Burnerz 3 of 5

❑ **Cockney Cab II/Chrome/OH5SP larger rear wheel.. $1.50**
❑ Cockney Cab II/Chrome/OH5SP larger rear wheel black windows $1.50
❑ Cockney Cab II/Chrome/OH5SP smaller rear wheel .. $3.00

CHROME BURNERZ 4 OF 5

❑ What-4-2/Chrome/PR5 blue flames $1.50

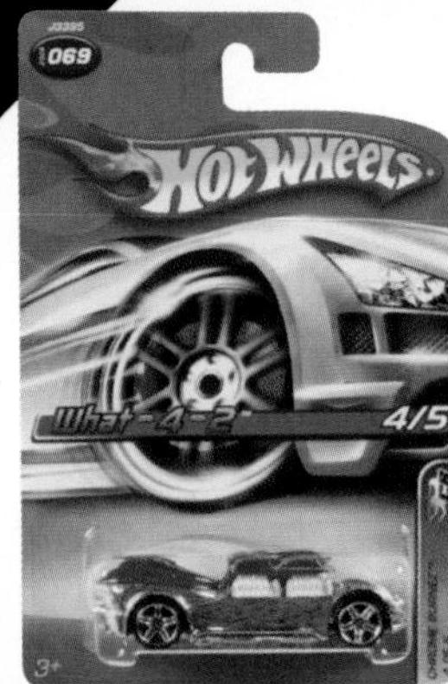

CHROME BURNERZ 4 OF 5

❑ What-4-2/Chrome/PR5 red flames chrome engine...... $1.50
❑ What-4-2/Chrome/PR5 red flames silver engine $1.50

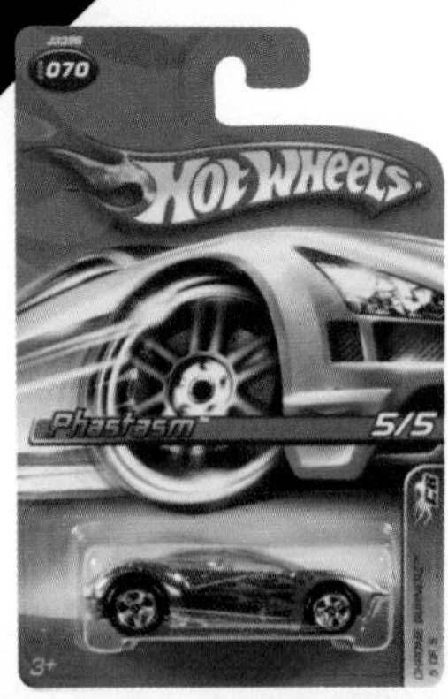

CHROME BURNERZ 5 OF 5

❑ Phastasm/Chrome/5SP black interior $12.00
❑ Phastasm/Chrome/5SP grey interior........................ $1.50

TAG RIDES 1 OF 5

❑ Dairy Delivery/Red/5SP.. $1.50

TAG RIDES 2 OF 5

2006 072

❑ 1964 Lincoln Continental/Green/WSP $1.50

TAG RIDES 3 OF 5

❑ Quadra-Sound/Purple/BLING $1.50

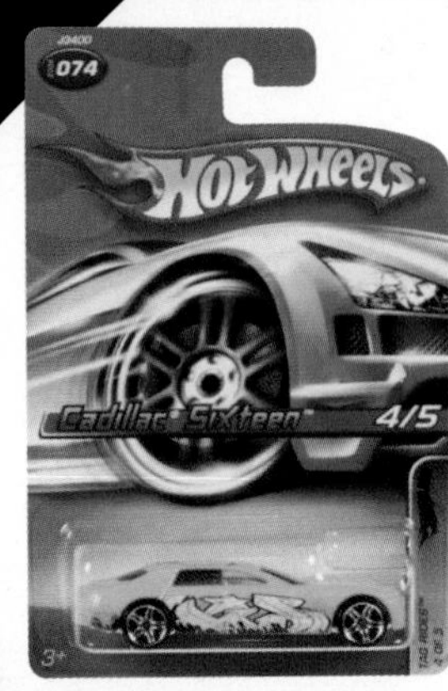

Tag Rides 4 of 5

2006 074

❑ Cadillac Sixteen/Yellow/PR5 .... $1.50

Tag Rides 5 of 5

❑ Hiway Hauler/M Silver/PR5.. $3.00

Spy Force 1 of 5

❑ Boom Box/Black/PR5 .... $1.50

Spy Force 2 of 5

❑ Jaguar XK8/M Dark Green/PR5 .... $1.50

Spy Force 3 of 5

❑ 2001 B Engineering Edonis/Dark Blue/WhitePR5 ...... $1.50

Spy Force 4 of 5

❑ **Combat Ambulance/M Blue-Grey/5SP...................... $1.50**
❑ Combat Ambulance/M Blue-Grey/White5SP................ $1.50

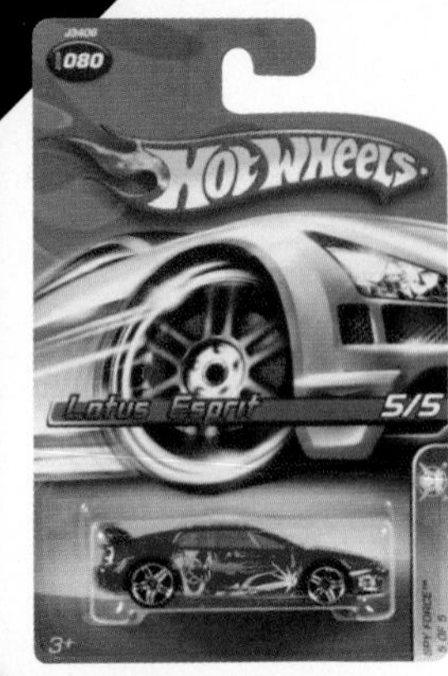

Spy Force 5 of 5

2006 080

- ❑ Lotus Espirit/M Dark Red/FTE $4.00
- **❑ Lotus Espirit/M Dark Red/GoldPR5 .... $1.50**

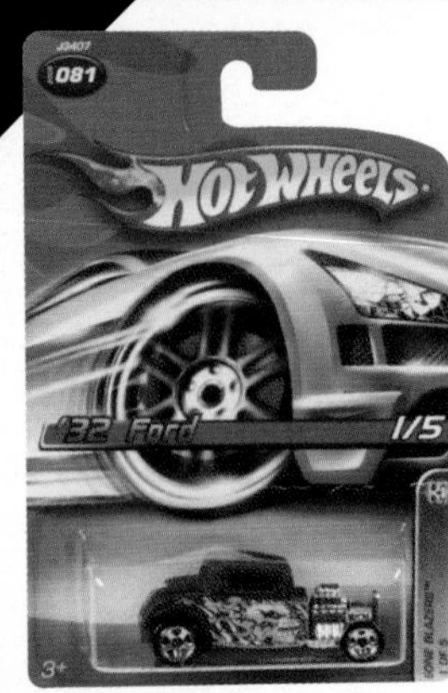

Bone Blazers 1 of 5

2006 081

- ❑ '32 Ford/Flat Black/5SP.. $1.50

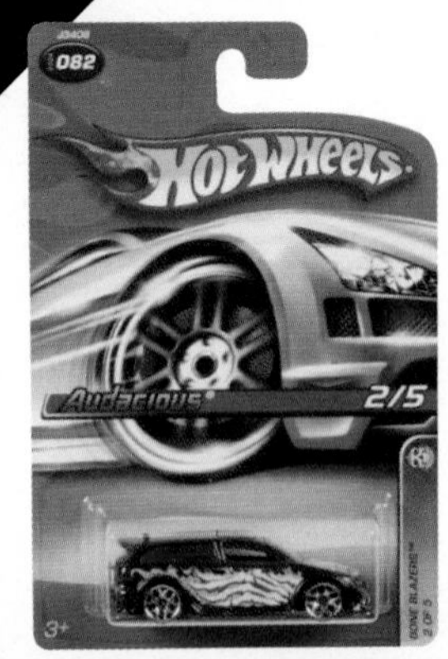

Bone Blazers 2 of 5

2006 082

- ❑ Audacious/Black/FTE $4.00
- **❑ Audacious/Black/GoldY5 .... $1.50**

BONE BLAZERS 3 OF 5

2006 083

- ❑ '57 Chevy Bel Air/M Grey/Red3SP $50.00
- ❑ **'57 Chevy Bel Air/M Grey/Red5SP $1.50**
- ❑ '57 Chevy Bel Air/M Grey/Red5SP HO $1.50

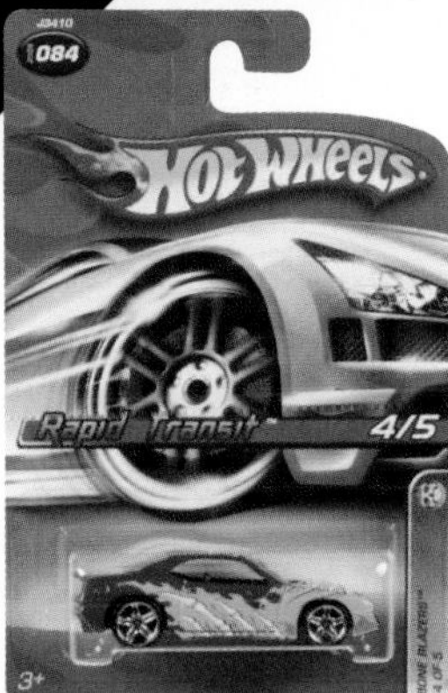

BONE BLAZERS 4 OF 5

2006 084

- ❑ Rapid Transit/M Red/PR5 .... $1.50

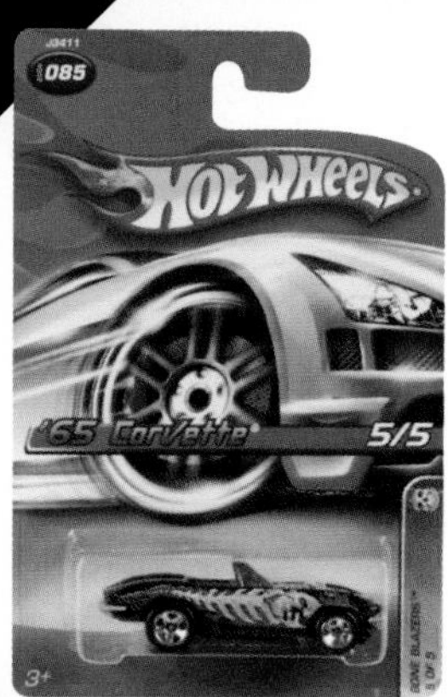

BONE BLAZERS 5 OF 5

2006 085

- ❑ '65 Corvette/Black/5SP $1.50
- ❑ '65 Corvette/Black/RL5SP $60.00
- ❑ **'65 Corvette/Black/Y5 .... $1.50**

Bone Blazers 5 of 5

2006 085

❑ '65 Corvette/M Purple/Gold5SP $1.50

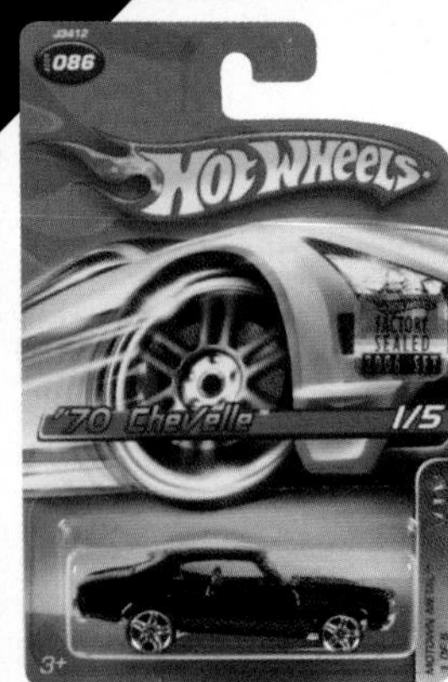

Motown Metal 1 of 5

2006 086

❑ 1970 Chevelle SS/Black/5SP $6.00
❑ 1970 Chevelle SS/Black/PR5 black interior $80.00
❑ **1970 Chevelle SS/Black/PR5 red interior $5.00**

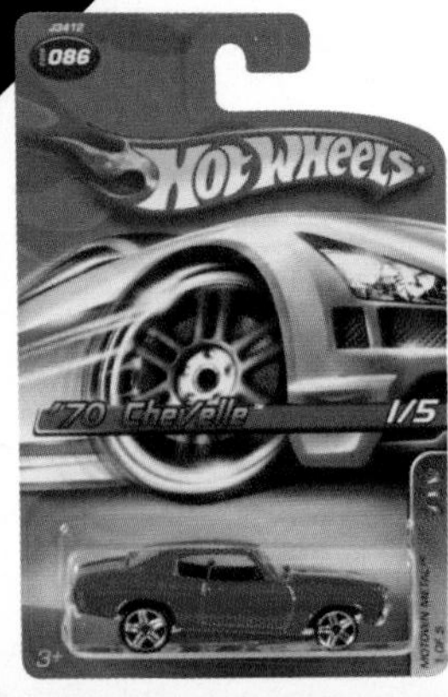

Motown Metal 1 of 5

2006 086

❑ 1970 Chevelle SS/Grey/PR5 (Kmart) $4.00
❑ **1970 Chevelle SS/Red/PR5.. $3.00**

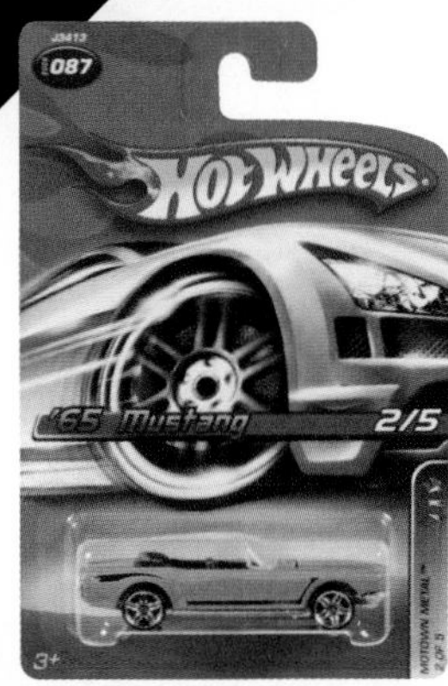

Motown Metal 2 of 5

2006 087

- ❑ '65 Mustang/Blue/5SP $5.00
- ❑ **'65 Mustang/Blue/PR5 .... $5.00**
- ❑ '65 Mustang/Blue/PR5 tinted windows $10.00

Motown Metal 2 of 5

2006 087

- ❑ **'65 Mustang/Pearl White/Gold10SP $3.00**
- ❑ '65 Mustang/Red/PR5 (Kmart) $5.00

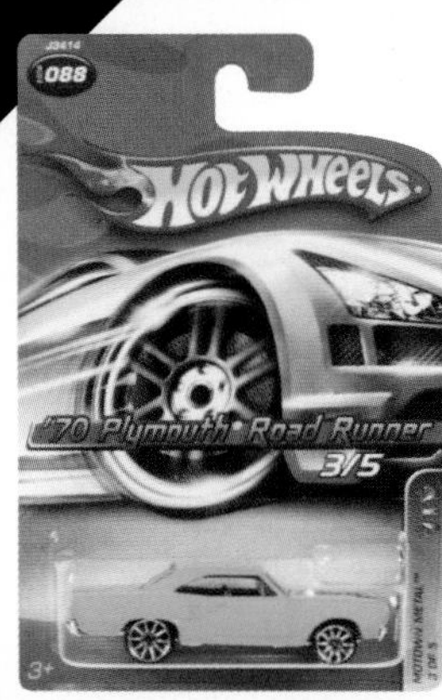

Motown Metal 3 of 5

2006 088

- ❑ **'70 Plymouth Road Runner/Lime Green/10SP $3.00**
- ❑ '70 Plymouth Road Runner/Lime Green/5SP $30.00
- ❑ '70 Plymouth Road Runner/M Dark Orange/10SP (Kmart) $30.00
- ❑ '70 Plymouth Road Runner/M Dark Orange/5SP (Kmart) $5.00

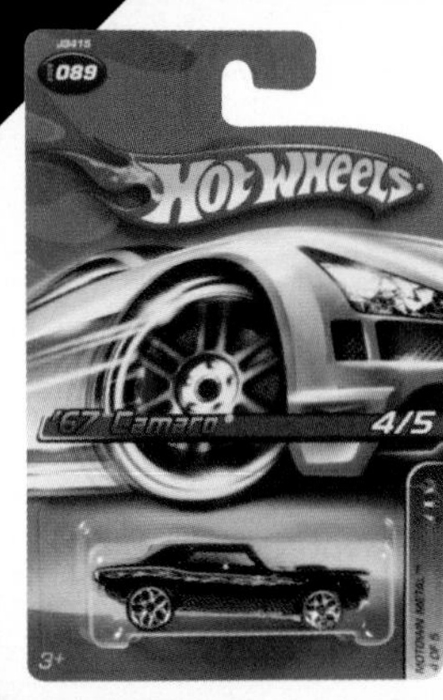

Motown Metal 4 of 5

2006 089

- ❑ 1967 Camaro/Black/5SP $5.00
- ❑ 1967 Camaro/Black/RL5SP $60.00
- **❑ 1967 Camaro/Black/Y5 .... $3.00**

Motown Metal 5 of 5

2006 090

- ❑ 1969 Pontiac GTO/Yellow/5SP $1.50

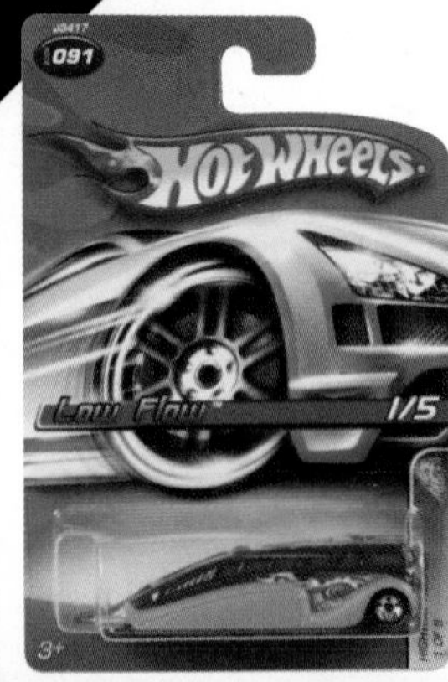

Highway Horror 1 of 5

2006 091

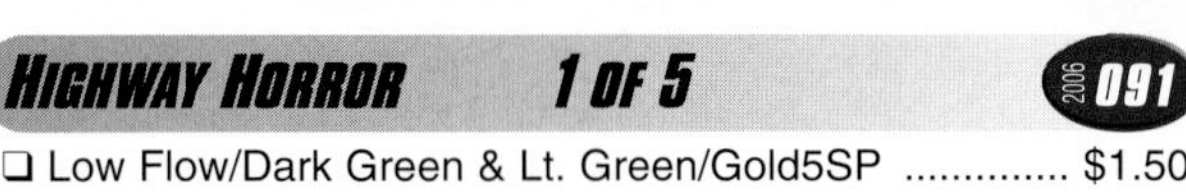

- ❑ Low Flow/Dark Green & Lt. Green/Gold5SP $1.50

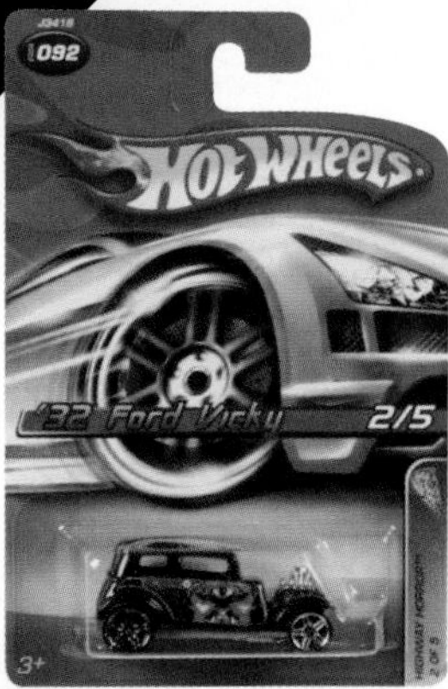

HIGHWAY HORROR 2 OF 5

2006 092

❑ '32 Ford Vicky/Black/PR5, rear BluePR5 .... $1.50

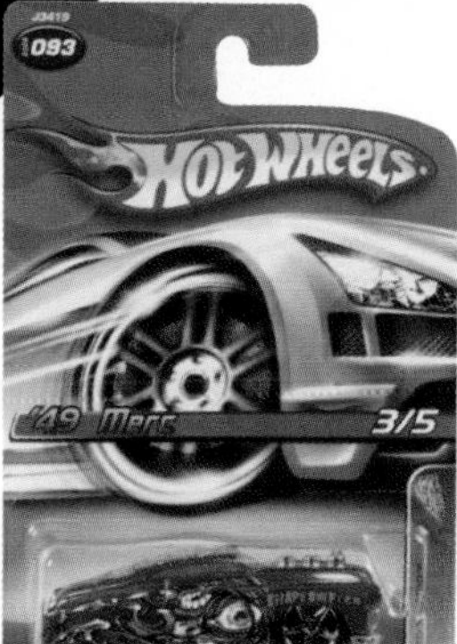

HIGHWAY HORROR 3 OF 5

2006 093

❑ '49 Merc/M Copper/Gold 5SP $1.50

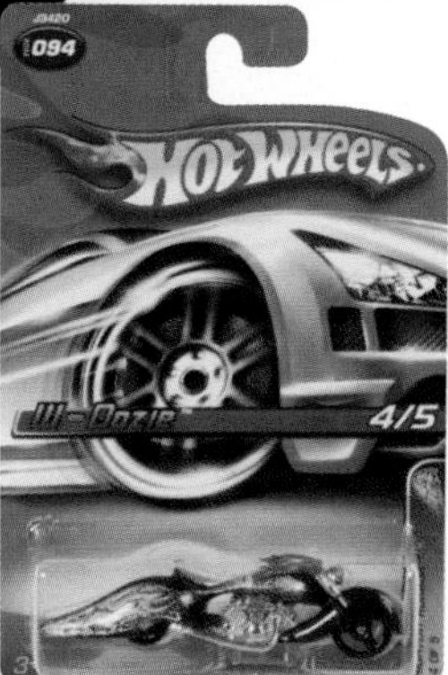

HIGHWAY HORROR 4 OF 5

2006 094

❑ W-Oozie/M Dark Blue/RedMC3 .... $1.50

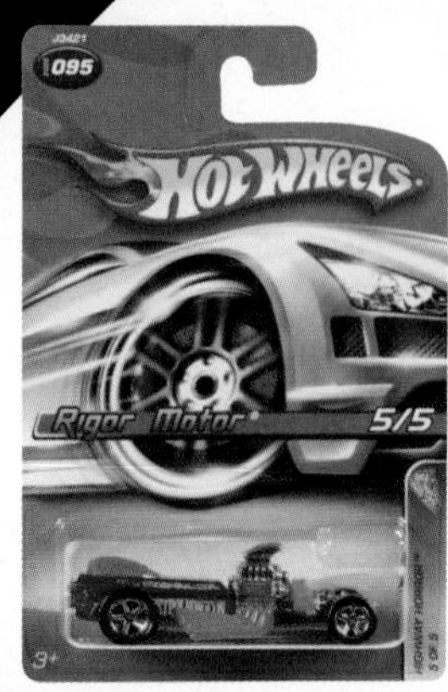

Highway Horror 5 of 5

2006 095

❑ Rigor Motor/M Magenta/Gold5SP $1.50

Red Line 1 of 5

2006 096

❑ Custom '69 Chevy/M Gold/RL5SP (Kmart) $5.00
❑ **Custom '69 Chevy/M Green/RL5SP $3.00**

Red Line 2 of 5

2006 097

❑ Ford GT40/M Yellow/RL5SP $1.50

Red Line 3 of 5

❑ 1968 Nova/M Green/RL5SP (Kmart) $5.00
❑ 1968 Nova/M Purple/RL5SP $3.00

Red Line 4 of 5

❑ Baja Bug/M Red/RL5SP $1.50

Red Line 5 of 5

❑ 1969 Pontiac Firebird T/A/M Blue/RL5SP $3.00
❑ 1969 Pontiac Firebird T/A/M Magenta/RL5SP $3.00

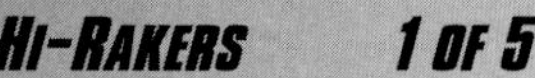

HI-RAKERS 1 OF 5

❑ Montezooma/Blue/BLING $1.50

HI-RAKERS 1 OF 5

❑ Montezooma/Green/BLING black base $1.50
❑ **Montezooma/Green/BLING chrome base $3.00**

HI-RAKERS 2 OF 5

❑ 1971 Buick Riviera/M Purple/PR5................................ $1.50

Hi-Rakers 3 of 5

❑ Monte Carlo/M Silver/GoldPR5 .... $1.50

Hi-Rakers 4 of 5

❑ '63 Chevy Impala/Green/BLING $1.50

Hi-Rakers 5 of 5

❑ Olds 442/M Black/Gold5SP... $1.50

WWE 1 of 5

- ❑ Baja Breaker/Grey Triple H/BlackOR5SP $3.00

WWE 2 of 5

- ❑ '65 Impala/M Green Eddie Guerrero/WSP $3.00

WWE 3 of 5

- ❑ Ballistik/Flat Black/BlueY5.. $12.00
- ❑ **Ballistik/Flat Black/BlueY5 Wrestlemania $3.00**

WWE 4 OF 5

❑ Power Panel/M Dark Red Batista/Gold5SP $5.00
❑ Power Panel/M Dark Red Batista/GoldOR5SP $3.00

WWE 5 OF 5

❑ Sir Ominous/M Dark Blue Hulk Hogan/RedPR5.......... $3.00

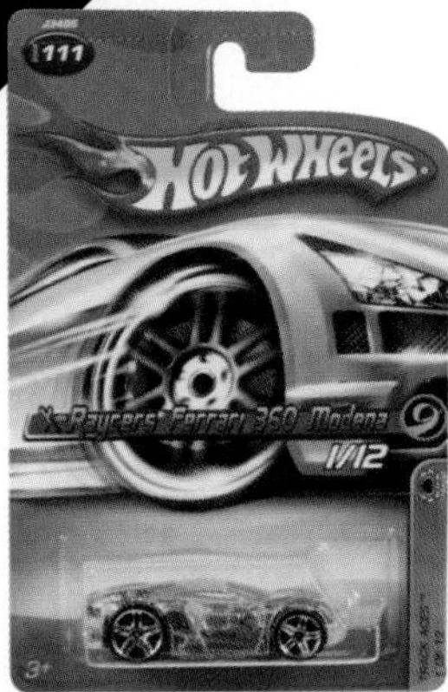

TRACK ACES 1 OF 12

❑ Ferrari 360 Modena/Clear/PR5 .... $1.50

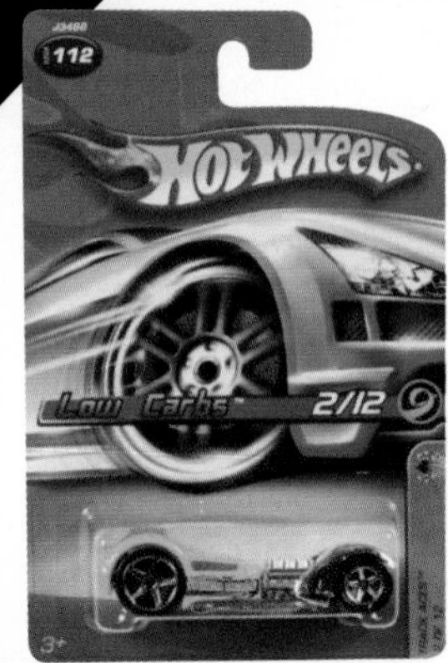

Track Aces 2 of 12

❑ Low Carbs/Yellow/5SP $1.50

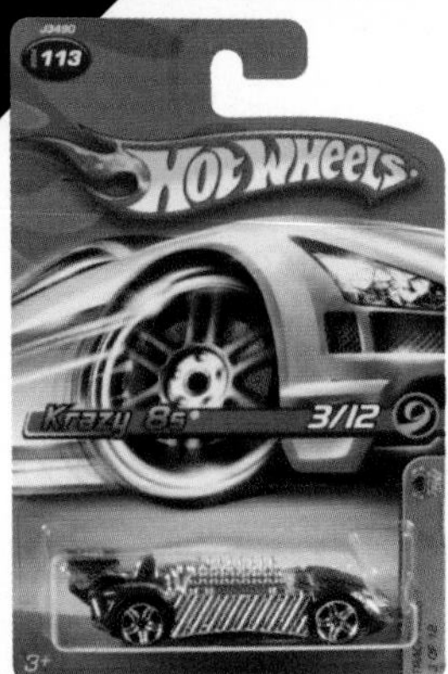

Track Aces 3 of 12

2006 113

❑ Krazy 8s/Purple/PR5 .... $1.50

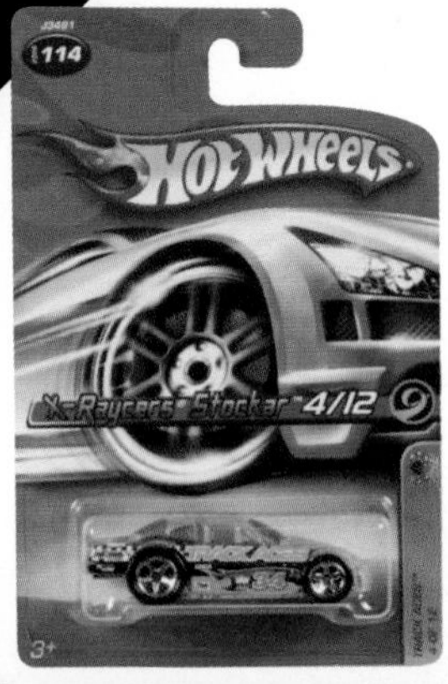

Track Aces 4 of 12

2006 114

❑ Stockar/Clear/5SP $1.50

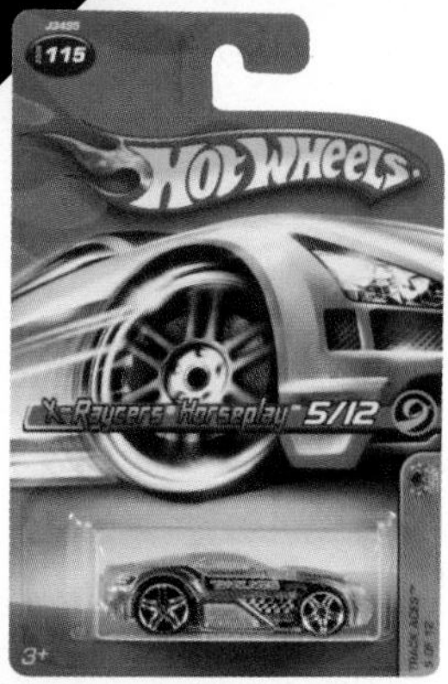

Track Aces 5 of 12

❑ Horseplay/Clear Yellow/PR5 .... $1.50

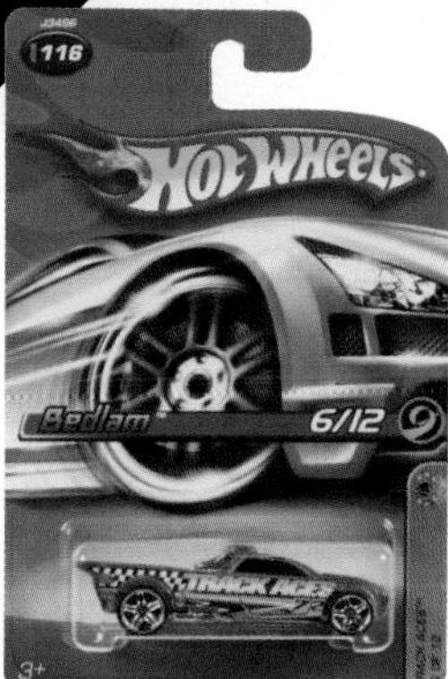

Track Aces 6 of 12

❑ Bedlam/Clear Green/FTE $4.00
❑ Bedlam/Clear Green/PR5 .... $1.50

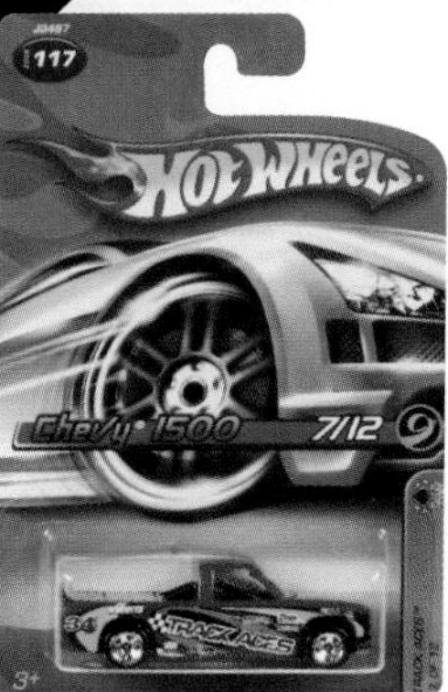

Track Aces 7 of 12

❑ Chevy 1500/Red/5SP $1.50

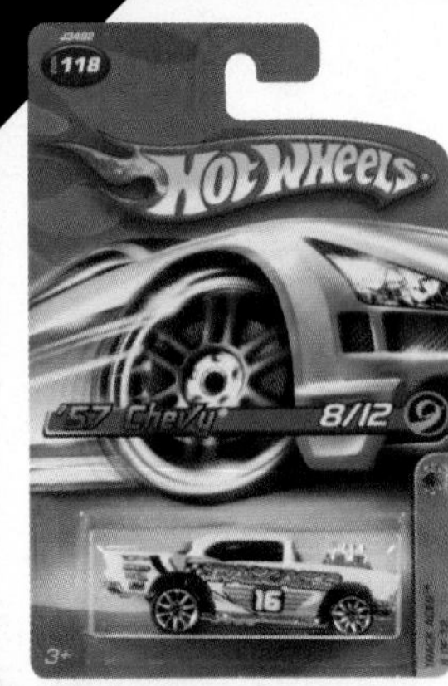

Track Aces 8 of 12

2006 118

- ❑ **'57 Chevy/Pearl White/5SP $5.00**
- ❑ '57 Chevy/Pearl White/10SP $3.00

Track Aces 9 of 12

2006 119

- ❑ Brutalistic/Pearl White/PR5 .... $1.50

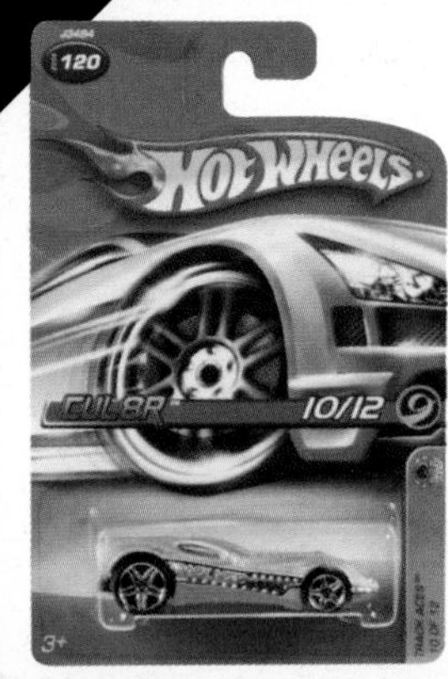

Track Aces 10 of 12

2006 120

- ❑ **CUL8R/M Silver/PR5 .... $1.50**
- ❑ CUL8R/Spectraflame Red/FTE (FTE Promo) $12.00

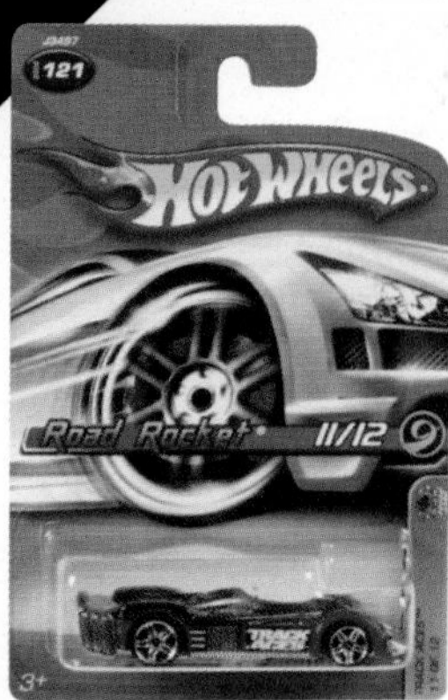

Track Aces 11 of 12

❑ Road Rocket/Red/5SP $3.00
❑ **Road Rocket/Red/PR5.. $1.50**

Track Aces 12 of 12

❑ Sling Shot/Blue/OH5SP.. $1.50

Hot Wheels

❑ Shredster/M Black & M Green/PR5 .... $1.50

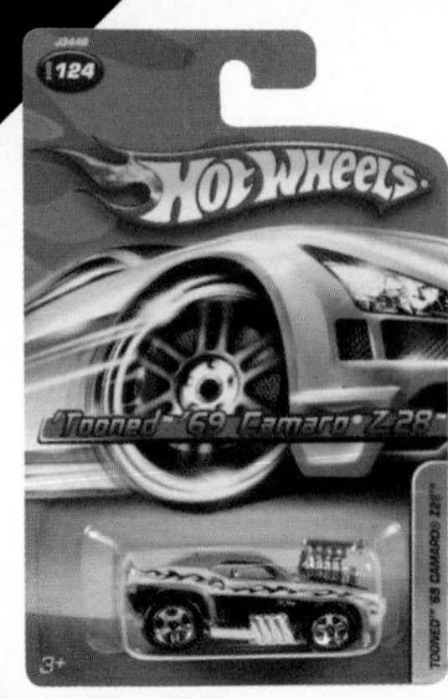

Hot Wheels

❑ **'Tooned '69 Camaro Z-28/M Green/5SP $3.00**
❑ 'Tooned '69 Camaro Z-28/M Purple/5SP (Kmart) $5.00

Hot Wheels

❑ **'Tooned '69 Camaro Z-28/M Yellow/5SP $5.00**
❑ 'Tooned '69 Camaro Z-28/M Yellow/FTE (Toys R Us Starter) $12.00

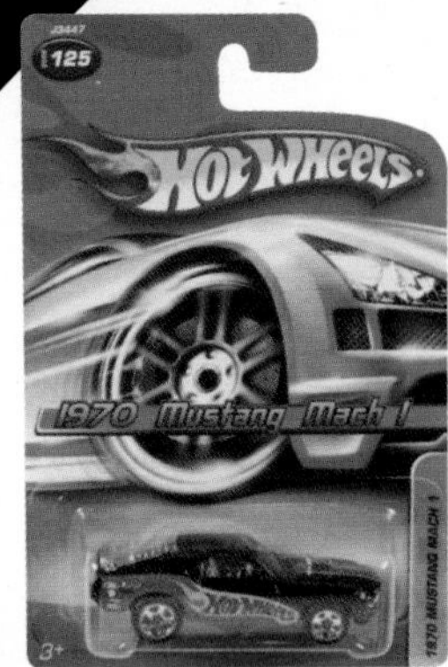

Hot Wheels

2006 125

❑ 1970 Mustang Mach 1/Black/5SP $3.00

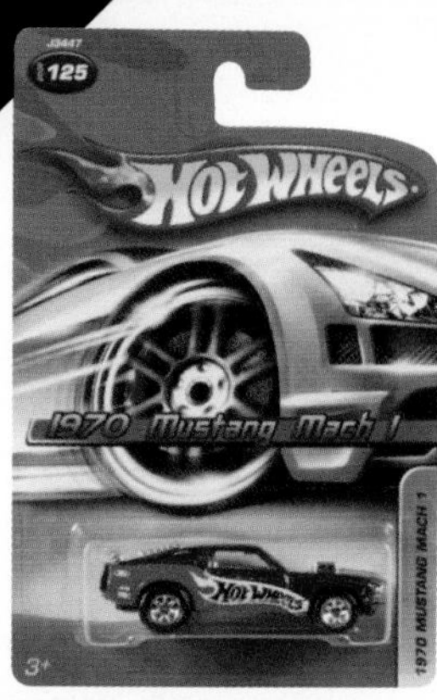

Hot Wheels 2006 125

- ❑ 1970 Mustang Mach 1/Blue/5SP $40.00
- ❑ **1970 Mustang Mach 1/Blue/7SP $3.00**

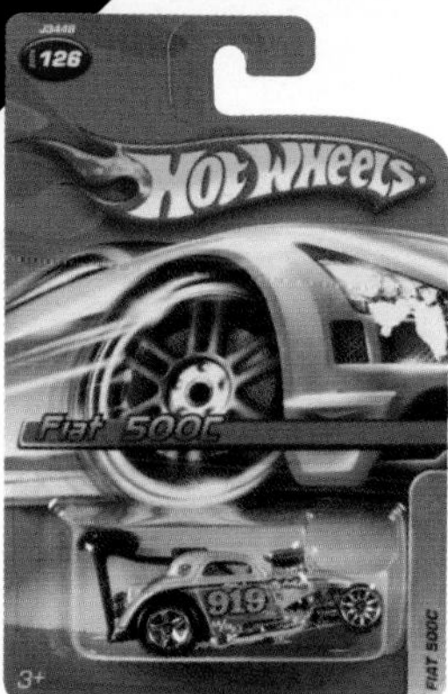

Hot Wheels 2006 126

- ❑ Fiat 500C/M Lt. Blue/10SP, 5SP rear $1.50

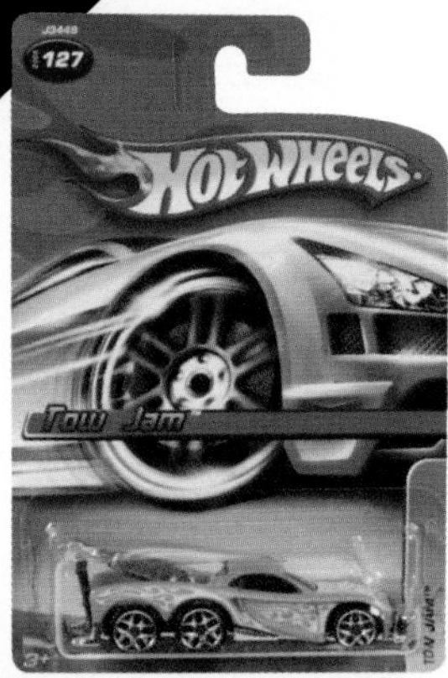

Hot Wheels 2006 127

- ❑ Tow Jam/M Lt. Blue/Y5 .... $3.00

Hot Wheels

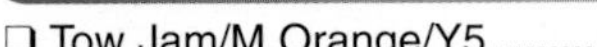

❑ Tow Jam/M Orange/Y5 .... $3.00

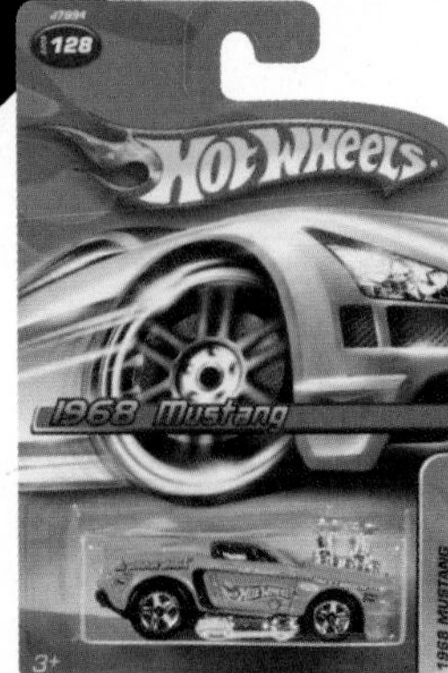

Hot Wheels

2006 128

❑ 1968 Mustang/M Copper/5SP $25.00
❑ 1968 Mustang/M Copper/FTE $20.00
❑ 1968 Mustang/M Lt. Olive Green/5SP black base $3.00
❑ 1968 Mustang/M Lt. Olive Green/5SP chrome base $15.00
❑ 1968 Mustang/Olive Green/5SP $3.00

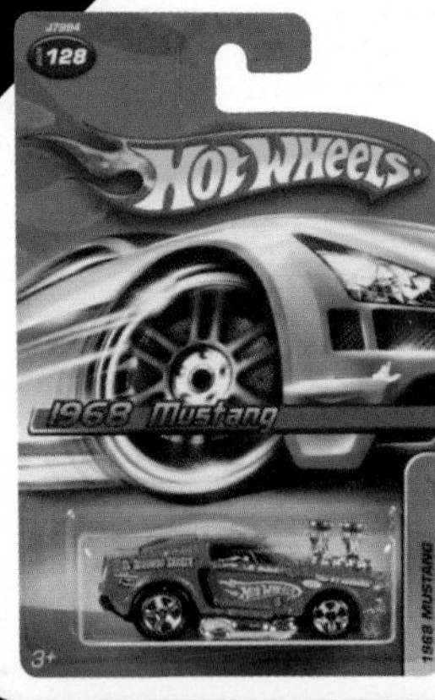

Hot Wheels

2006 128

❑ 1968 Mustang/M Orange/FTE..................................... $6.00
❑ 1968 Mustang/M Orange/5SP $3.00

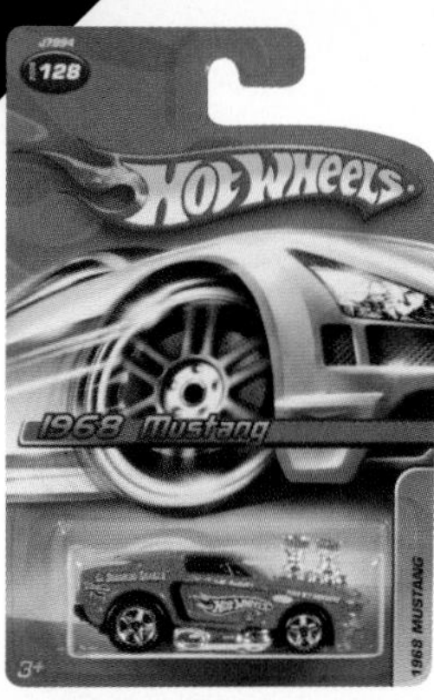

Hot Wheels

2006 128

❑ 1968 Mustang/M Pink/5SP $3.00
❑ **1968 Mustang/M Pink/5SP Tam cams $3.00**

Hot Wheels

2006 129

❑ Lotus Elise 340R/M Yellow/WSP................................. $1.50

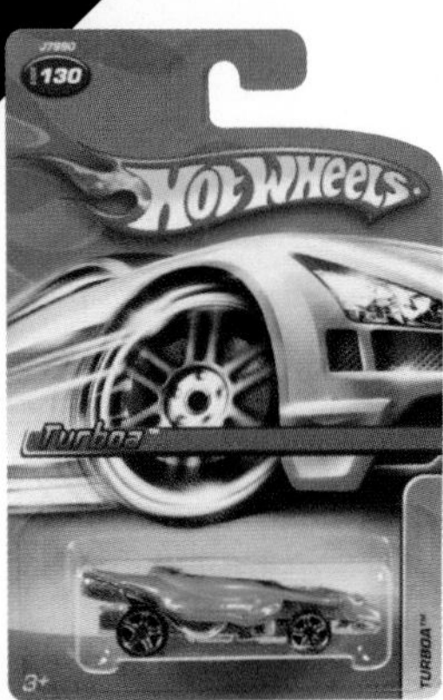

Hot Wheels

2006 130

❑ Turboa/Green/GreenPR5 .... $1.50

Hot Wheels

- ❑ Turboa/M Copper/GoldPR5 .... $1.50
- ❑ Turboa/M Lt. Copper/GoldPR5 .... $1.50

Hot Wheels

- ❑ **Mitsubishi Eclipse/M Lt. Blue/Y5 .... $1.50**
- ❑ Mitsubishi Eclipse/M Lt. Blue/Y5 5 tampos $8.00

Hot Wheels

- ❑ **Pikes Peak Celica/Black/PR5 black interior $1.50**
- ❑ Pikes Peak Celica/Black/PR5 no tampo rear quarter .. $1.50
- ❑ Pikes Peak Celica/Black/PR5 orange interior $1.50

Hot Wheels

- ❑ Honda Civic Type R/Black/FTE $4.00
- ❑ **Honda Civic Type R/Black/PR5 .... $1.50**

Hot Wheels

- ❑ Honda Civic Type R/Pearl White/PR5 .... $1.50

Hot Wheels

- ❑ Twin Mill II/M Blue/5SP $3.00
- ❑ **Twin Mill II/M Blue/Y5 .... $1.50**

HOT WHEELS

❑ Super Modified/M Dark Green/WSP $1.50

HOT WHEELS

❑ Super Modified/M Red/WSP $1.50

HOT WHEELS

❑ Swoop Coupe/M Purple & Grey/5SP $5.00
❑ **Swoop Coupe/M Purple & Grey/SK5, 5SP rear........ $1.50**

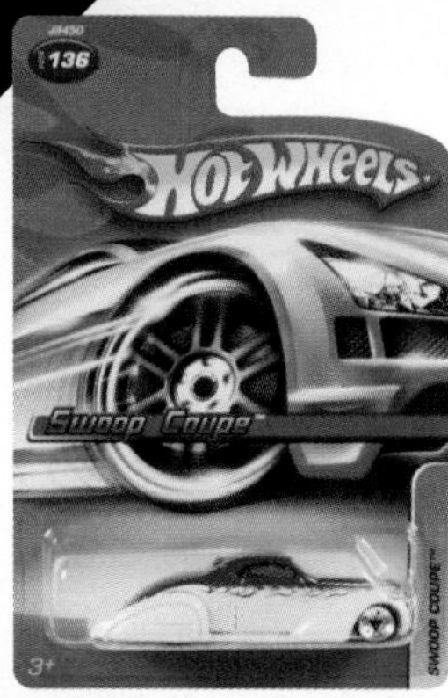

HOT WHEELS

2006 136

❑ Swoop Coupe/White & Red/SK5, 5SP rear $1.50

HOT WHEELS

2006 136

❑ Swoop Coupe/Yellow & M Green/SK5, 5SP rear $1.50

HOT WHEELS

2006 137

❑ Blast Lane/M Dark Red/MC3 .... $3.00

❑ Blast Lane/Yellow/MC3 .... $3.00

HOT WHEELS

❑ Shadow Jet/M Purple/5SP $1.50

HOT WHEELS

❑ Ford GT90 Concept/M Black/3SP................................ $1.50

Hot Wheels

- ❑ L'Bling/M Dark Red/PR5 .... $1.50

Hot Wheels

- ❑ Dodge Ram 1500/M Magenta/PR5 .... $1.50

Hot Wheels

- ❑ Dodge Ram 1500/Orange/PR5 .... $1.50

❑ **'40 Ford Truck/Flat Black/Blue5SP............................ $1.50**
❑ '40 Ford Truck/Grey/5SP.. $30.00
❑ '40 Ford Truck/Grey/Blue5SP $1.50

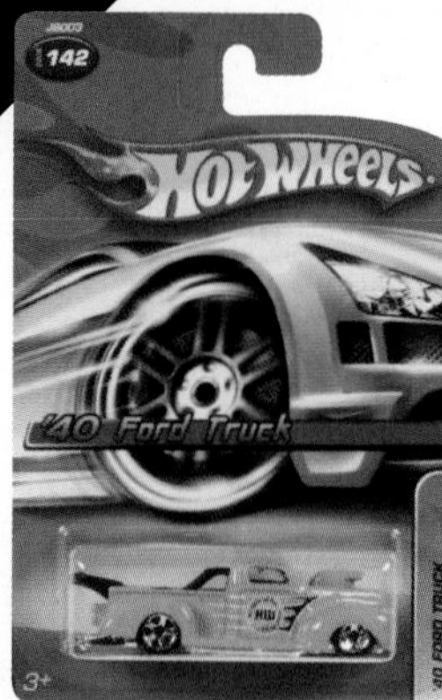

Hot Wheels

2006 142

❑ **'40 Ford Truck/Yellow/5SP.. $1.50**
❑ '40 Ford Truck/Yellow/Y5.. $8.00

Hot Wheels

❑ Trak-Tune/Clear Green/FTE $4.00
❑ **Trak-Tune/Clear Green/Y5.. $1.50**

Hot Wheels

❑ Trak-Tune/Clear Purple/Y5 .... $1.50

Hot Wheels

❑ **Bugatti Veyron/Blue-Grey/10SP $1.50**
❑ Bugatti Veyron/Blue-Grey/FTE $4.00

Hot Wheels

❑ Hammered Coupe/M Magenta/Gold5SP $1.50

Hot Wheels

❑ Hammered Coupe/M Red/Gold5SP $1.50

Hot Wheels

❑ Roll Cage/Lime Green/OR5SP $1.50

Hot Wheels

❑ Sharkruiser/Black/BlueY5 .... $1.50

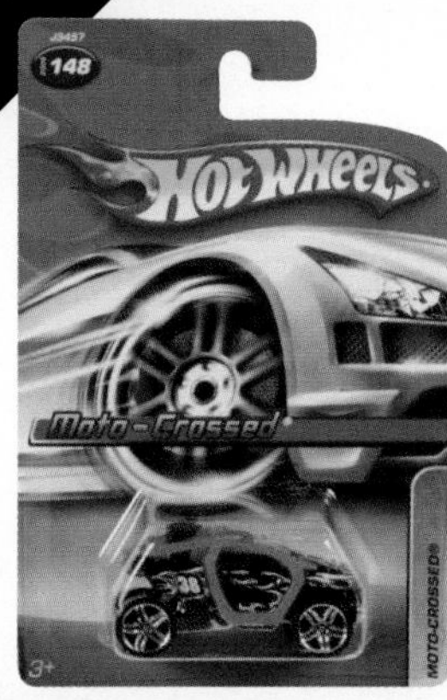

Hot Wheels

- ❑ Moto-Crossed/Black/5SP $40.00
- ❑ **Moto-Crossed/Black/PR5 .... $1.50**

Hot Wheels

- ❑ Ferrari 360 Modena/M Dark Red/PR5 .... $1.50

Hot Wheels

- ❑ Deuce Roadster/M Lt. Blue/5SP $1.50

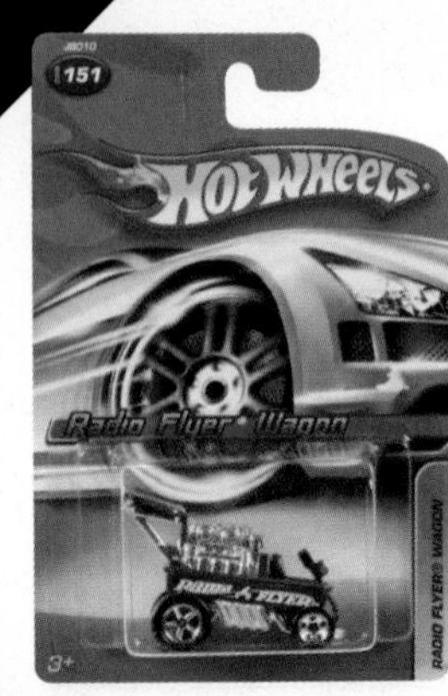

Hot Wheels

❑ Radio Flyer Wagon/Blue/5SP black spoiler $3.00

❑ Radio Flyer Wagon/Blue/5SP chrome spoiler.......... $1.50

Hot Wheels

❑ Way 2 Fast/Silver/5SP $3.00

Hot Wheels

❑ Way 2 Fast/Yellow/5SP $3.00

HOT WHEELS

2006 153

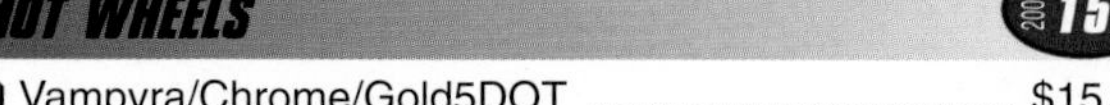

❑ Vampyra/Chrome/Gold5DOT $15.00

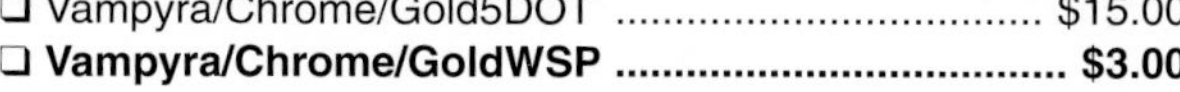

❑ **Vampyra/Chrome/GoldWSP $3.00**

HOT WHEELS

❑ Corvette C6/Blue/PR5 (Kmart) $3.00
❑ Corvette C6/Blue/PR5 (Kmart) tinted windows $3.00
❑ **Corvette C6/White/PR5 .... $1.50**

HOT WHEELS

❑ 'Tooned 1969 Pontiac GTO/Black & Red/5SP $1.50

Hot Wheels

2006 156

❑ Vairy 8/Flat Black/5SP (Wal-Mart) $1.50
❑ Vairy 8/Flat Blue/5SP $1.50

Hot Wheels

2006 156

❑ Vairy 8/Flat Dark Green/5SP $3.00

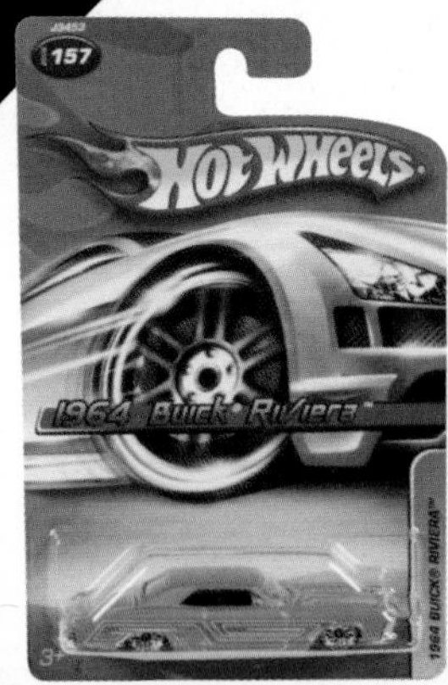

Hot Wheels

2006 157

❑ 1964 Buick Riviera/Green/WSP $1.50

Hot Wheels

❑ 1964 Buick Riviera/Red/WSP $1.50

Hot Wheels

❑ Fore Wheeler/Black & Red/5SP $1.50

Hot Wheels

❑ Fore Wheeler/M Red/5SP $1.50

Hot Wheels

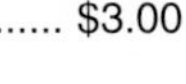

❑ 1947 Chevy Fleetline/Flat Black/WSP $3.00

Hot Wheels

❑ Itso-Skeenie/Magenta/PR5 .... $1.50

Hot Wheels

❑ Rocket Box/Flat Black/PR5 .... $1.50

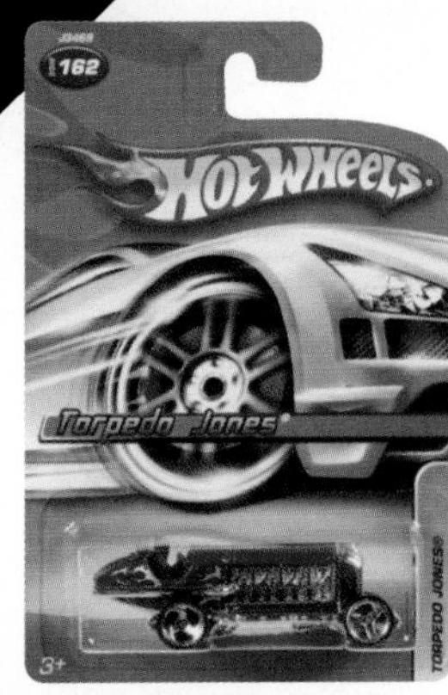

HOT WHEELS

2006 162

- ❑ **Torpedo Jones/Dark Red/3SP $3.00**
- ❑ Torpedo Jones/Dark Red/3SP silver flames $1.50
- ❑ Torpedo Jones/Dark Red/5SP..................................... $1.50
- ❑ Torpedo Jones/Dark Red/WSP $25.00

HOT WHEELS

2006 162

- ❑ Torpedo Jones/Dark Yellow/Gold5SP $1.50

HOT WHEELS

2006 163

- ❑ Toyota Celica/Black/Y5 black inetrior $5.00
- ❑ **Toyota Celica/Black/Y5 chrome inetrior $1.50**

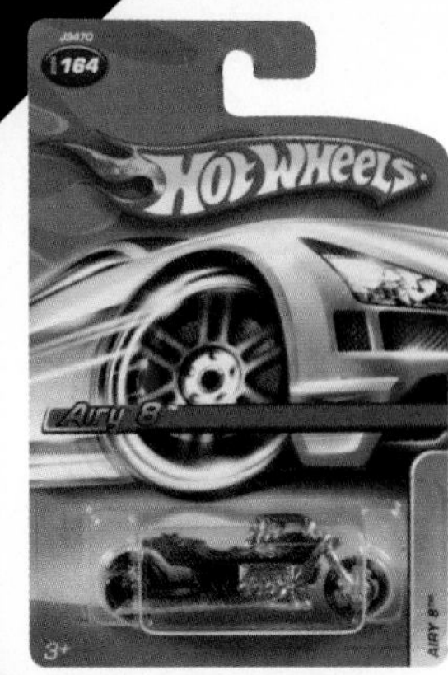

Hot Wheels

❑ Airy 8/Flat Black/RedMC3 .... $1.50

Hot Wheels

❑ Airy 8/Purple/MC3 .... $1.50

Hot Wheels

❑ Morris Cooper/Dark Red/PR5 .... $1.50

Hot Wheels

- ❑ Pikes Peak Tacoma/Pearl White/Red10SP $1.50

Hot Wheels

- ❑ **Mega-Duty/Copper/Gold5DOT $1.50**
- ❑ Mega-Duty/Copper/Gold5SP...................................... $25.00
- ❑ Mega-Duty/Copper/GoldOR5SP $3.00

Hot Wheels

- ❑ Tor-Speedo/Blue/FTE $4.00
- ❑ **Tor-Speedo/Blue/PR5 .... $1.50**

Hot Wheels

❑ Talbot Lago/M Grey/WSP $1.50

Hot Wheels

❑ 1941 Willys Coupe/Flat Black/Gold5SP black base $3.00

❑ **1941 Willys Coupe/Flat Black/Gold5SP gold chrome base $1.50**

Hot Wheels

❑ Monoposto/Silver/PR5.. $1.50

Hot Wheels

❑ '69 El Camino/Grey/Gold5SP $6.00

Hot Wheels

❑ '69 El Camino/Yellow/5SP (Toys R Us Starter) $6.00

Hot Wheels

❑ Hummer H3T Concept/M Grey/OR5SP $1.50

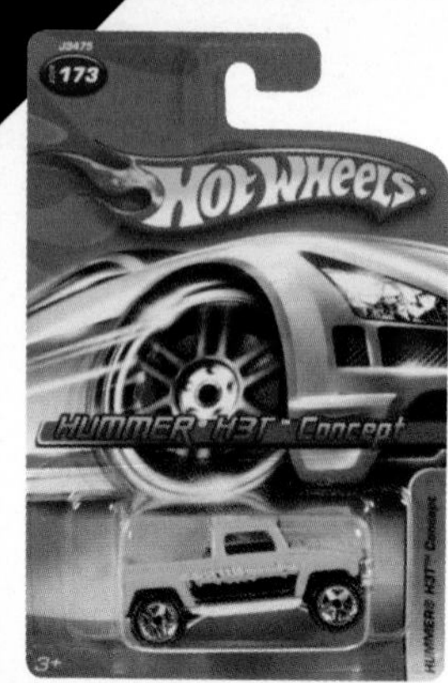

HOT WHEELS 2006 173

❑ Hummer H3T Concept/Yellow/OR5SP $1.50

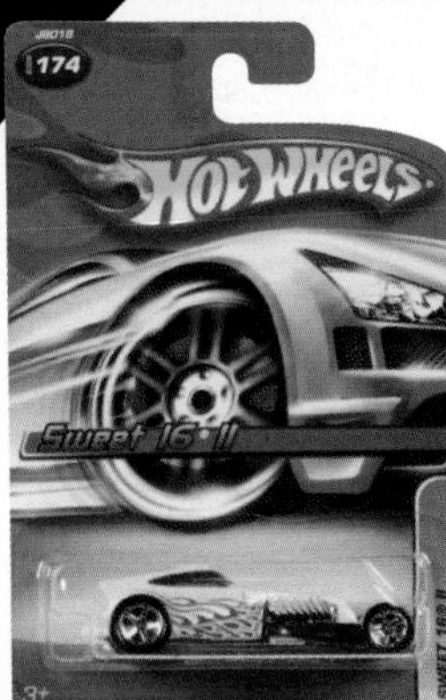

HOT WHEELS 2006 174

❑ Sweet 16 II/Pearl White/5SP $1.50

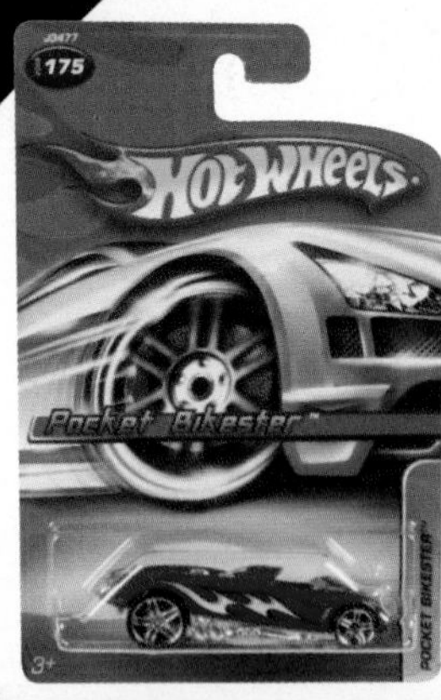

HOT WHEELS 2006 175

❑ Pocket Bikester/Red/FTE $4.00
❑ Pocket Bikester/Red/PR5 .... $1.50

Hot Wheels

- ❑ 1968 Dodge Dart/M Black/5SP $30.00
- ❑ **1968 Dodge Dart/M Black/10SP $3.00**

Hot Wheels

- ❑ 1932 Bugatti Type 50/M Green/Gold5DOT $1.50

Hot Wheels

- ❑ Arachnorod/Grey/PR5 .... $1.50

Hot Wheels

❑ Jester/Black/BluePR5 .... $1.50

Hot Wheels

❑ Saleen S7/Dark Blue/PR5 .... $1.50

Hot Wheels

❑ 1963 Thunderbird/Pearl White/WSP $1.50

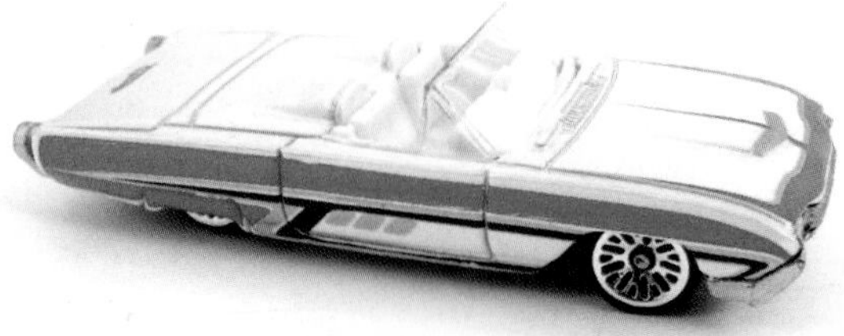

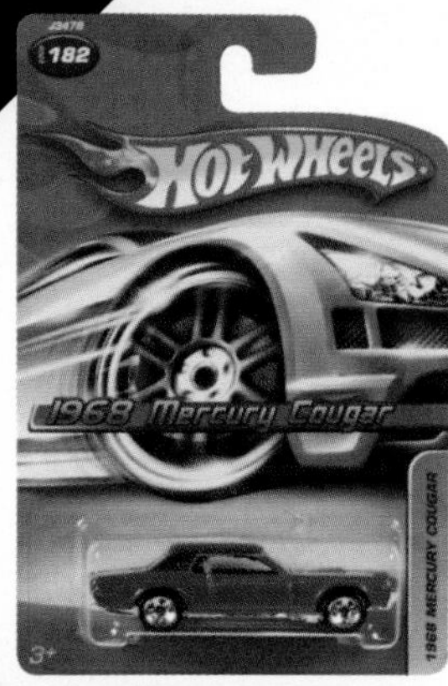

Hot Wheels

2006 182

❑ 1968 Mercury Cougar/M Green/5SP............................ $1.50

Hot Wheels

2006 182

❑ 1968 Mercury Cougar/Orange/5SP.............................. $1.50

Hot Wheels

2006 183

❑ Scorchin' Scooter/M Green/MC3................................. $3.00

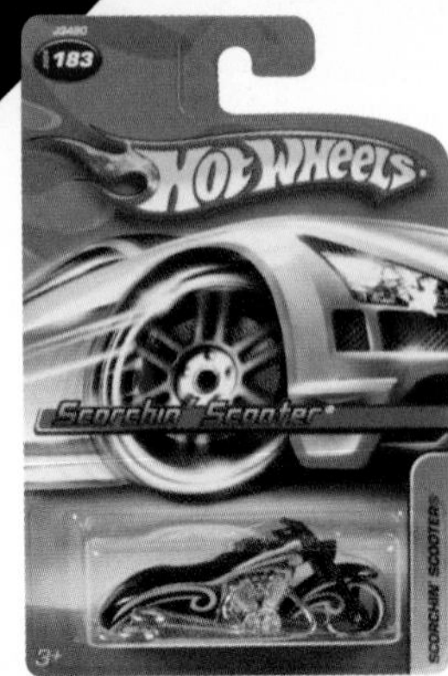

Hot Wheels

- ❑ **Scorchin' Scooter/M Purple/GoldMC3 black handlebars $3.00**
- ❑ Scorchin' Scooter/M Purple/GoldMC3 grey handlebars $10.00

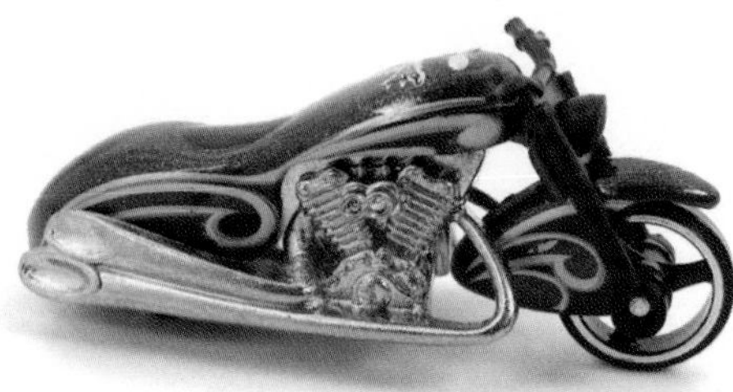

Hot Wheels

- ❑ 2005 Ford Mustang GT/M Grey/PR5 .... $25.00
- ❑ **2005 Ford Mustang GT/M Grey/Y5............................ $1.50**

Hot Wheels

- ❑ 2005 Ford Mustang GT/Yellow/PR5 .... $1.50

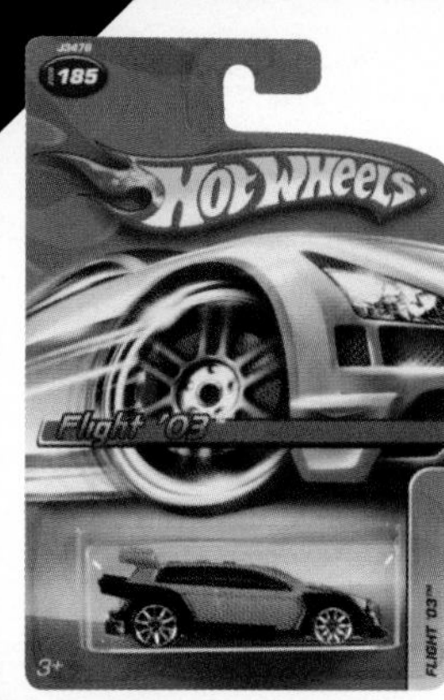

HOT WHEELS 2006 185

- ❑ Flight '03/M Gold/5SP $10.00
- **❑ Flight '03/M Gold/10SP $1.50**
- ❑ Flight '03/M Gold/PR5 .... $10.00

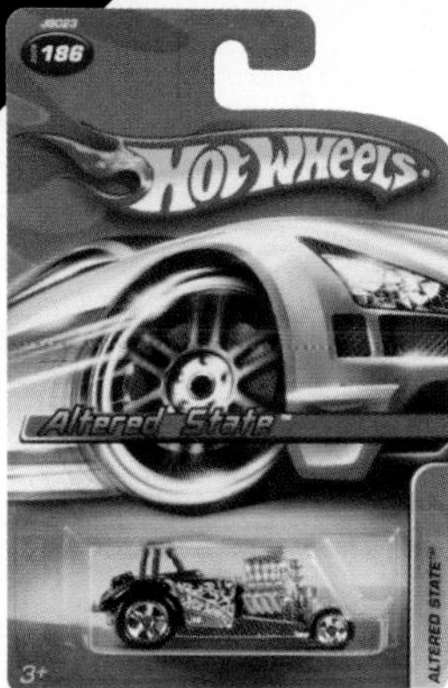

HOT WHEELS 2006 186

- ❑ Altered State/Black/5SP $1.50

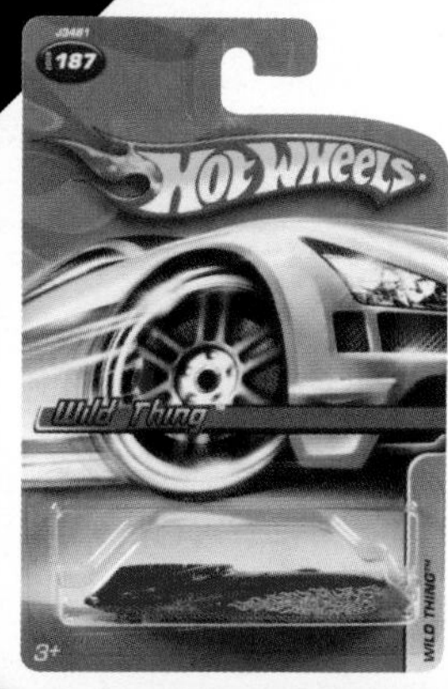

HOT WHEELS 2006 187

- ❑ Wild Thing/Dark Red/Mini $1.50

Hot Wheels

❑ Sinistra/Black/GoldPR5 .... $1.50

Hot Wheels

❑ Oscar Mayer Wienermobile/Yellow & Red/Gold5SP.... $1.50

Hot Wheels

❑ **3-Window '34/Flat Black/5SP $1.50**
❑ 3-Window '34/Grey/5SP $1.50

HOT WHEELS 2006 191

- ❑ Old Number 5.5/Red/5SP $1.50
- ❑ Old Number 5.5/Red/OH5SP $3.00
- ❑ **Old Number 5.5/Yellow/5SP $1.50**

HOT WHEELS 2006 192

- ❑ Lotus Project M250/Green/5SP $1.50

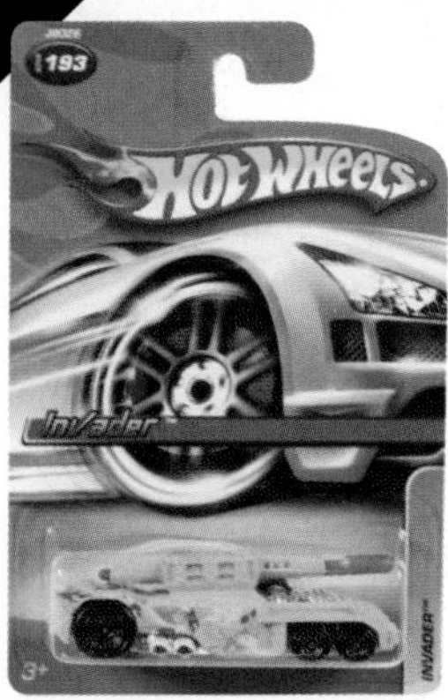

HOT WHEELS 2006 193

- ❑ **Invader/Tan/Black5SP $1.50**
- ❑ Invader/Tan/BlackPR5.. $8.00

Hot Wheels

❑ Enzo Ferrari/Black/GoldOH5SP $1.50

Hot Wheels

❑ Ferrari 333SP/Black/5SP $1.50

Hot Wheels

❑ Shock Factor/Salmon Red/OR5SP $1.50

Hot Wheels 2006 197

- ❑ VW Bug/Black/5SP (Wal-Mart Red) $30.00
- ❑ **VW Bug/Black/GoldY5 .... $1.50**
- ❑ VW Bug/White/5SP (Wal-Mart) $3.00

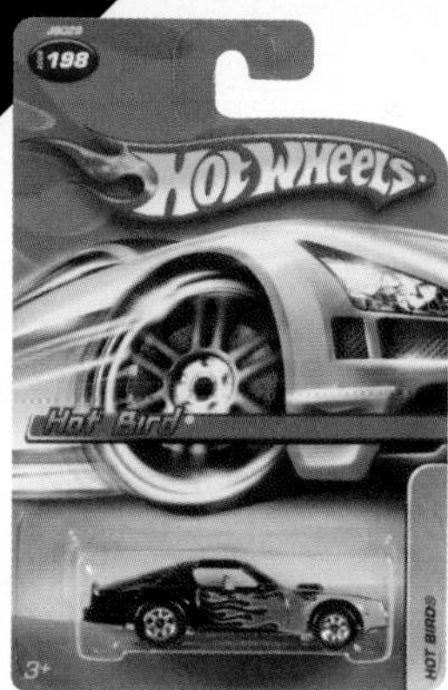

Hot Wheels 2006 198

- ❑ Hot Bird/Black/5SP $10.00
- ❑ **Hot Bird/Black/7SP $1.50**
- ❑ Hot Bird/M Purple/5SP $1.50

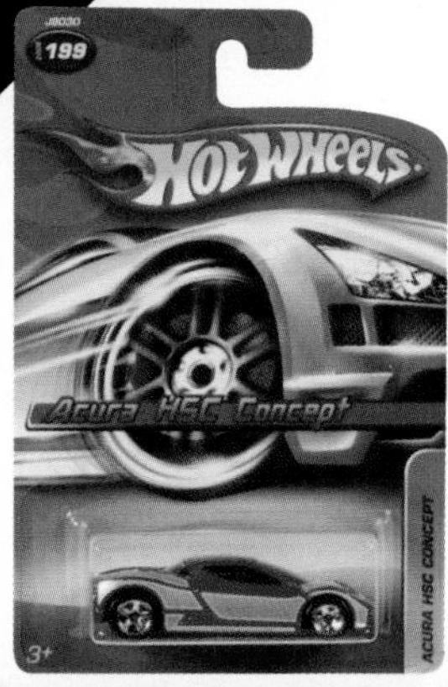

Hot Wheels 2006 199

- ❑ Acura HSC Concept/M Red/5SP................................. $1.50

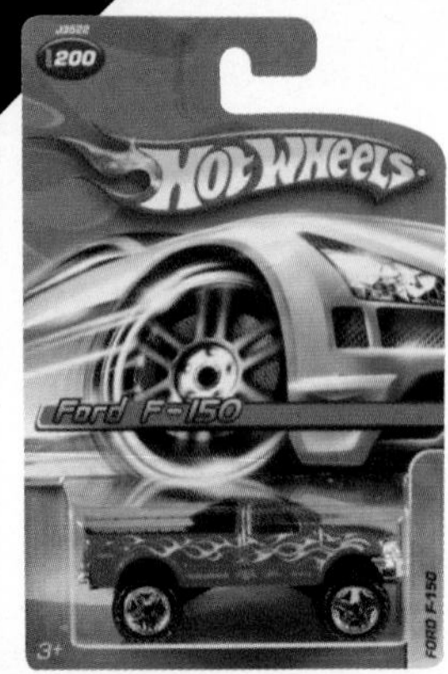

Hot Wheels 2006 200

❑ Ford F-150/M Red/OR5SP $1.50

Hot Wheels 2006 201

❑ Ferrari 575 GTC/Grey/PR5 .... $1.50

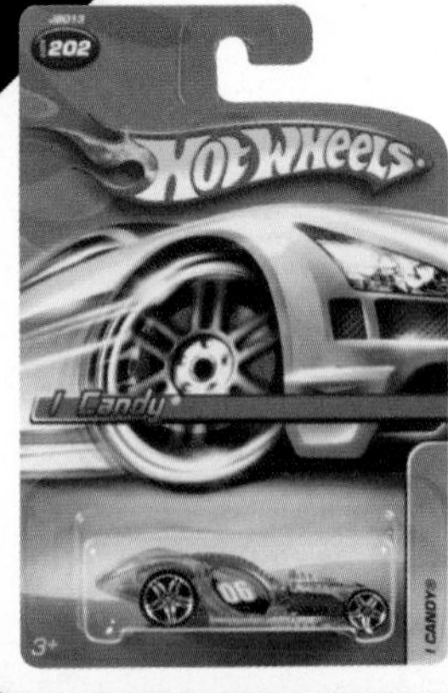

Hot Wheels 2006 202

❑ I Candy/M Green/PR5.. $1.50

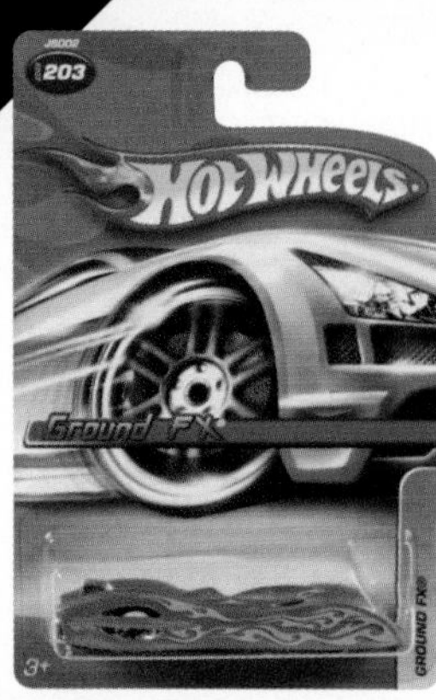

HOT WHEELS 2006 203

❑ Ground FX/M Green/BlackSK5 .... $3.00
❑ Ground FX/M Green/SK5 .... $1.50

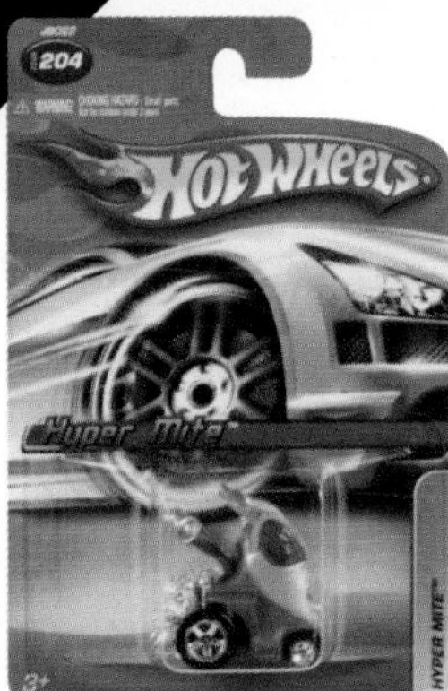

HOT WHEELS 2006 204

❑ Hyper Mite/M Silver & Blue/5SP $1.50

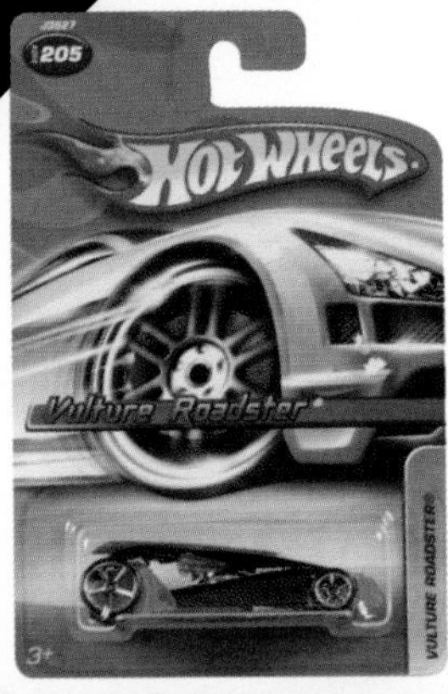

HOT WHEELS 2006 205

❑ Vulture Roadster/Black/OH5SP $1.50

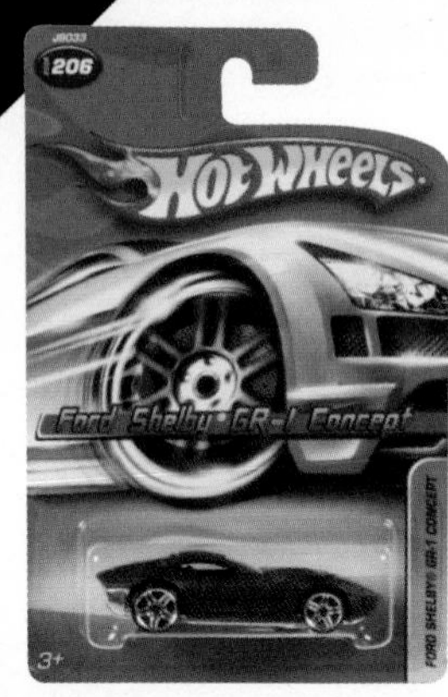

Hot Wheels

❑ **Ford Shelby GR-1 Concept/Flat Black/PR5 .... $1.50**
❑ Ford Shelby GR-1 Concept/M Dark Red/PR5 .... $1.50

Hot Wheels

❑ Batmobile/Flat Black/GoldPR5 .... $1.50

Hot Wheels

❑ **GMC Motorhome/Black/5SP $3.00**
❑ GMC Motorhome/Black/PR5 .... $15.00
❑ GMC Motorhome/White/5SP (Kmart) $60.00
❑ GMC Motorhome/White/PR5 (Kmart) $5.00

Hot Wheels 2006 209

- ❑ **MS-T Suzuka/Orange/Blue10SP................................ $1.50**
- ❑ MS-T Suzuka/Orange/BluePR5 .... $1.50

Hot Wheels 2006 210

- ❑ 8 Crate/Dark Blue/5SP $3.00

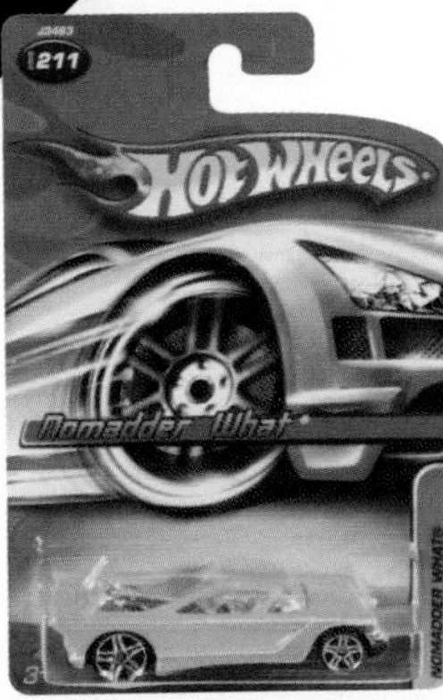

Hot Wheels 2006 211

- ❑ Nomadder What/M Yellow/5SP $1.50
- ❑ **Nomadder What/M Yellow/PR5 .... $1.50**

2006

Hot Wheels

❑ Shelby Cobra 427 S/C/M Gray/5SP $1.50

Hot Wheels

❑ Greased Lightnin'/Black/GoldPR5................................ $1.50

Hot Wheels

❑ Poison Arrow/Smoke Tinted/Micro5SP $1.50

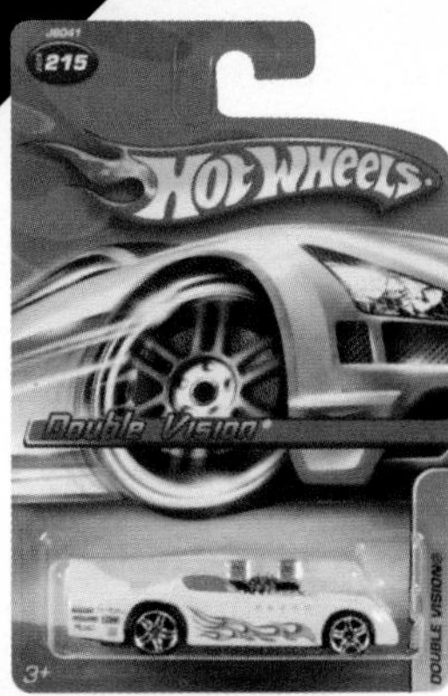

HOT WHEELS 2006 215

❑ Double Vision/Pearl White/PR5 .... $1.50

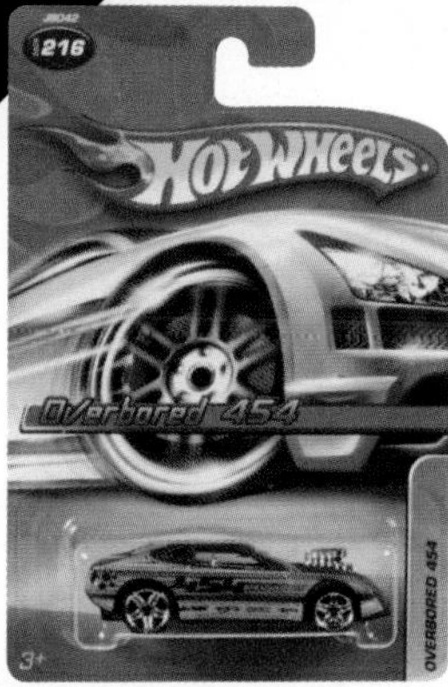

HOT WHEELS 2006 216

❑ Overbored 454/Black/PR5 .... $1.50

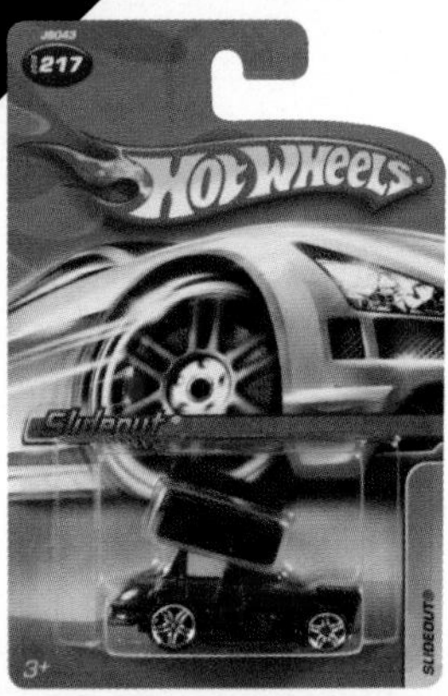

HOT WHEELS 2006 217

❑ Slideout/M Blue/PR5 .... $1.50

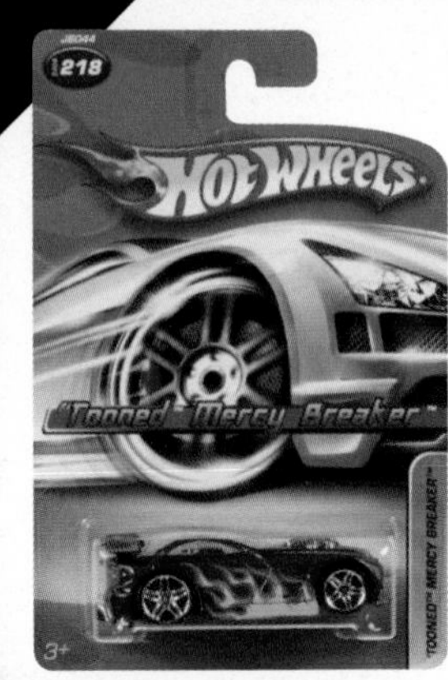

Hot Wheels

2006 218

❑ 'Tooned Mercy Breaker/Dark Blue/PR5 .... $1.50

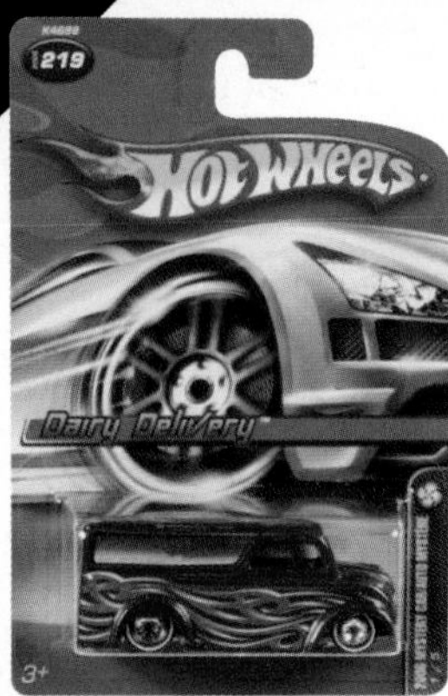

2006 Mystery Car 1 of 5

2006 219

❑ Dairy Delivery/Dark Blue/WLRR $40.00

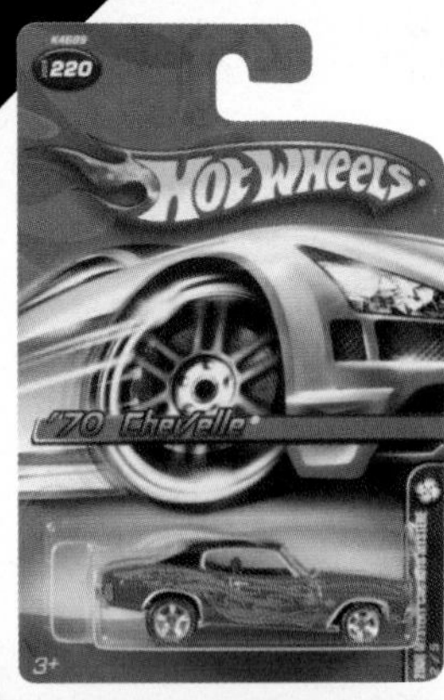

2006 Mystery Car 2 of 5

2006 220

❑ '70 Chevelle/M Orange/RLRR5SP $25.00

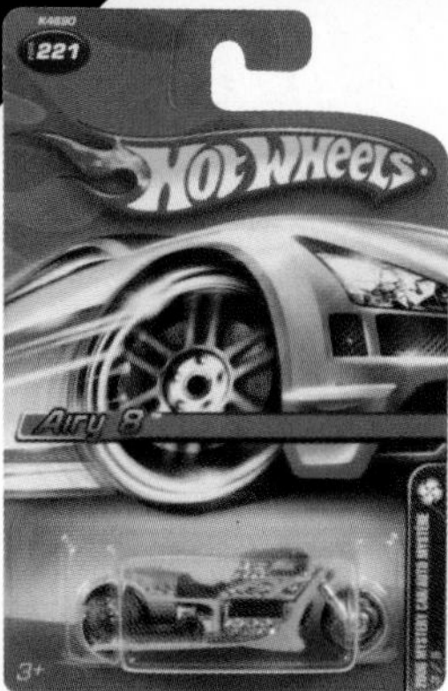

2006 Mystery Car 3 of 5

❑ Airy 8/Yellow/GoldMC3 .... $15.00

2006 Mystery Car 4 of 5

❑ '55 Chevy Panel/M Purple/RLRR5SP $30.00

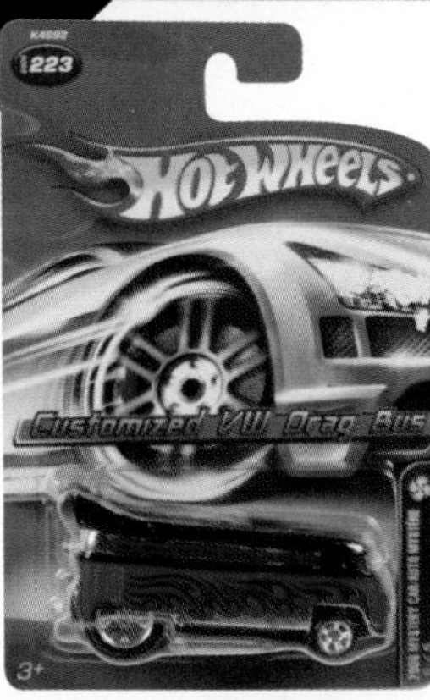

2006 Mystery Car 5 of 5

❑ Customized VW Drag Bus/Chrome & Black/RR5SP (10th Anniversary) $50.00

2007 HOT WHEELS PRICE GUIDE

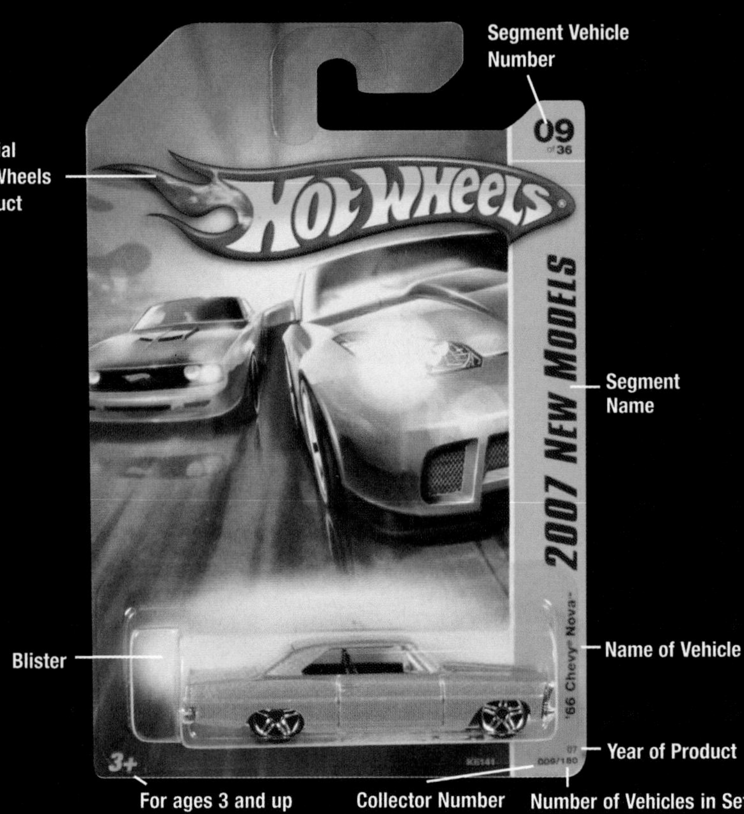

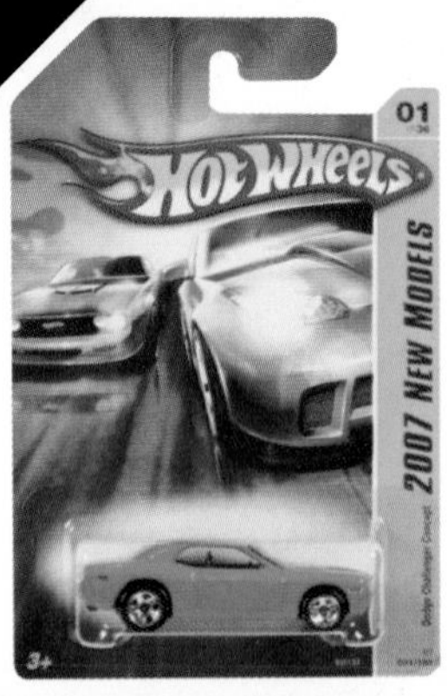

2007 NEW MODELS 1 OF 36

- ❑ **Dodge Challenger Concept/Green/5SP $3.00**
- ❑ Dodge Challenger Concept/Green/PR5 .... $1.50

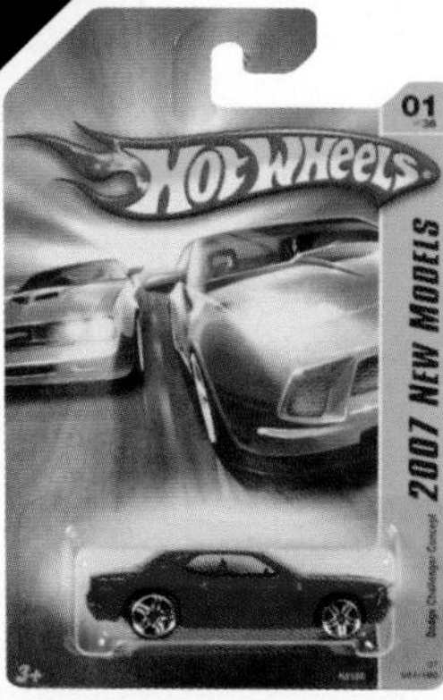

2007 New Models 1 of 36

❑ Dodge Challenger Concept/M Dark Red/PR5 .... $1.50

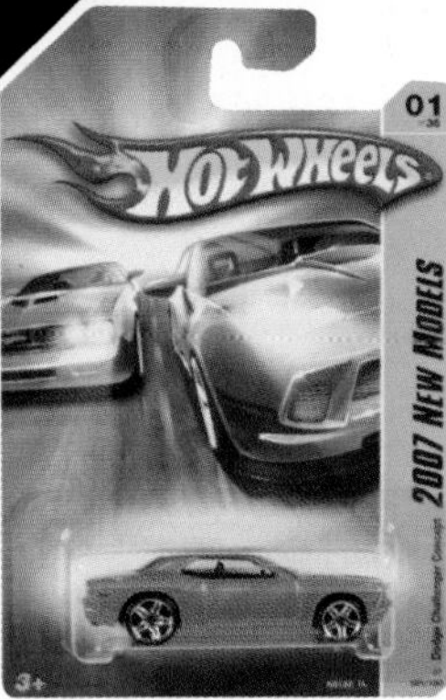

2007 New Models 1 of 36

❑ Dodge Challenger Concept/M Grey/PR5 .... $1.50

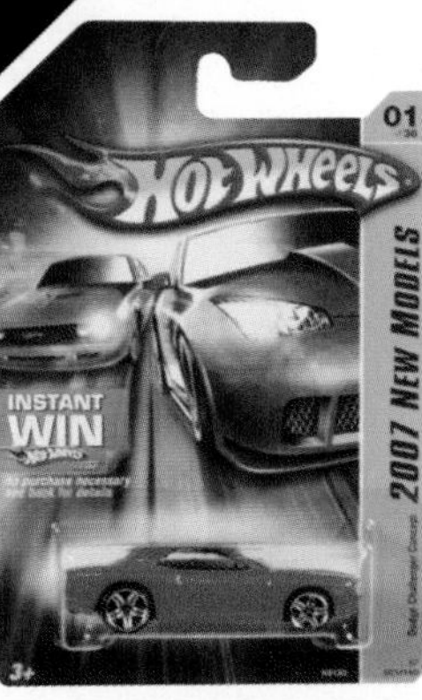

2007 New Models 1 of 36

❑ Dodge Challenger Concept/M Orange/PR5 .... $1.50

2007

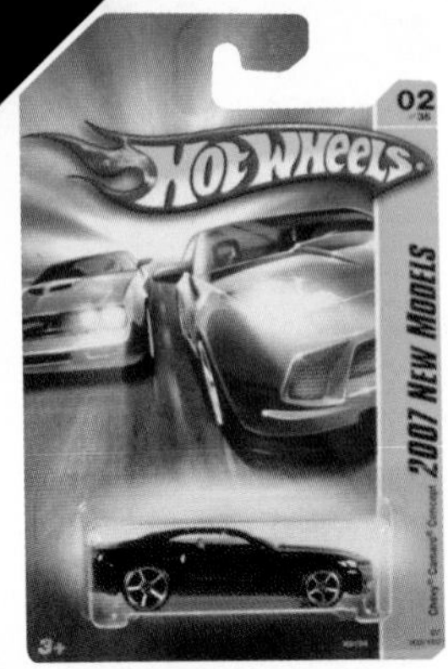

2007 New Models 2 of 36

❑ Chevy Camaro Concept/Black/OH5SP $1.50

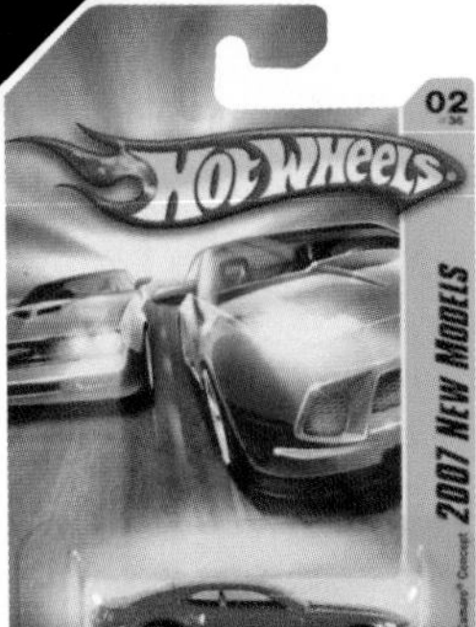

2007 New Models 2 of 36

❑ Chevy Camaro Concept/M Orange/OH5SP (K-Mart) .. $5.00

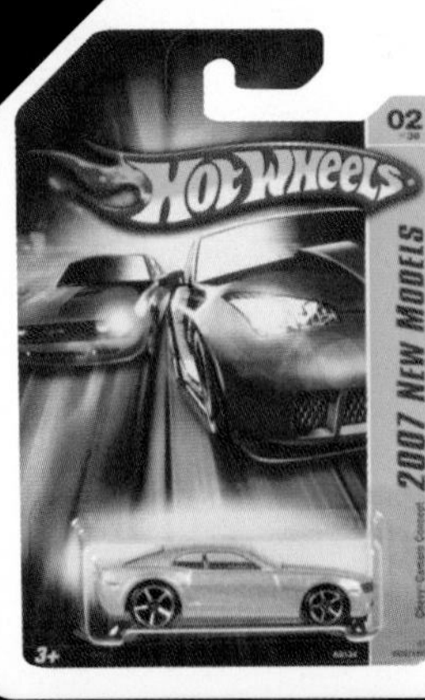

2007 New Models 2 of 36

❑ **Chevy Camaro Concept/M Silver/OH5SP black base $1.50**
❑ Chevy Camaro Concept/M Silver/OH5SP chrome base $1.50

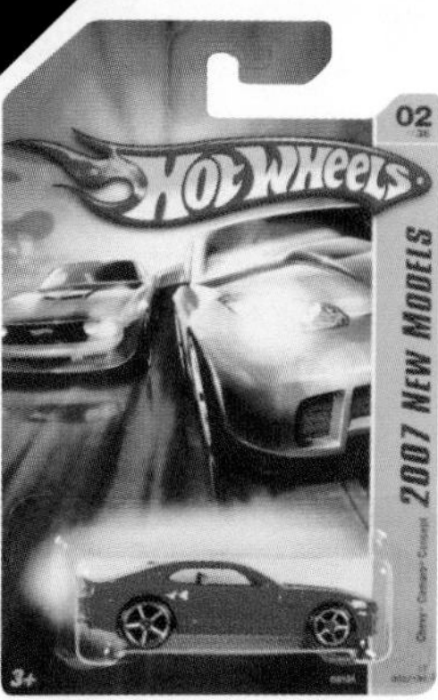

2007 New Models 2 of 36

2007 002

- ❑ Chevy Camaro Concept/Red/5SP $5.00
- **❑ Chevy Camaro Concept/Red/OH5SP........................ $1.50**

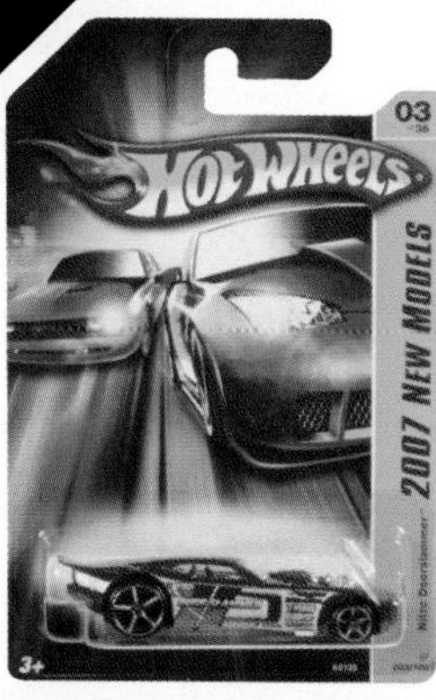

2007 New Models 3 of 36

2007 003

- ❑ Nitro Doorslammer/M Burgundy/GoldOH5SP.............. $1.50

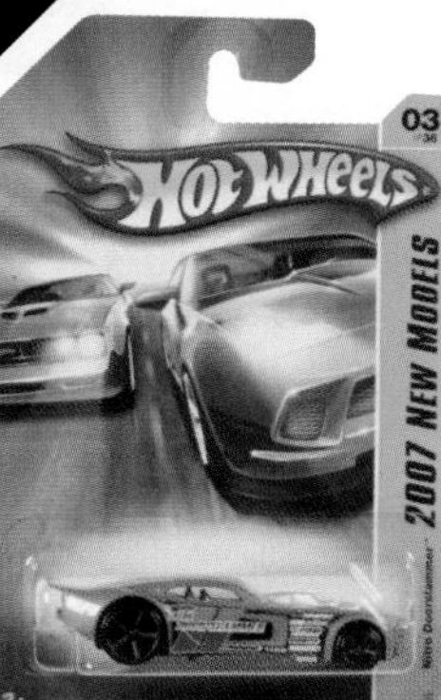

2007 New Models 3 of 36

2007 003

- ❑ Nitro Doorslammer/M Gold/RedOH5SP $1.50

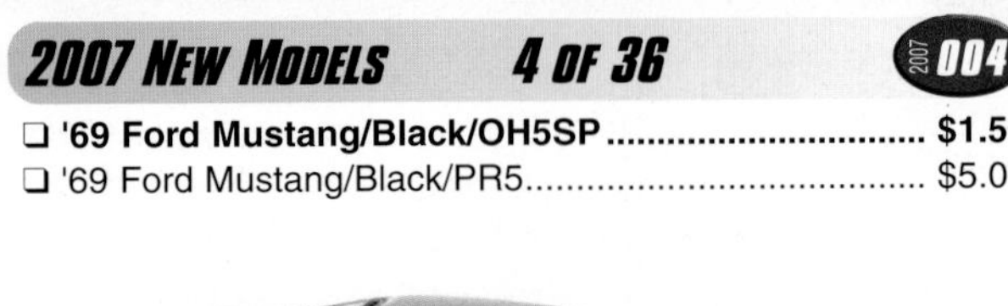

2007 New Models 4 of 36 2007 004

- ❑ **'69 Ford Mustang/Black/OH5SP $1.50**
- ❑ '69 Ford Mustang/Black/PR5.. $5.00

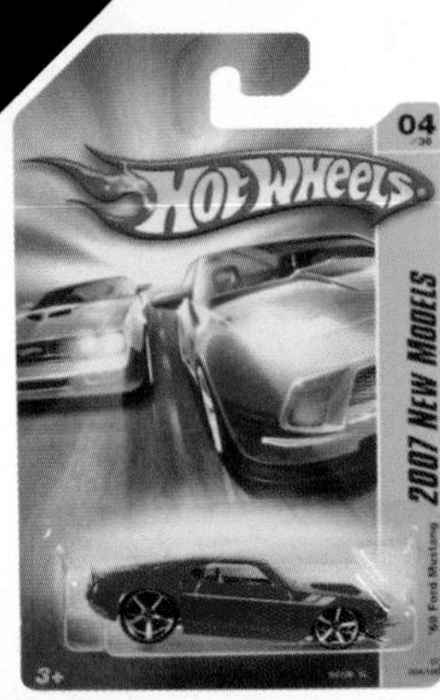

2007 New Models 4 of 36 2007 004

- ❑ '69 Ford Mustang/M Dark Red/5SP $1.50
- ❑ **'69 Ford Mustang/M Dark Red/OH5SP $1.50**

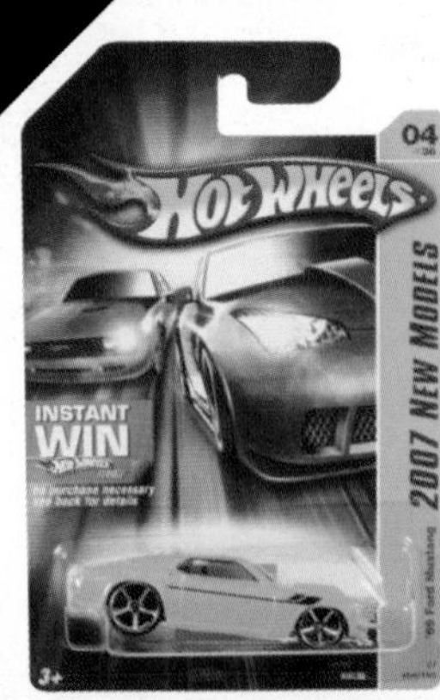

2007 New Models 4 of 36 2007 004

- ❑ '69 Ford Mustang/M Dark Yellow/OH5SP $1.50

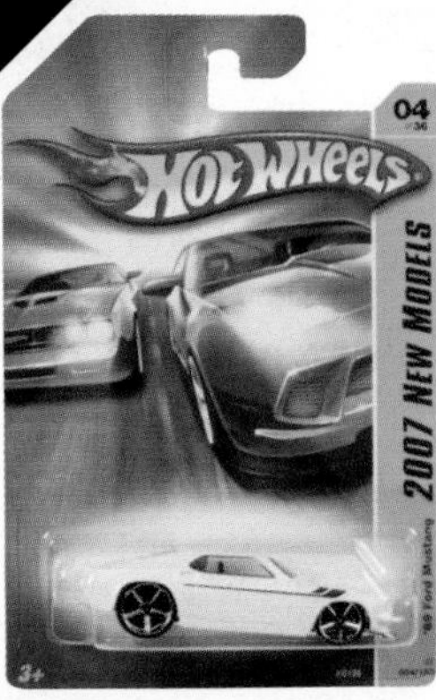

2007 NEW MODELS 4 OF 36

2007 004

- ❑ **'69 Ford Mustang/Pearl White/OH5SP $1.50**
- ❑ '69 Ford Mustang/Pearl White/PR5.............................. $5.00

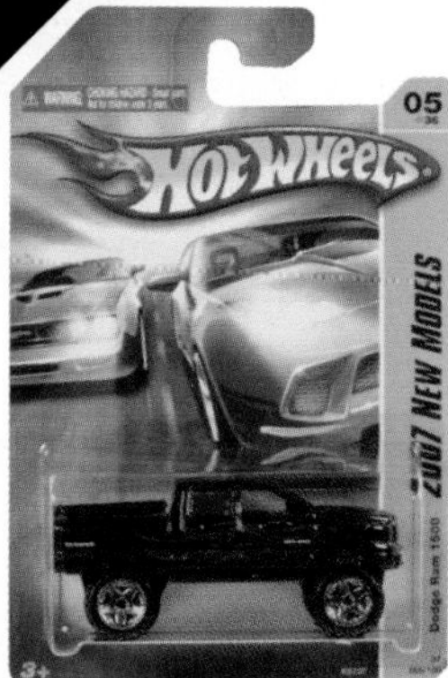

2007 NEW MODELS 5 OF 36

- ❑ Dodge Ram 1500/Black/OR5SP $3.00

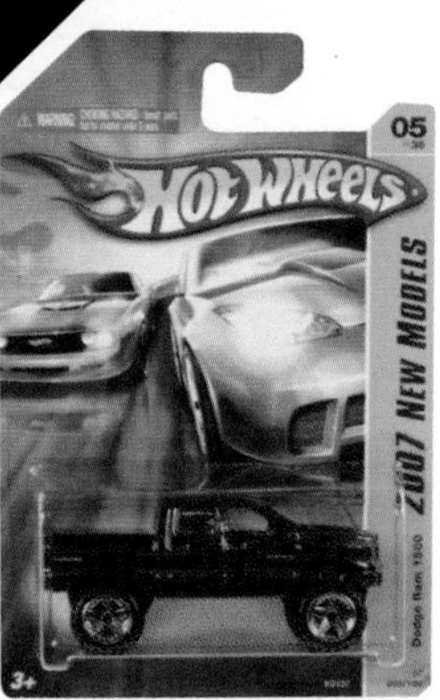

2007 NEW MODELS 5 OF 36

- ❑ Dodge Ram 1500/M Dark Purple/OR5SP.................... $3.00

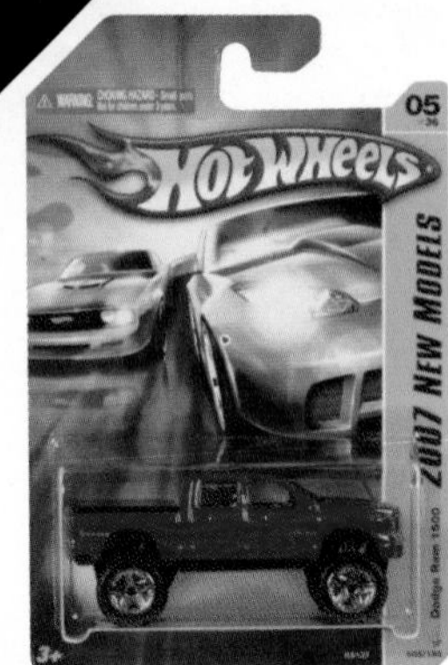

2007 New Models 5 of 36

❑ Dodge Ram 1500/M Dark Red/OR5SP $3.00

2007 New Models 5 of 36

❑ Dodge Ram 1500/Pearl Yellow/OR5SP (K-Mart) $3.00

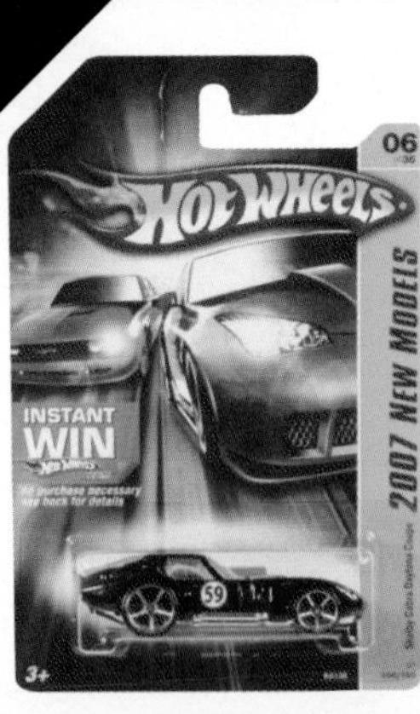

2007 New Models 6 of 36

❑ Shelby Cobra Daytona Coupe/M Dark Blue/OH5SP .. $1.50

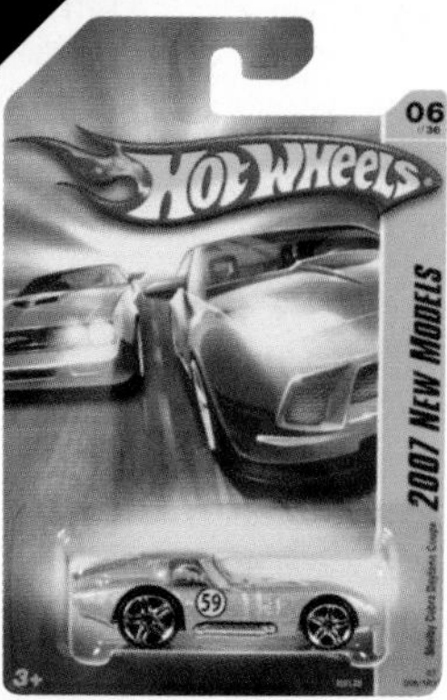

2007 New Models 6 of 36

❑ **Shelby Cobra Daytona Coupe/M Silver/PR5 large 59 $1.50**
❑ Shelby Cobra Daytona Coupe/M Silver/PR5 small 59 $3.00

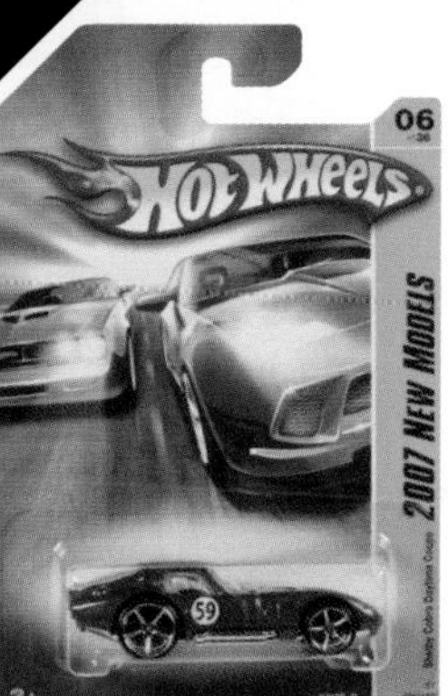

2007 New Models 6 of 36

❑ Shelby Cobra Daytona Coupe/M Teal/OH5SP $1.50

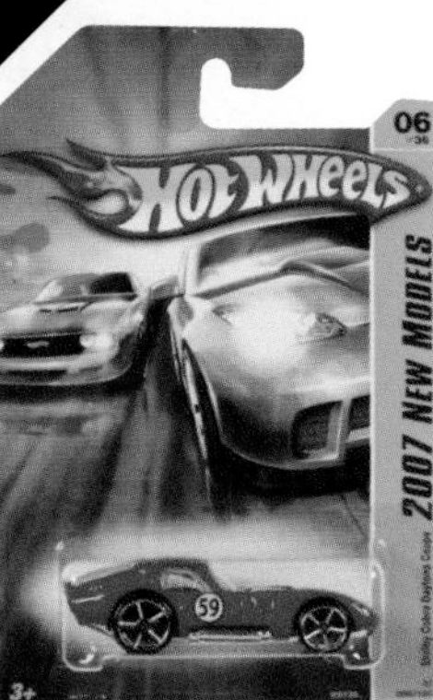

2007 New Models 6 of 36

❑ **Shelby Cobra Daytona Coupe/Red/OH5SP.............. $1.50**
❑ Shelby Cobra Daytona Coupe/Red/PR5...................... $3.00

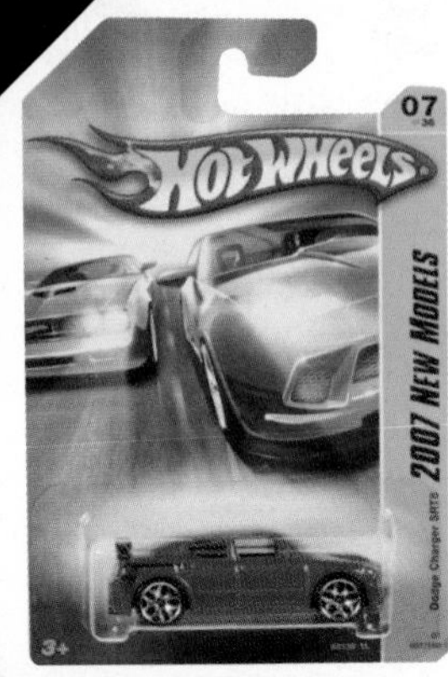

2007 New Models 7 of 36

❑ Dodge Charger SRT8/M Orange/Y5 .... $1.50

2007 New Models 7 of 36

❑ Dodge Charger SRT8/M Red-Orange/Y5 orange spoiler $1.50
❑ Dodge Charger SRT8/M Red-Orange/Y5 red spoiler .. $5.00

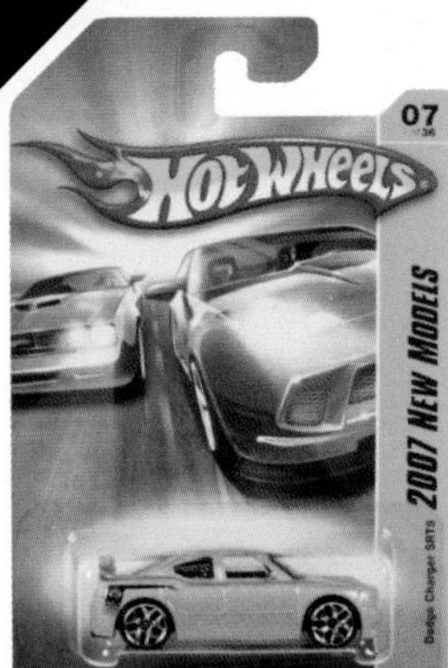

2007 New Models 7 of 36

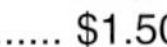

❑ Dodge Charger SRT8/M Silver/Y5 .... $1.50

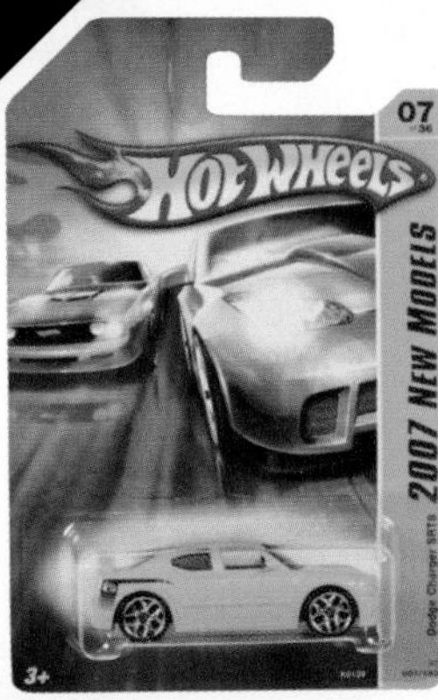

2007 New Models 7 of 36

2007 007

❑ Dodge Charger SRT8/M Yellow/Y5 .... $1.50

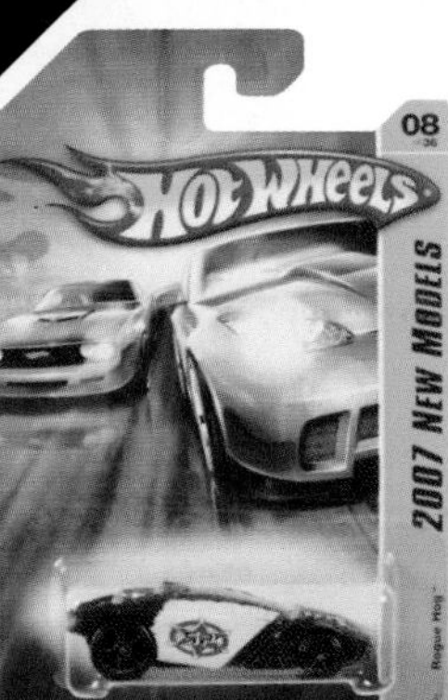

2007 New Models 8 of 36

2007 008

❑ Rogue Hog/Black/BlackOH5SP $1.50

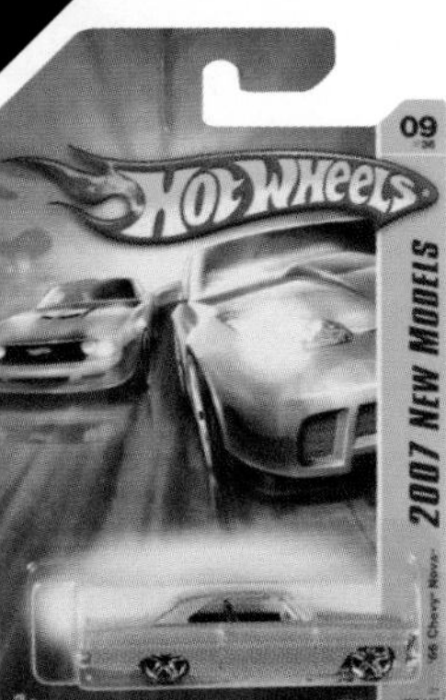

2007 New Models 9 of 36

2007 009

❑ '66 Chevy Nova/Champagne/PR5 .... $1.50

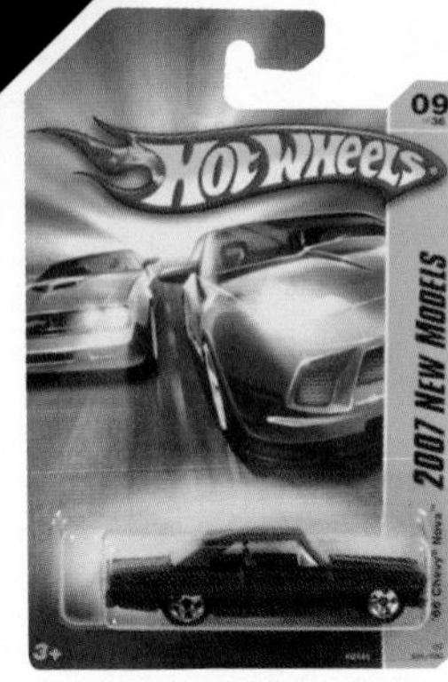

2007 New Models 9 of 36

- ❑ '66 Chevy Nova/Flat Black/5SP black base $3.00
- **❑ '66 Chevy Nova/Flat Black/5SP chrome base.......... $1.50**

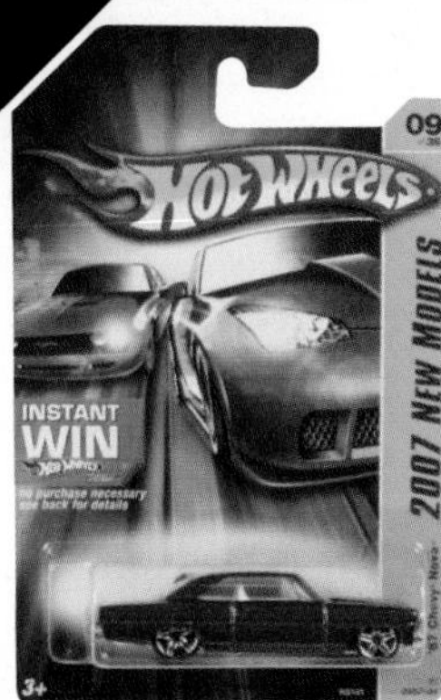

2007 New Models 9 of 36

- ❑ '66 Chevy Nova/M Blue/PR5.. $1.50

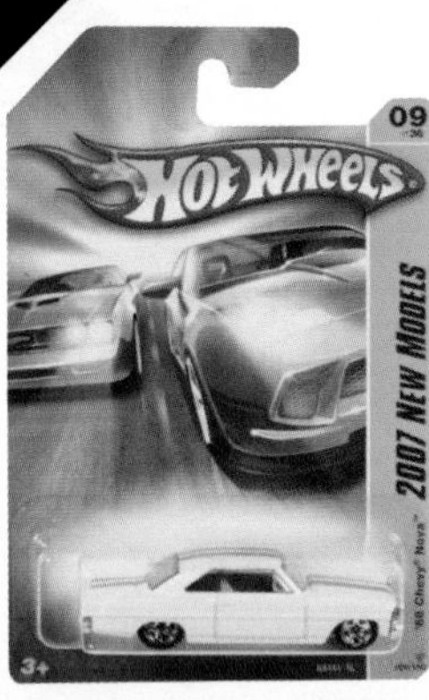

2007 New Models 9 of 36

- ❑ '66 Chevy Nova/Pearl White/5SP $3.00

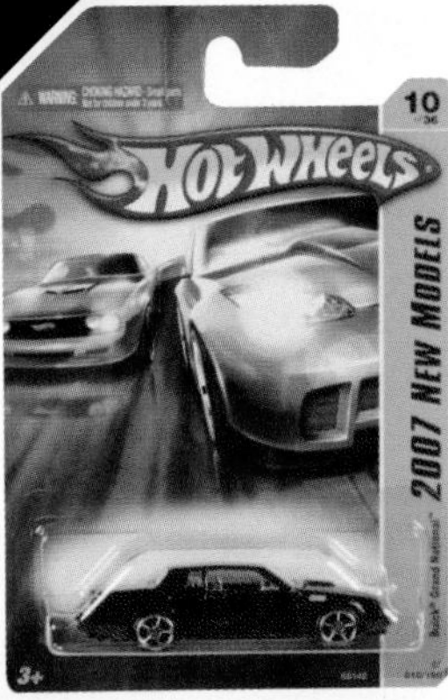

2007 New Models 10 of 36

- ❑ Buick Grand National/Black/5SP................................ $15.00
- ❑ **Buick Grand National/Black/OH5SP $1.50**

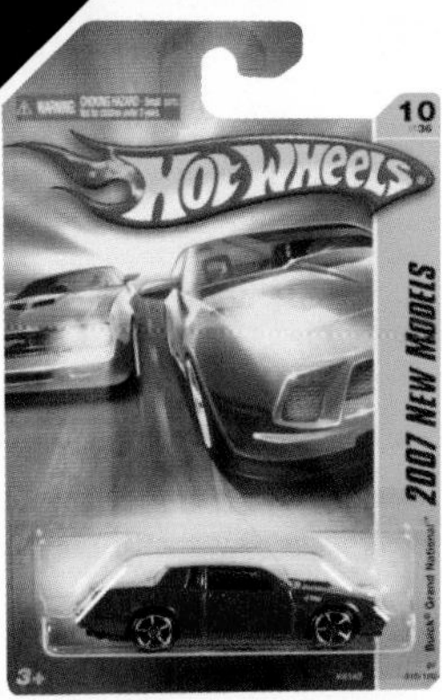

2007 New Models 10 of 36

- ❑ Buick Grand National/M Blue/OH5SP (K-Mart).......... $20.00

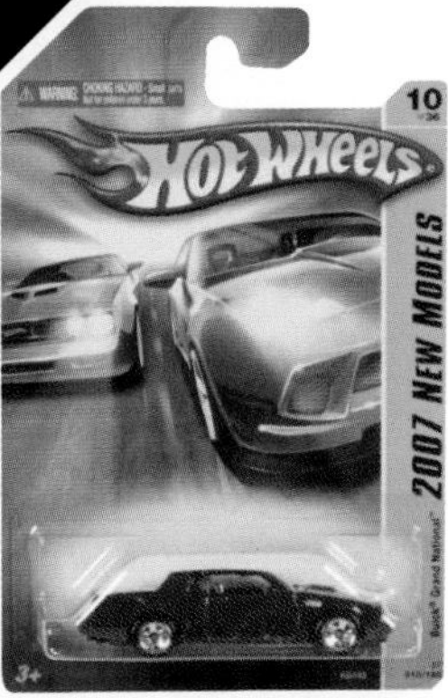

2007 New Models 10 of 36

- ❑ Buick Grand National/M Burgundy/5SP $1.50

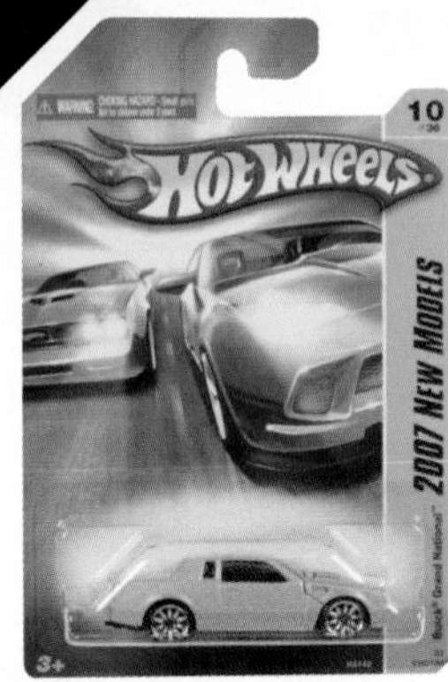

2007 New Models 10 of 36

- ❑ **Buick Grand National/Silver/10SP black interior $1.50**
- ❑ Buick Grand National/Silver/10SP chrome interior $25.00
- ❑ Buick Grand National/Silver/Y5 chrome inetrior $12.00
- ❑ Buick Grand National/Silver/Y5 black interior $125.00

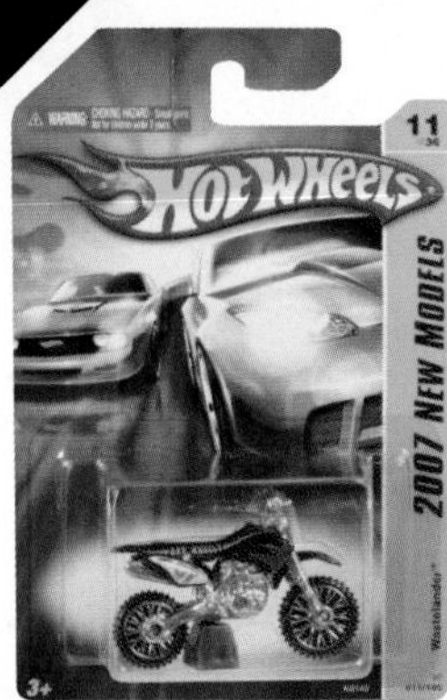

2007 New Models 11 of 36

- ❑ Wastelander/Black/BlackORMC $3.00
- ❑ **Wastelander/Black/GoldORMC $1.50**

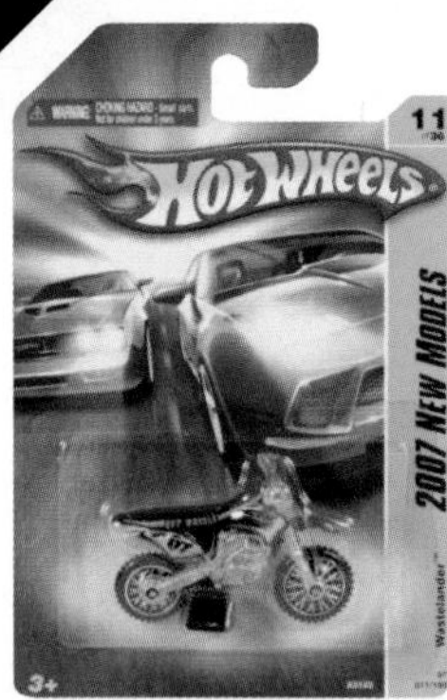

2007 New Models 11 of 36

- ❑ Wastelander/Dark Olive Green/ORMC $1.50

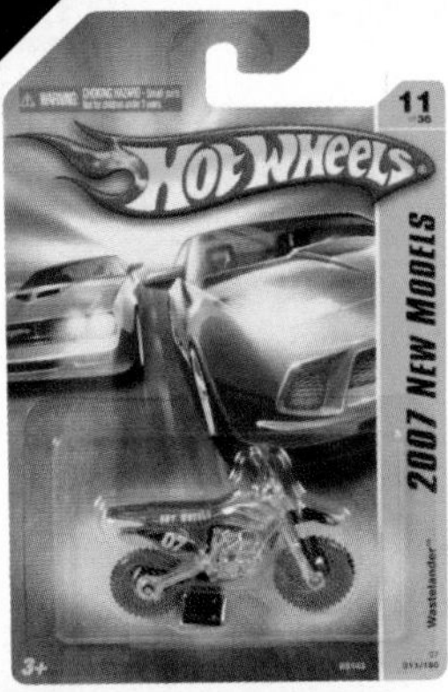

2007 New Models 11 of 36

❑ Wastelander/Grey/RedORMC $1.50

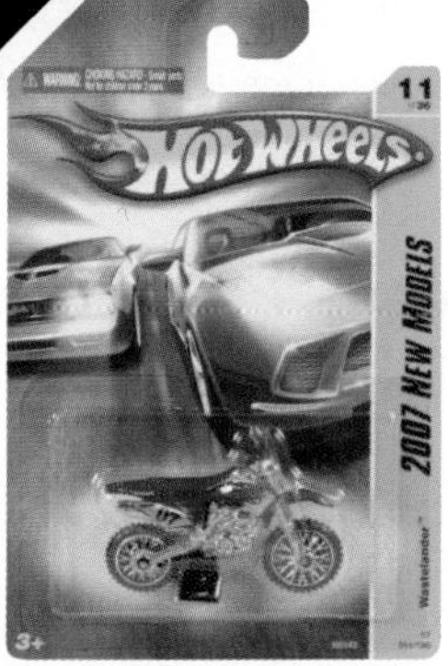

2007 New Models 11 of 36

❑ Wastelander/M Red/ORMC $1.50

2007 New Models 12 of 36

❑ Straight Pipes/Black/5SP black interior $30.00
❑ **Straight Pipes/Black/5SP red interior $1.50**

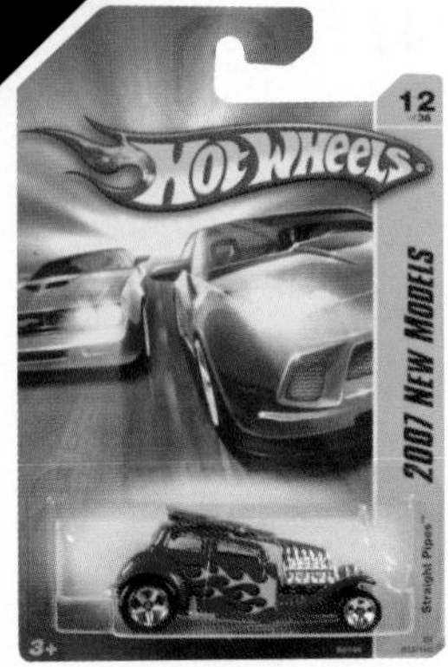

2007 New Models 12 of 36

❑ Straight Pipes/M Red/5SP $1.50

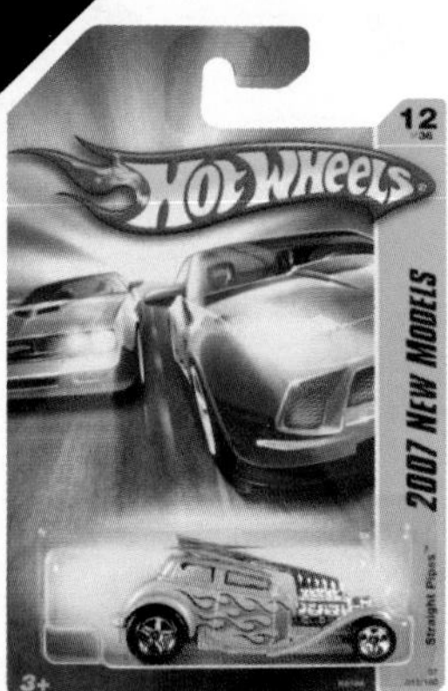

2007 New Models 12 of 36

❑ Straight Pipes/M Silver/5SP $1.50

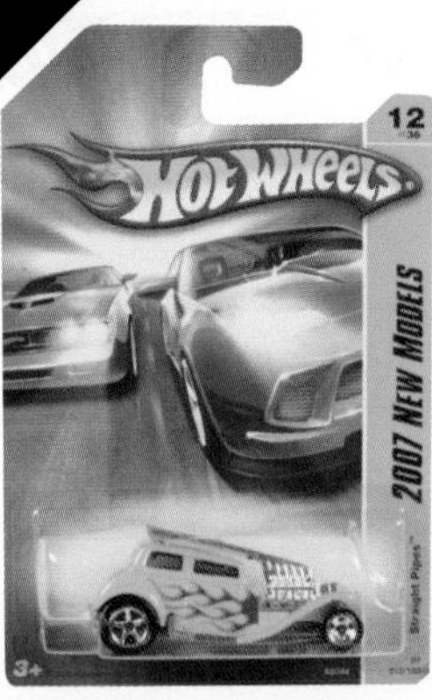

2007 New Models 12 of 36

❑ Straight Pipes/Yellow/5SP $1.50

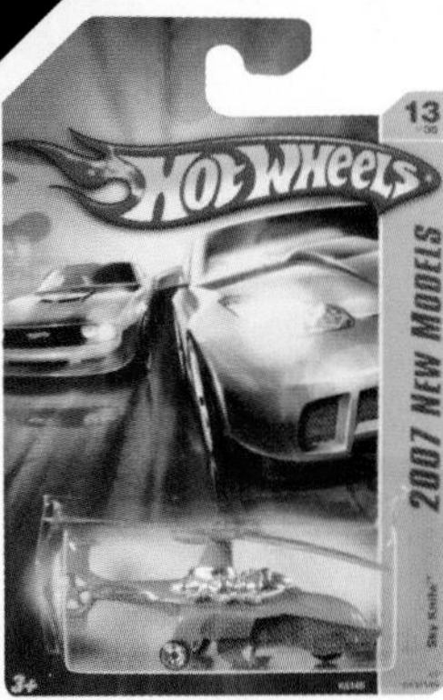

2007 New Models 13 of 36

❑ Sky Knife/Antifreeze Green/Micro5SP $1.50

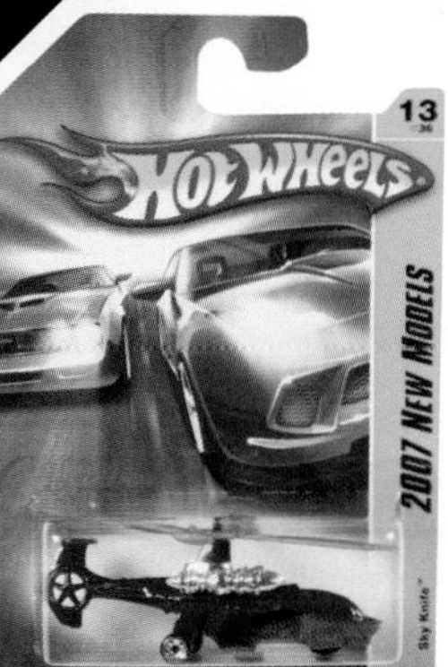

2007 New Models 13 of 36

❑ Sky Knife/Blue/Micro5SP $1.50

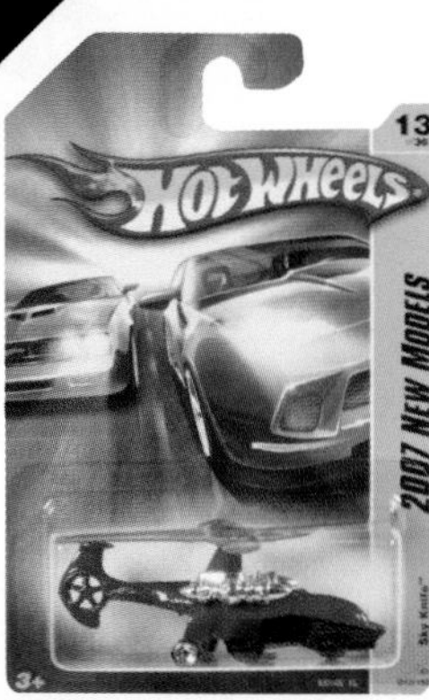

2007 New Models 13 of 36

❑ Sky Knife/M Red/Micro5SP $1.50

2007 New Models 14 of 36

❑ Ferrari 599 GTB/Black/PR5 .... $1.50

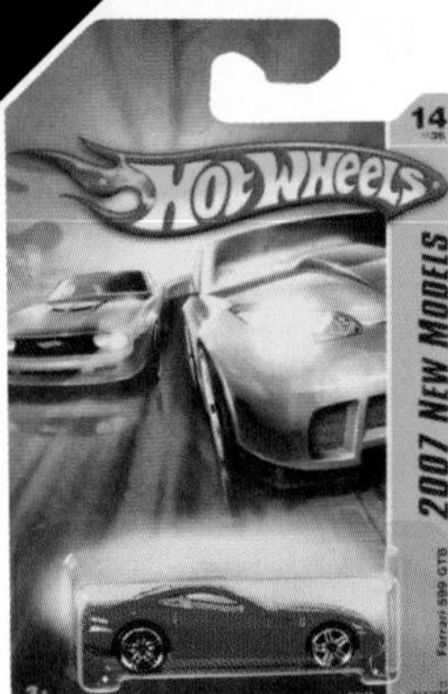

2007 New Models 14 of 36

2007 014

❑ **Ferrari 599 GTB/Red/PR5 .... $1.50**
❑ Ferrari 599 GTB/Red/PR5 orange headlights.............. $1.50

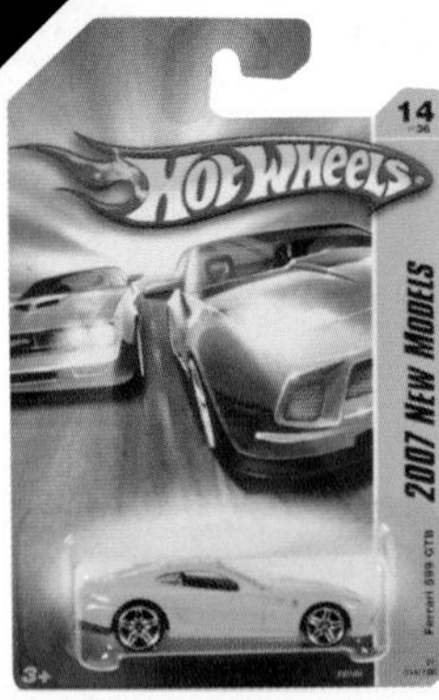

2007 New Models 14 of 36

❑ Ferrari 599 GTB/Yellow/PR5....................................... $1.50

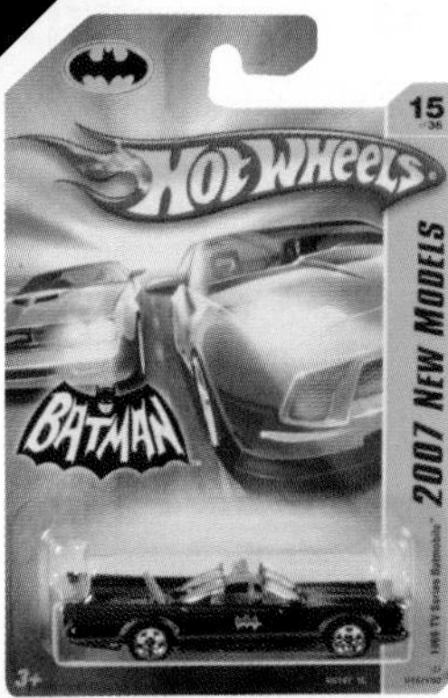

2007 New Models 15 of 36

- ❑ '66 Batmobile/Black/5SP $5.00

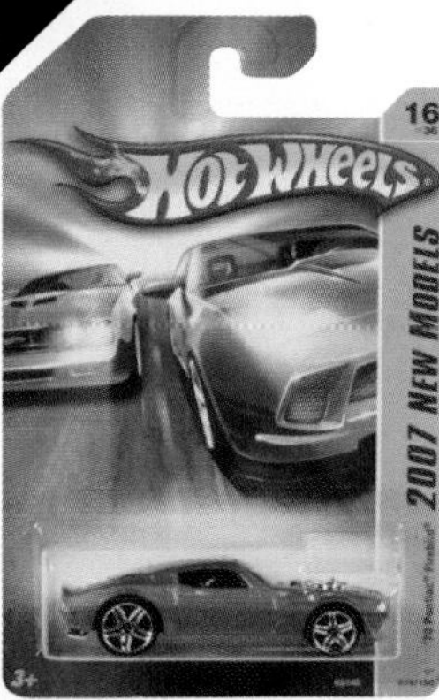

2007 New Models 16 of 36

- ❑ **'70 Pontiac Firebird/M Blue/PR5 .... $1.50**
- ❑ '70 Pontiac Firebird/M Blue/PR5 scum bum $5.00

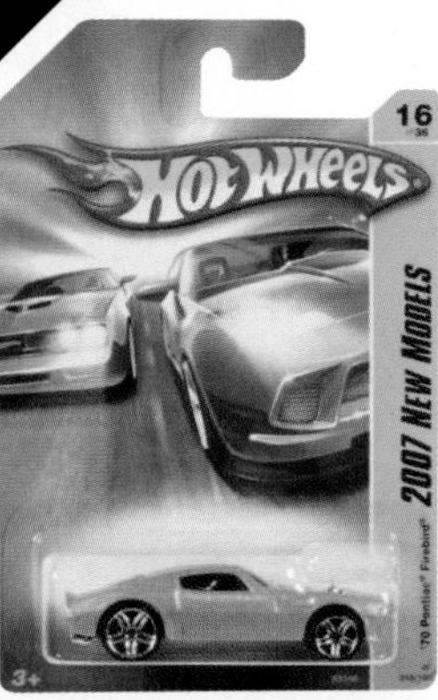

2007 New Models 16 of 36

- ❑ '70 Pontiac Firebird/M Gold/PR5................................ $1.50

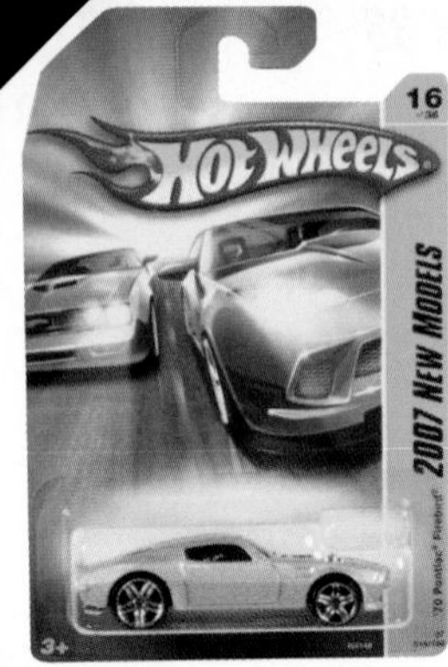

2007 New Models 16 of 36

2007 016

❑ '70 Pontiac Firebird/M Silver/PR5 (K-Mart) $5.00

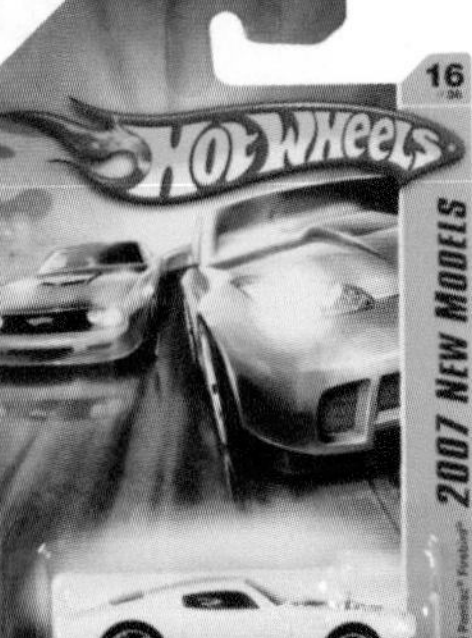

2007 New Models 16 of 36

2007 016

❑ '70 Pontiac Firebird/Pearl White/PR5 .... $1.50

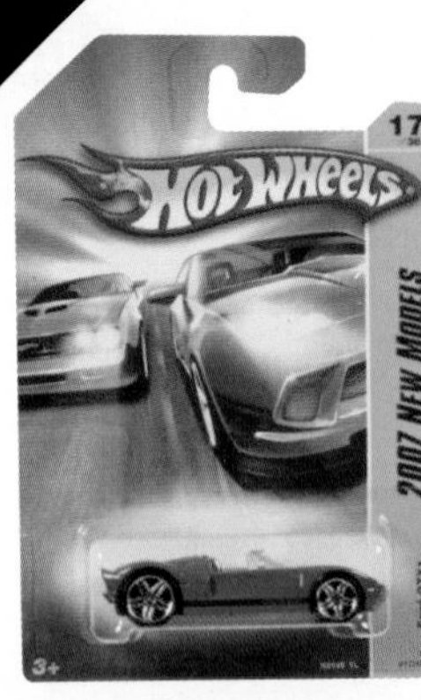

2007 New Models 17 of 36

❑ Ford GTX1/Blue/5SP.. $15.00
❑ Ford GTX1/Blue/OH5SP $1.50
❑ Ford GTX1/Blue/PR5 .... $1.50

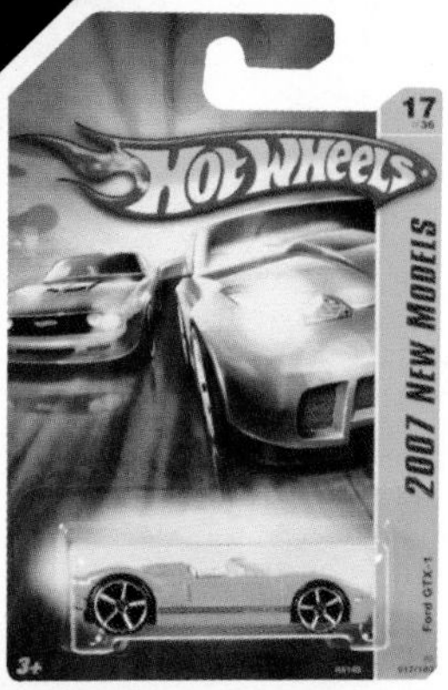

2007 New Models 17 of 36

❑ Ford GTX1/M Dark Yellow/OH5SP $1.50

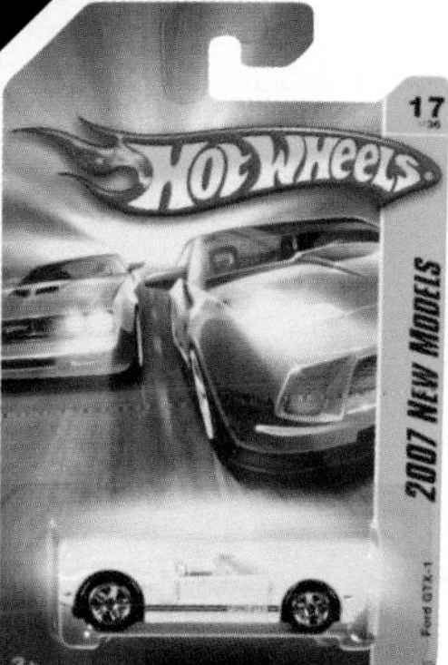

2007 New Models 17 of 36

❑ **Ford GTX1/Pearl White/5SP $1.50**
❑ Ford GTX1/Pearl White/OH5SP $30.00

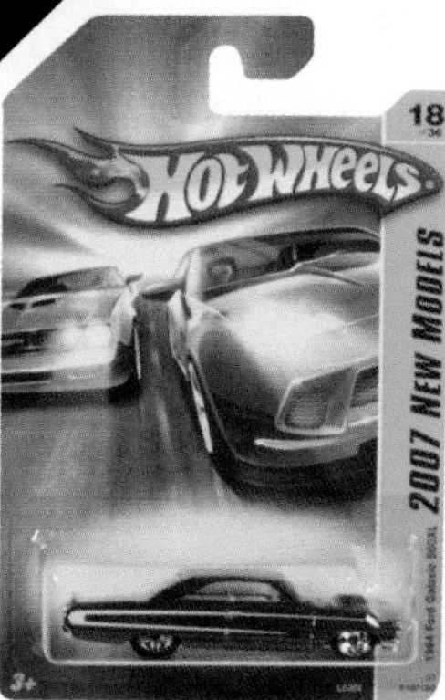

2007 New Models 18 of 36

❑ 1964 Ford Galaxie 500XL/M Blue/5SP $1.50

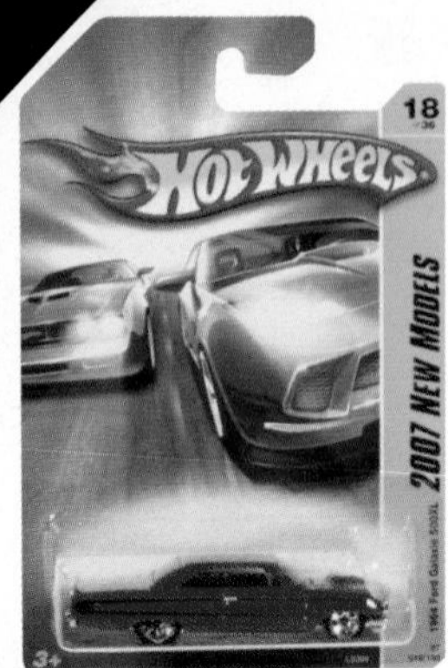

2007 New Models 18 of 36

❑ 1964 Ford Galaxie 500XL/M Dark Red/5SP $3.00

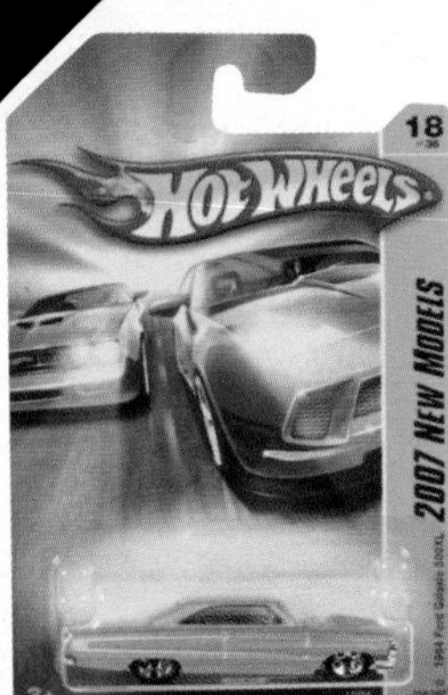

2007 New Models 18 of 36

❑ 1964 Ford Galaxie 500XL/M Powder Blue/5SP $1.50

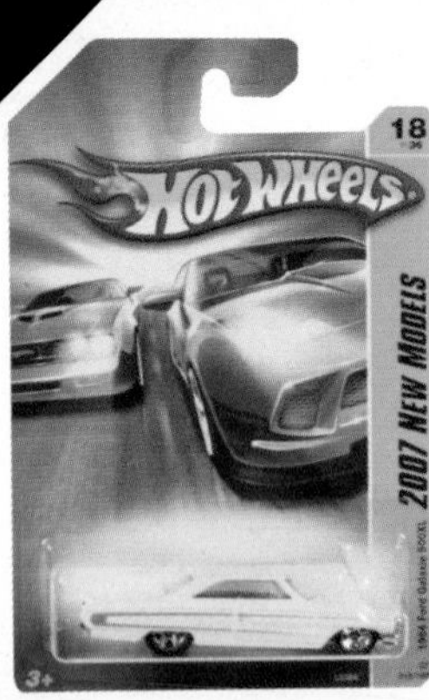

2007 New Models 18 of 36

❑ 1964 Ford Galaxie 500XL/Pearl White/5SP (K-Mart) .. $5.00

2007 NEW MODELS 19 OF 36

❑ CCM Country Club Muscle/Champagne/PR5 .... $1.50

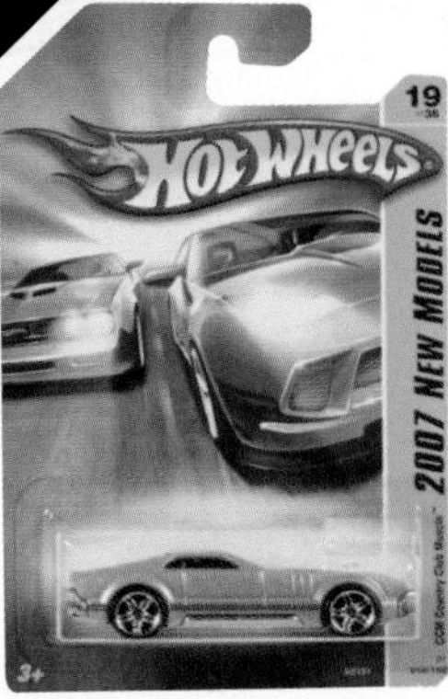

2007 NEW MODELS 20 OF 36

❑ Chevy Silverado/M Black/OH5SP $3.00

2007 NEW MODELS 20 OF 36

❑ Chevy Silverado/M Blue/OH5SP $1.50

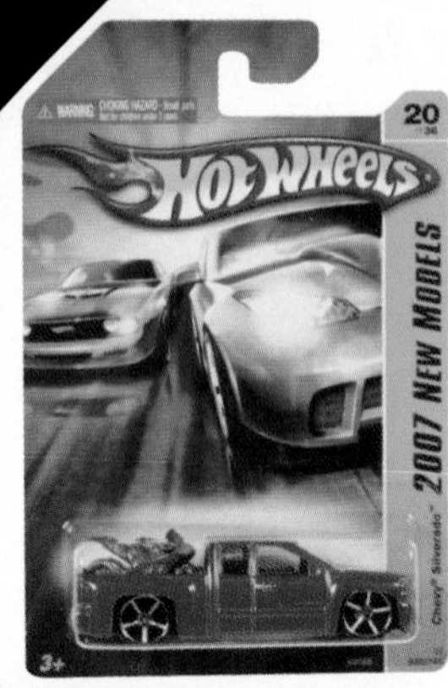

2007 New Models 20 of 36

❑ Chevy Silverado/M Dark Orange/OH5SP $3.00

2007 New Models 20 of 36

❑ Chevy Silverado/M Dark Red/OH5SP.......................... $3.00

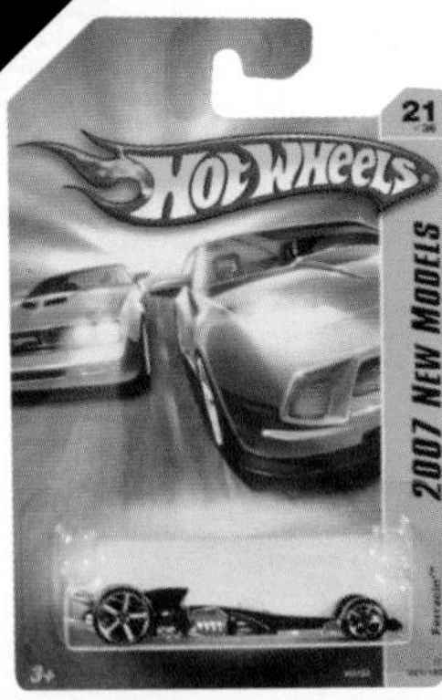

2007 New Models 21 of 36

❑ Nitro Scorcher (Ferracin')/M Blue/OH5SP $3.00

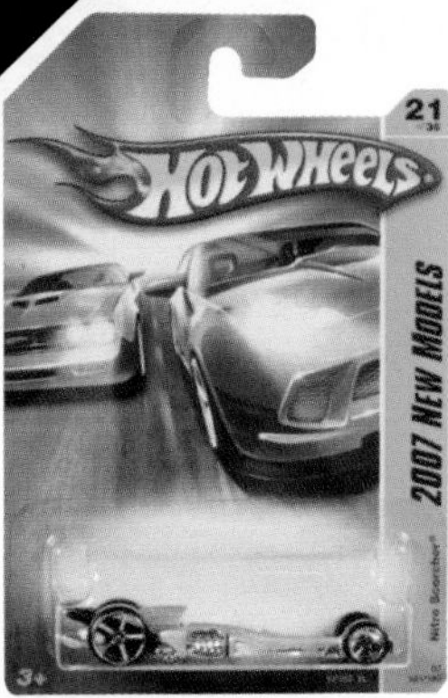

2007 New Models 21 of 36

- ❑ Nitro Scorcher (Ferracin')/M Silver/OH5SP.................. $1.50
- ❑ Nitro Scorcher (Ferracin')/Red/OH5SP $1.50
- ❑ Ferracin' (Nitro Scorcher)/Red/OH5SP ferracin' base.. $1.50
- **❑ Ferracin' (Nitro Scorcher)/Red/OH5SP nitro base .. $1.50**

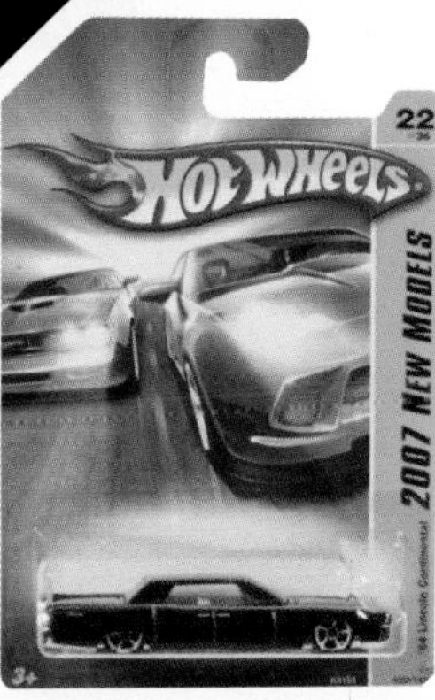

2007 New Models 22 of 36

- ❑ '64 Lincoln Continental/M Dark Blue/White5SP $20.00
- **❑ '64 Lincoln Continental/M Dark Blue/WhiteOH5SP $1.50**

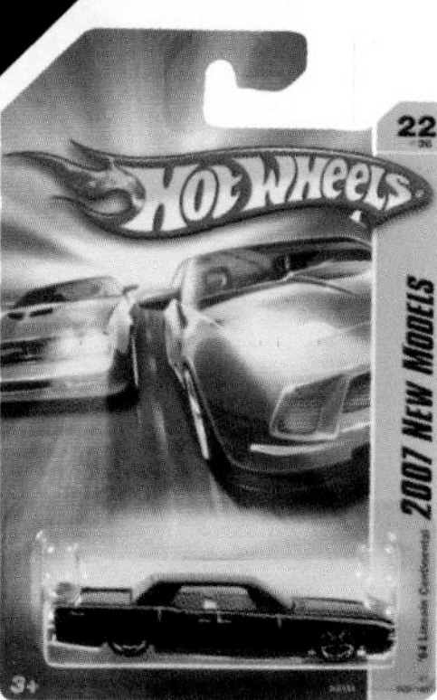

2007 New Models 22 of 36

- **❑ '64 Lincoln Continental/M Dark Purple/WSP $1.50**
- ❑ '64 Lincoln Continental/Pearl White/GoldOH5SP $1.50
- ❑ '64 Lincoln Continental/Silver/White5SP $200.00

2007 NEW MODELS 23 OF 36

❑ Ferrari 250 LM/Powder Blue/10SP $1.50

2007 NEW MODELS 23 OF 36

2007 023

❑ Ferrari 250 LM/Red/WSP $1.50

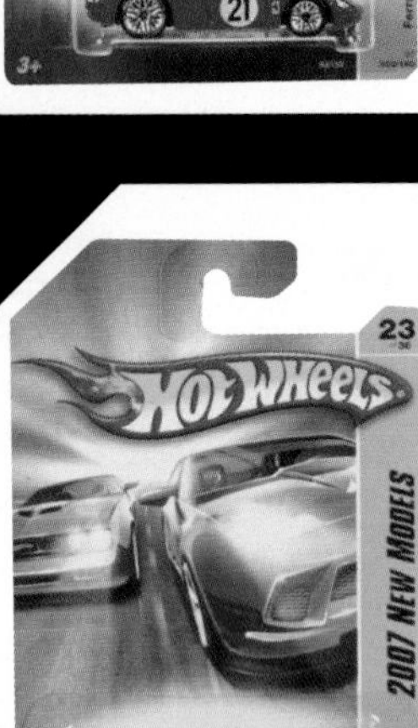

2007 NEW MODELS 23 OF 36

2007 023

❑ Ferrari 250 LM/Yellow/WSP black base $3.00

❑ **Ferrari 250 LM/Yellow/WSP chrome base $1.50**

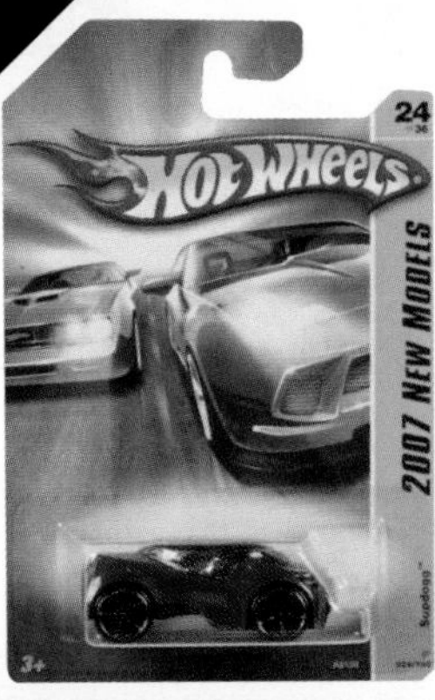

2007 New Models 24 of 36

❑ Supdogg/M Brown/GoldOH5SP $1.50

2007 New Models 25 of 36

❑ Solar Reflex/Gold Chrome/Y5 .... $1.50

2007 New Models 26 of 36

❑ Buzz Bomb/Black/OH5SP $1.50

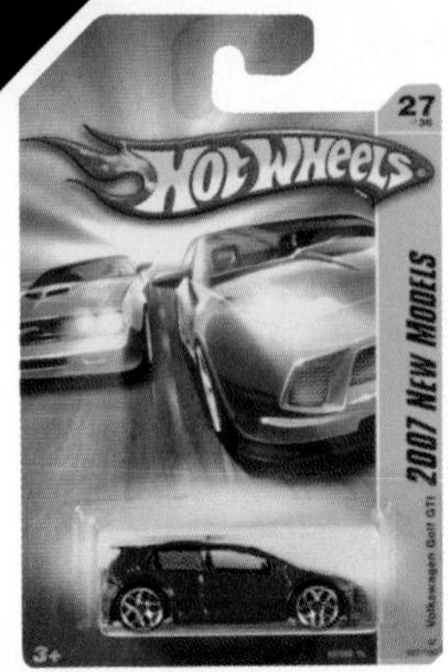

2007 New Models 27 of 36

❑ Volkswagen Golf GTI/M Blue/Y5 black base $1.50
❑ **Volkswagen Golf GTI/M Blue/Y5 chrome base........ $1.50**

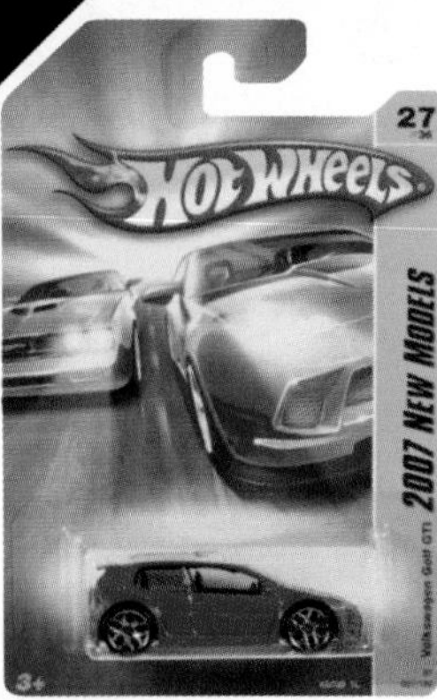

2007 New Models 27 of 36

❑ Volkswagen Golf GTI/M Dark Orange/CopperY5 (K-Mart) $5.00

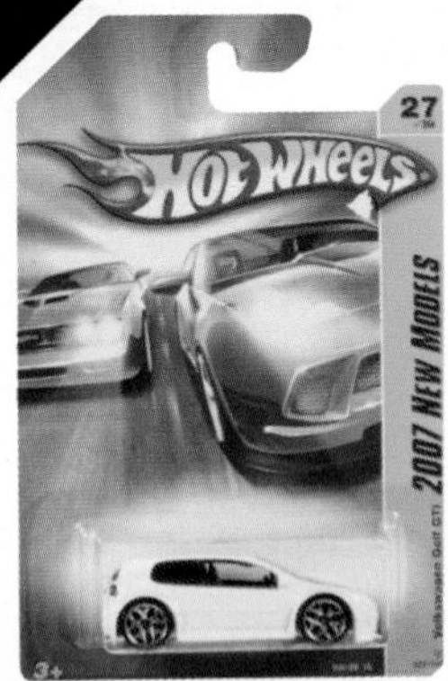

2007 New Models 27 of 36

❑ Volkswagen Golf GTI/Pearl White/Y5 .... $1.50

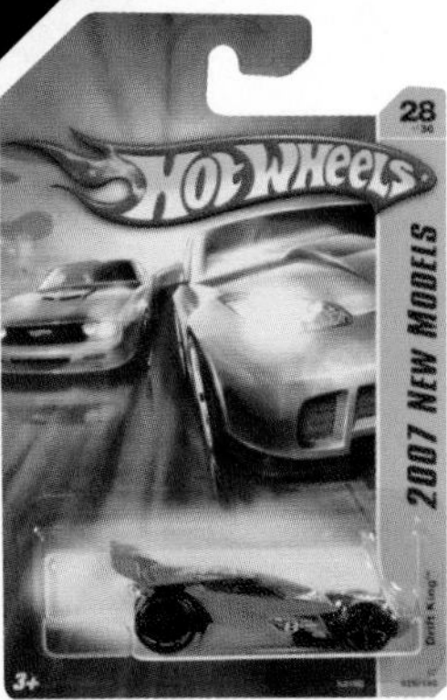

2007 New Models 28 of 36

❑ Drift King/M Gold/RedOH5SP $1.50

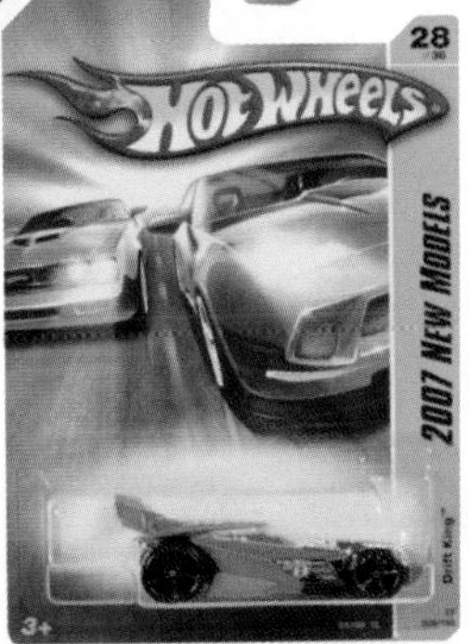

2007 New Models 28 of 36

❑ Drift King/M Lt. Green/RedOH5SP $1.50

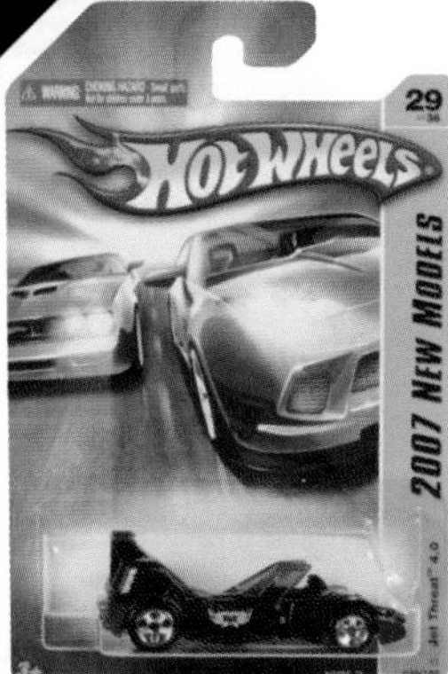

2007 New Models 29 of 36

❑ Jet Threat 4.0/M Black/10SP $3.00
❑ Jet Threat 4.0/M Black/5SP $1.50
❑ Jet Threat 4.0/M Black/OH5SP $1.50

❑ Jet Threat 4.0/M Silver/CopperOH5SP $1.50

❑ Jet Threat 4.0/Red/10SP $1.50

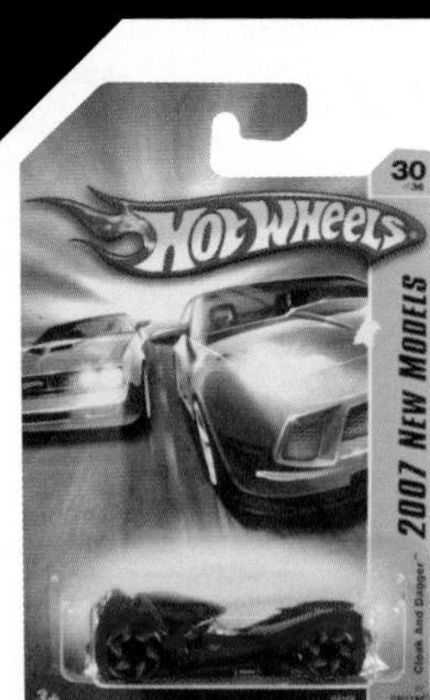

2007 New Models 30 of 36

❑ Cloak And Dagger/Black Clear w/Green/OH5SP $1.50

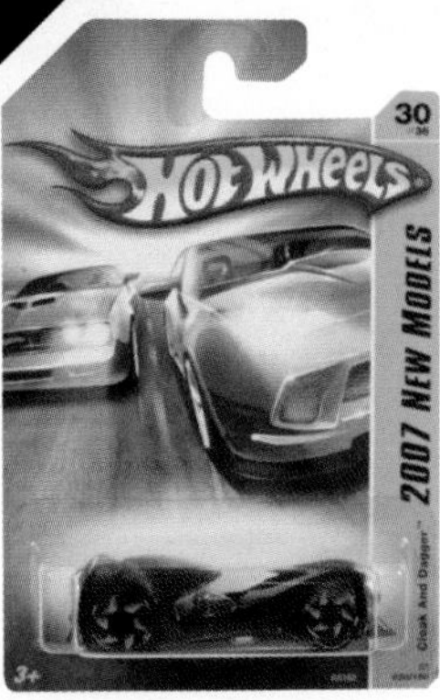

2007 New Models 30 of 36

❑ Cloak And Dagger/Red Clear w/Blue/OH5SP (K-Mart) $5.00

2007 New Models 31 of 36

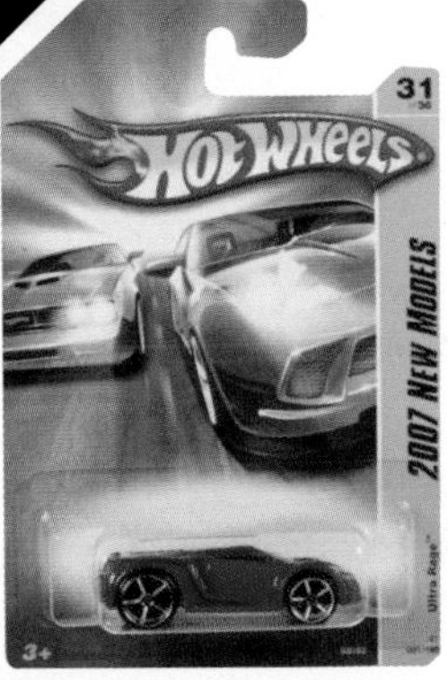

❑ Ultra Rage/Red/OH5SP $1.50

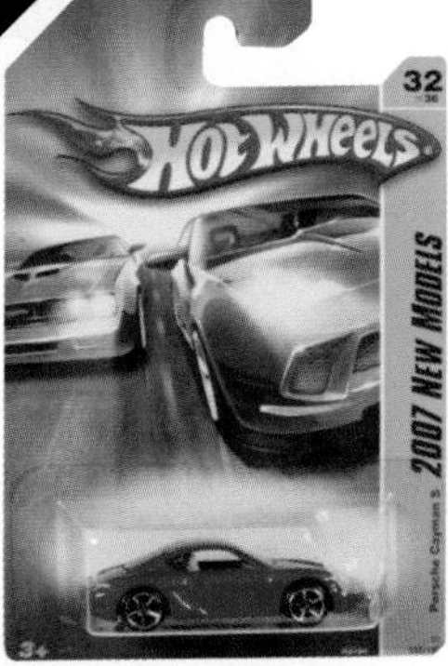

2007 New Models 32 of 36

❑ Porsche Cayman S/M Red/OH5SP $1.50

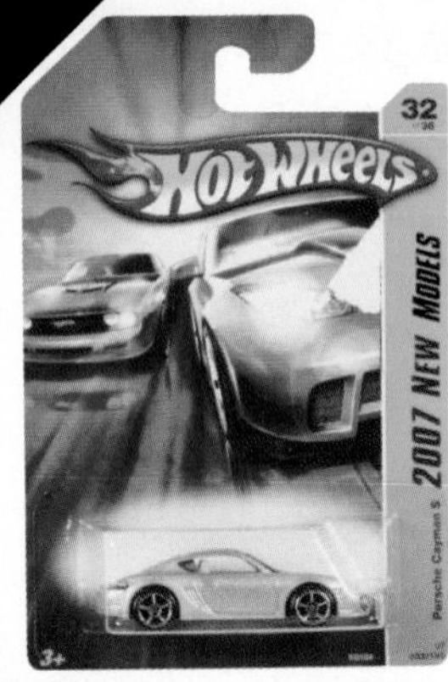

2007 New Models 32 of 36

❑ Porsche Cayman S/M Silver/OH5SP $1.50

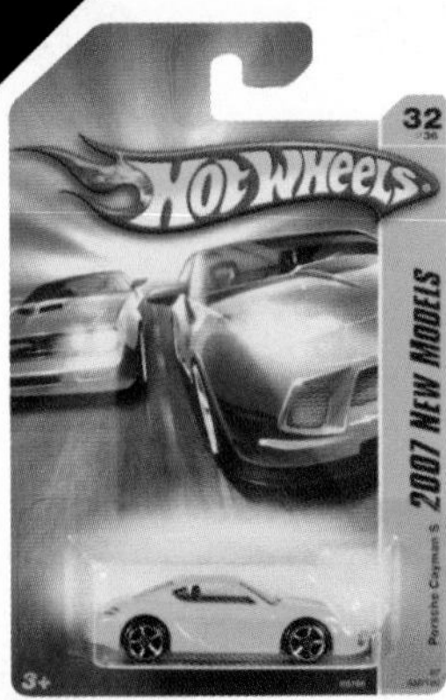

2007 New Models 32 of 36

❑ Porsche Cayman S/Pearl Yellow/OH5SP $1.50

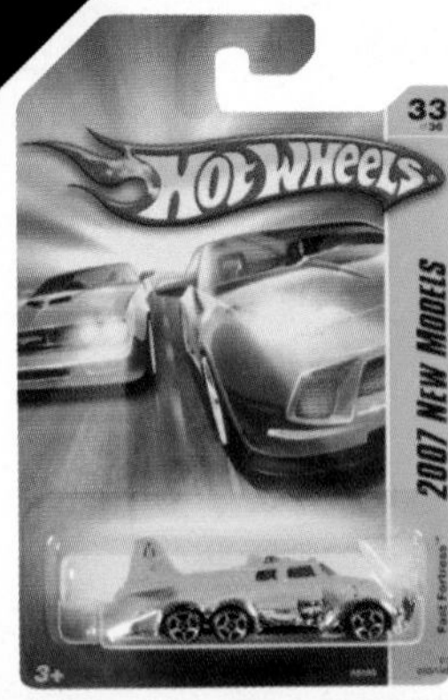

2007 New Models 33 of 36

❑ Fast Fortress/Flat Grey/5SP $1.50
❑ Fast Fortress/Flat Grey/OH5SP $1.50

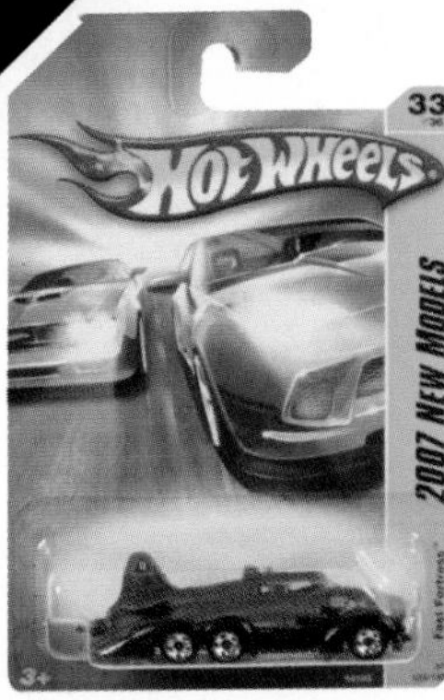

2007 New Models 33 of 36

❑ Fast Fortress/Olive Green/5SP $1.50

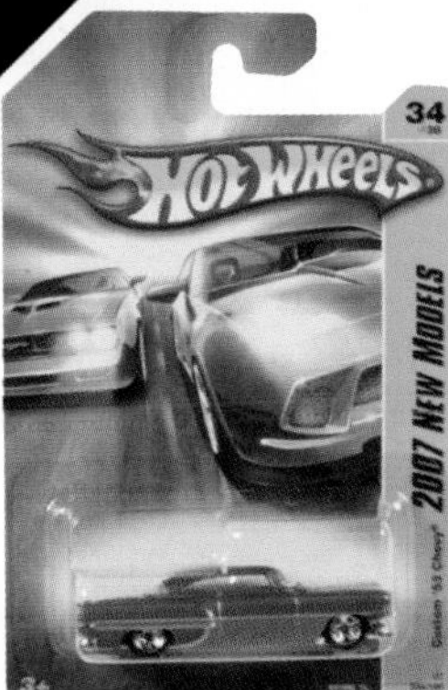

2007 New Models 34 of 36

2007 034

❑ Custom '53 Chevy/M Copper/5SP (K-Mart) $5.00

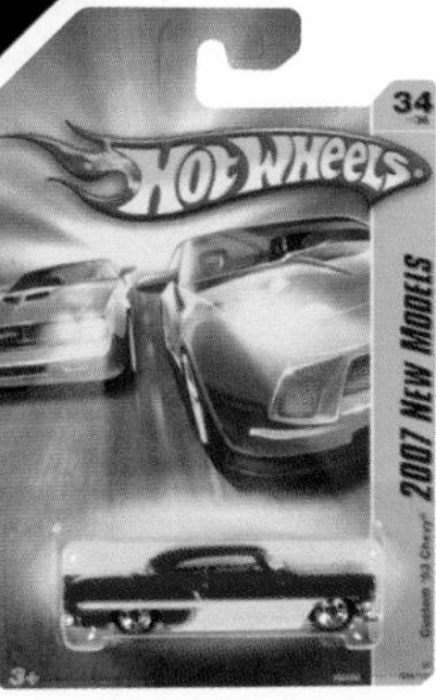

2007 New Models 34 of 36

❑ Custom '53 Chevy/M Dark Red/5SP $3.00

2007

 2007 New Models 34 of 36 

❑ Custom '53 Chevy/M Purple/5SP $3.00

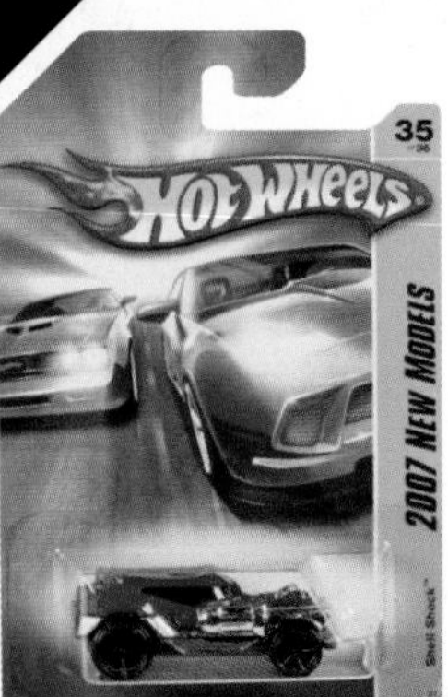

2007 New Models 35 of 36 

❑ Shell Shock/M Red/RedOH5SP $1.50

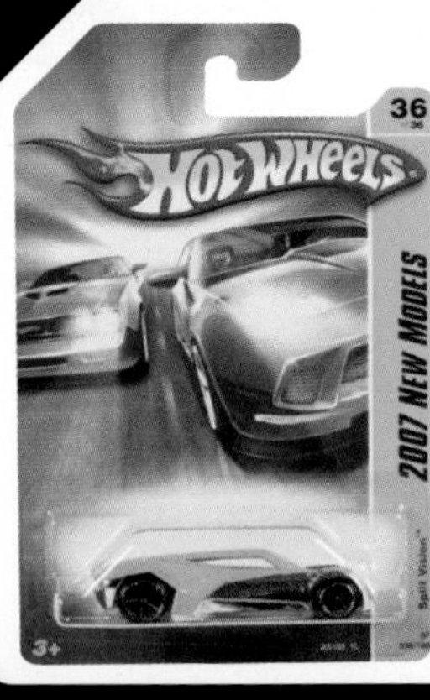

2007 New Models 36 of 36 

❑ Split Vision/Pearl Yellow/OH5SP................................. $1.50

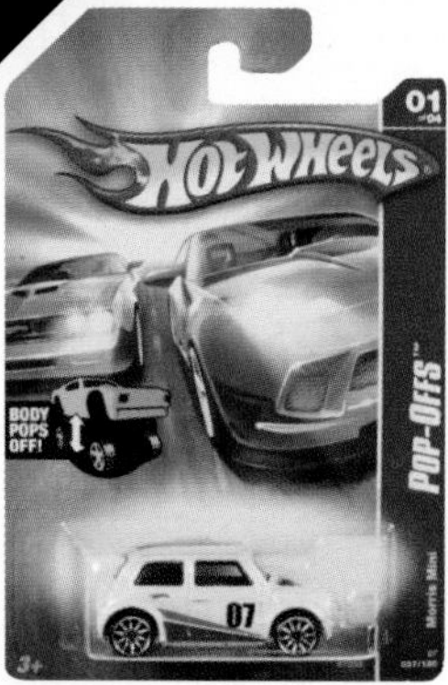

Pop-Offs 1 of 4 — 2007 037

❑ Morris Mini/Pearl White/10SP $3.00

Pop-Offs 2 of 4 — 2007 038

❑ Hyperliner/Flat Black/BlackOH5SP $1.50

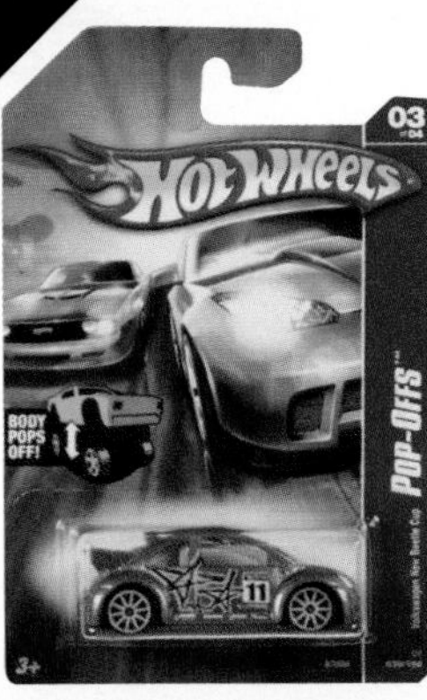

Pop-Offs 3 of 4 — 2007 039

❑ Volkswagen New Beetle Cup/M Teal/10SP.................. $3.00

❑ **Volkswagen New Beetle Cup/M Teal/Yellow10SP $3.00**

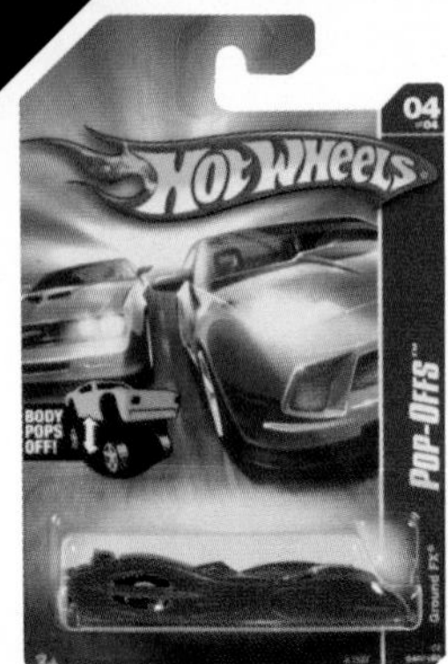

❑ Ground FX/M Purple/SK5 .... $1.50

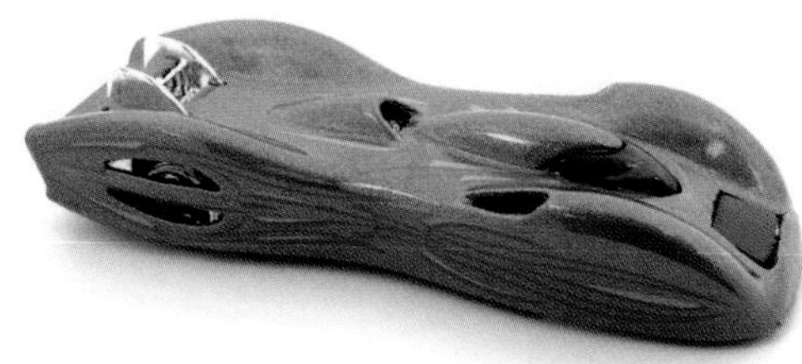

CAMARO 1 OF 4

❑ '69 Camaro Conv./M Dark Red/5SP chrome Malaysia base $3.00
❑ '69 Camaro Conv./M Dark Red/5SP chrome Thailand base $3.00
❑ '69 Camaro Conv./M Dark Red/PR5 black Malaysia base .. $3.00
❑ '69 Camaro Conv./M Dark Red/PR5 chrome Malaysia base $3.00
❑ '69 Camaro Conv./M Dark Red/PR5 chrome Thailand base $3.00

CAMARO 2 OF 4

❑ '67 Camaro/M Dark Blue/5SP $3.00
❑ '67 Camaro/M Dark Blue/PR5 .... $8.00

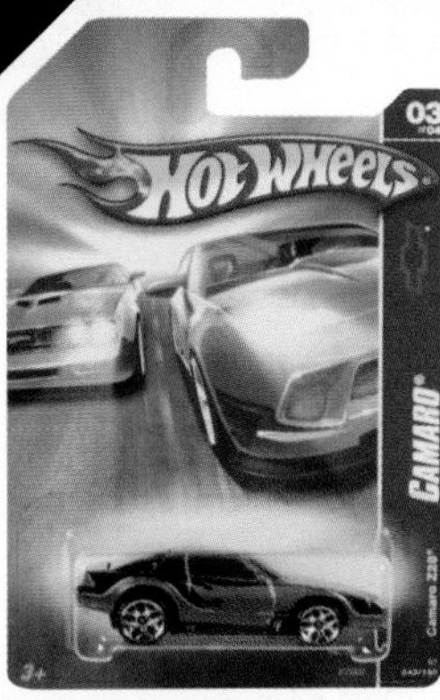

Camaro 3 of 4

2007 043

- ❑ **Camaro Z28/M Grey/5SP $1.50**
- ❑ Camaro Z28/M Grey/Y5 .... $3.00
- ❑ Camaro Z28/M Grey/Y5 black Malaysia base $3.00

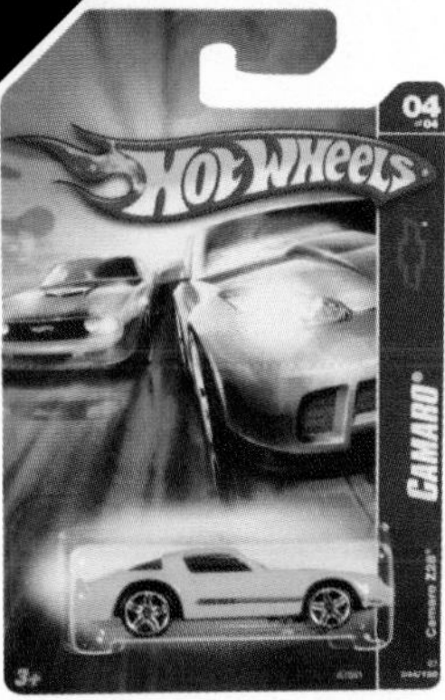

Camaro 4 of 4

2007 044

- ❑ Camaro Z28/M Yellow/PR5 .... $1.50

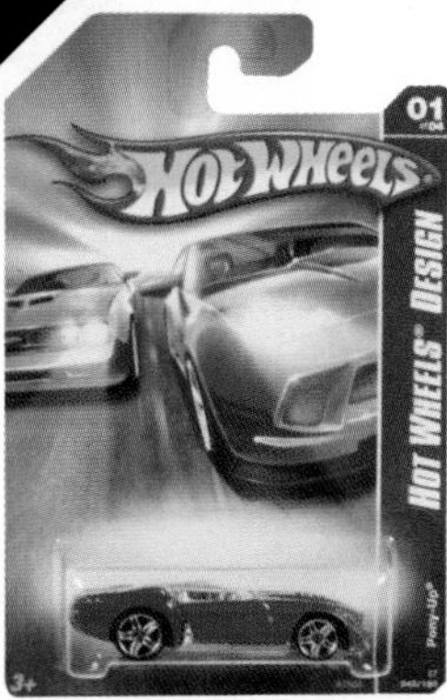

Hot Wheels Design 1 of 4

2007 045

- ❑ Pony-Up/M Dark Orange/PR5 .... $1.50

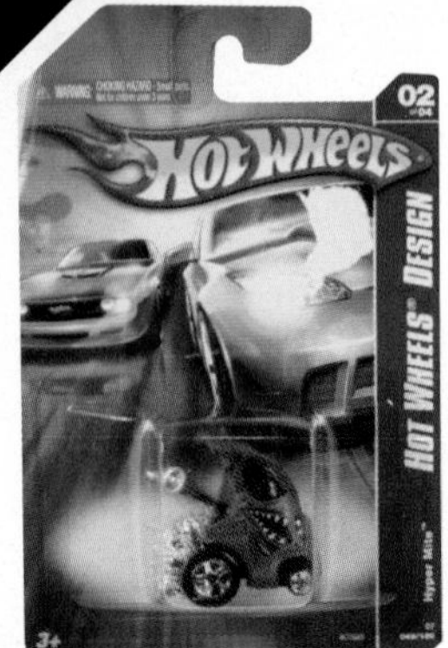

Hot Wheels Design 2 of 4

❑ Hyper Mite/Dark Olive Green/5SP $1.50

Hot Wheels Design 3 of 4

❑ Asphalt Assault/M Green/10SP $1.50

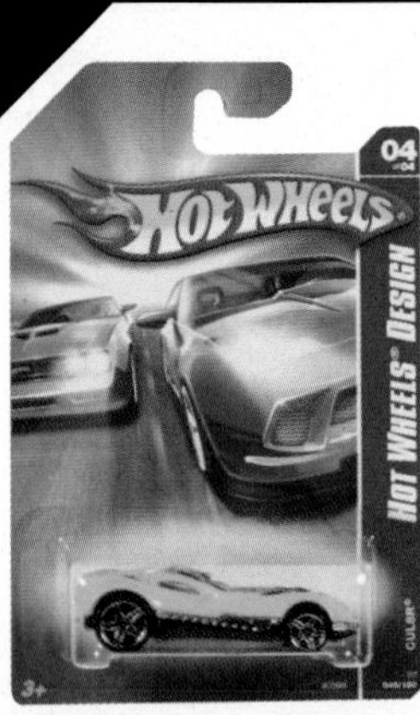

Hot Wheels Design 4 of 4

❑ **CUL8R/Pearl Yellow/GoldOH5SP $1.50**
❑ CUL8R/Pearl Yellow/GoldPR5 .... $1.50

Taxi Rods 1 of 4

❑ Cockney Cab II/M Gold/5SP $1.50

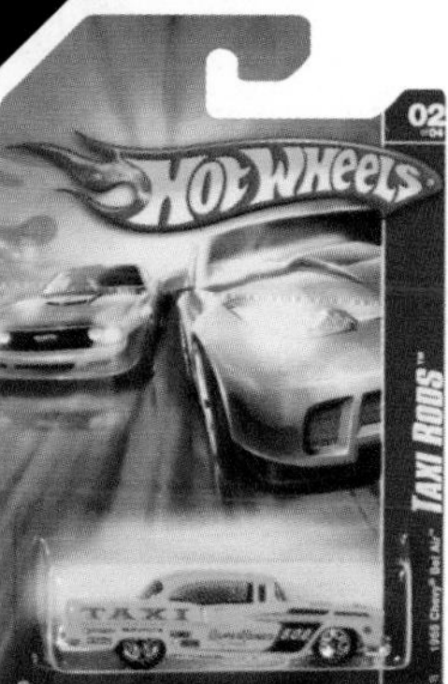

Taxi Rods 2 of 4

❑ '55 Chevy/Yellow/5SP $3.00

Taxi Rods 3 of 4

❑ '70 Plymouth Road Runner/M Black/5SP black TAXI .. $3.00
❑ '70 Plymouth Road Runner/M Black/5SP grey TAXI $3.00
❑ '70 Plymouth Road Runner/M Black/OH5SP $3.00

TAXI RODS 4 OF 4

❑ **1964 Chevy Impala/M Yellow/GoldWSP clear windows $1.50**
❑ 1964 Chevy Impala/M Yellow/GoldWSP tinted windows $3.00

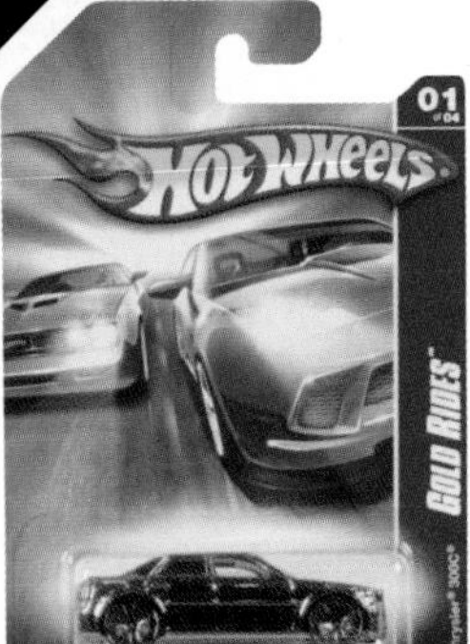

GOLD RIDES 1 OF 4

❑ Chrysler 300C/Gold Chrome/GoldBLING $1.50

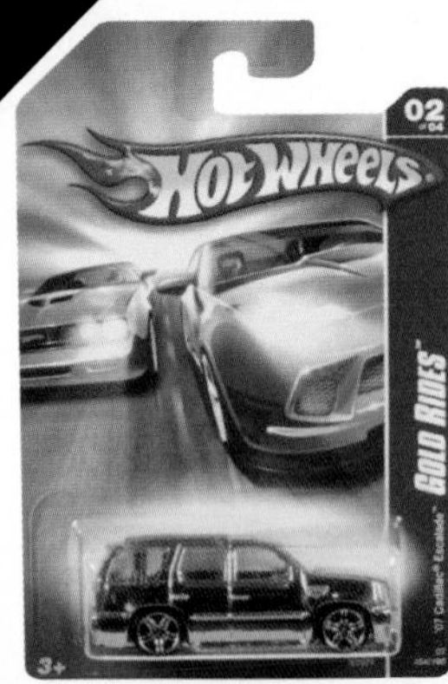

GOLD RIDES 2 OF 4

❑ '07 Cadillac Escalade/Gold Chrome/GoldPR5 .... $1.50

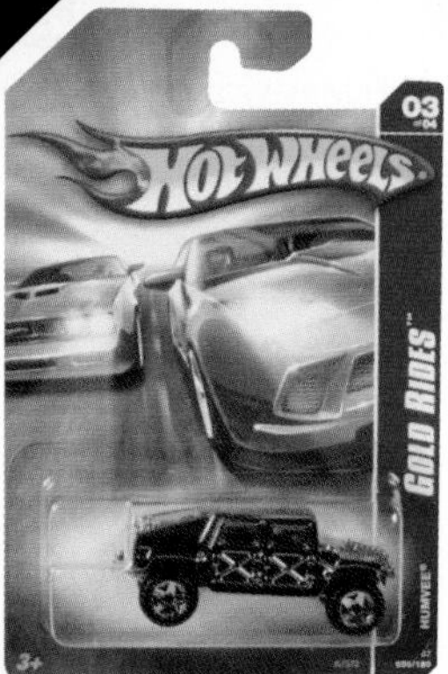

Gold Rides 3 of 4

❑ Humvee/Gold Chrome/GoldOR5SP $1.50

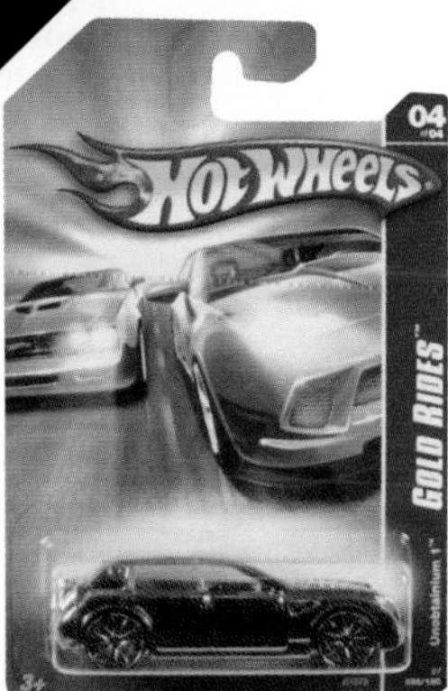

Gold Rides 4 of 4

❑ Unobtainium 1/Gold Chrome/GoldBLING $1.50

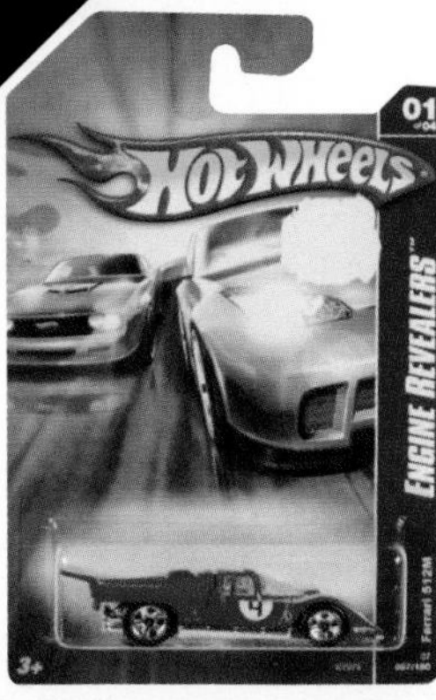

Engine Revealers 1 of 4

❑ **Ferrari 512M/M Red-Orange/5SP $1.50**
❑ Ferrari 512M/M Red-Orange/PR5 Malaysia base........ $1.50
❑ Ferrari 512M/M Red-Orange/PR5 Thailand base $1.50

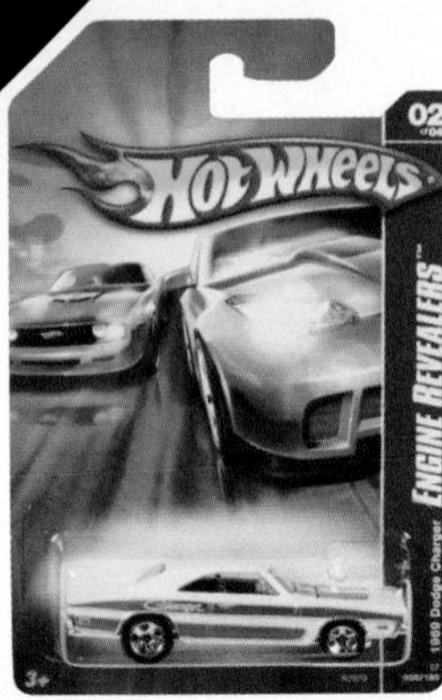

Engine Revealers 2 of 4

❑ 1969 Dodge Charger/Pearl White/5SP Malaysia Base $3.00
❑ 1969 Dodge Charger/Pearl White/5SP Thailand Base $3.00

Engine Revealers 3 of 4

❑ '58 Corvette/M Dark Grey/5SP $1.50

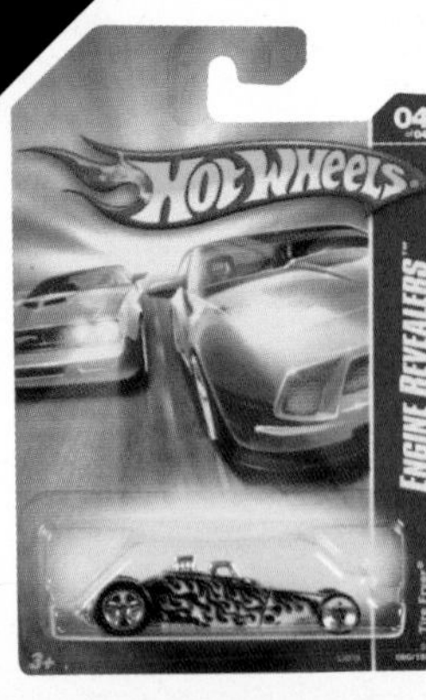

Engine Revealers 4 of 4

❑ Tire Fryer/Black/OH5SP $3.00
❑ Tire Fryer/Black/SK5 front, 5SP rear $1.50

HUMMER 1 OF 4

❑ Hummer H2/Champagne/OR5SP Malaysia base........ $1.50
❑ **Hummer H2/Champagne/OR5SP Thailand base...... $1.50**

HUMMER 2 OF 4

❑ Hummer H3T Concept/M Dark Blue/OR5SP $1.50

HUMMER 3 OF 4

❑ Hummer H3/Red/GoldOH5SP Malaysia base $1.50
❑ **Hummer H3/Red/GoldOH5SP Thailand base $1.50**

HUMMER 4 OF 4

2007 064

❑ Hummer H2/M Grey/BLING $1.50

STREET BEAST II 1 OF 4

❑ Preying Menace/Black/PR5.. $1.50

STREET BEAST II 2 OF 4

❑ Sharkruiser/Grey/3SP $1.50

2007

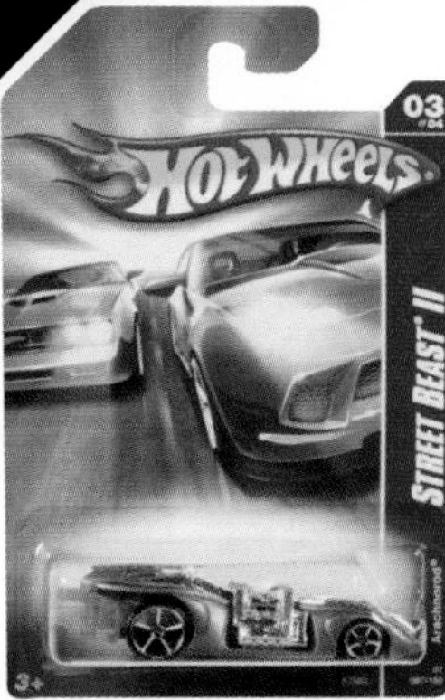

STREET BEAST II 3 OF 4

2007 067

- ❑ Arachnorod/Blue-Grey/5SP Malaysia base.................. $8.00
- ❑ Arachnorod/Blue-Grey/5SP Thailand base $8.00
- ❑ Arachnorod/Blue-Grey/OH5SP Malaysia base $1.50
- ❑ **Arachnorod/Blue-Grey/OH5SP Thailand base $1.50**

STREET BEAST II 4 OF 4

2007 068

- ❑ Rodzilla/Purple/GoldPR5... $1.50

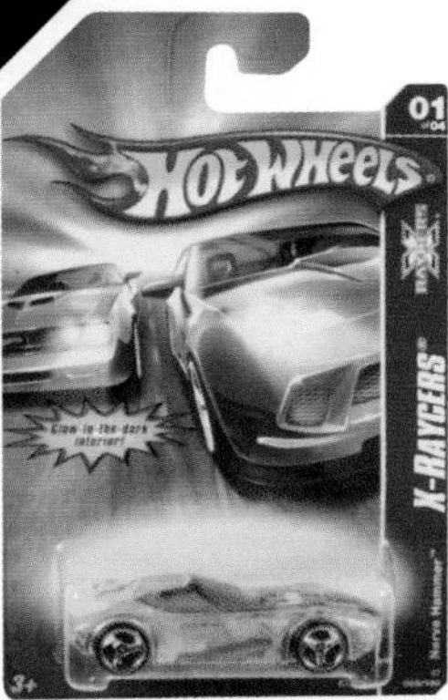

X-RAYCERS 1 OF 4

2007 069

- ❑ Nerve Hammer/Clear/3SP... $1.50

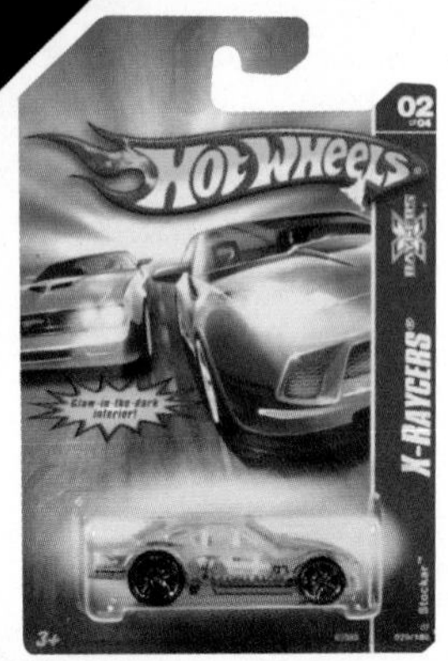

X-RAYCERS 2 OF 4

2007 070

❑ Stockar/Clear/BluePR5 .... $1.50

X-RAYCERS 3 OF 4

2007 071

❑ Phastasm/Clear/GreenOH5SP $12.00

❑ Phastasm/Clear/GreenPR5 .... $1.50

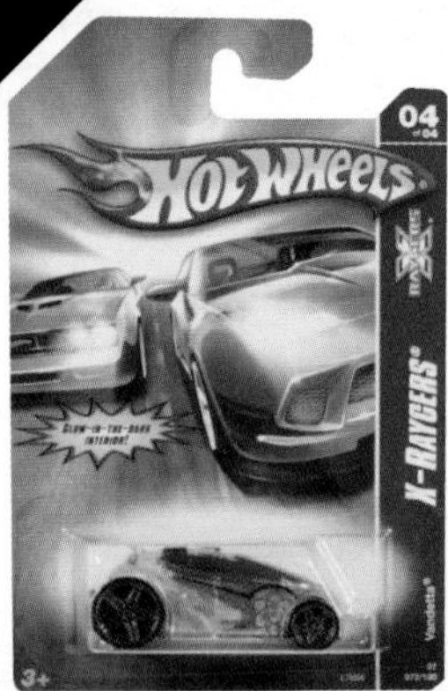

X-RAYCERS 4 OF 4

2007 072

❑ Vandetta/Clear/RedPR5 .... $1.50

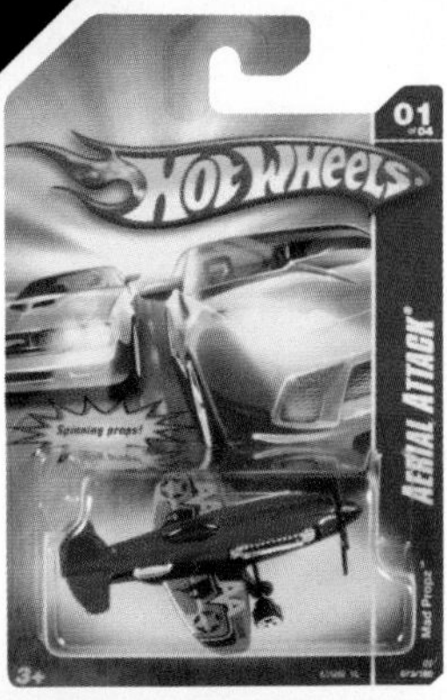

Aerial Attack 1 of 4

❑ Mad Propz/M Orange/Micro5SP $1.50

Aerial Attack 2 of 4

❑ Killer Copter/Olive Green $3.00

Aerial Attack 3 of 4

❑ Poison Arrow/Clear Red/GoldMicro5SP $1.50

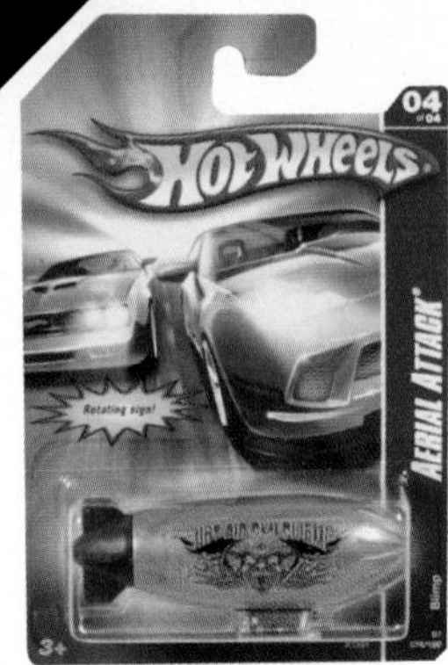

Aerial Attack 4 of 4

2007 076

❏ Blimp/Silver $1.50

Hot Wheels Racing 1 of 4

2007 077

❏ 1941 Willys Coupe/M Dark Blue/5SP $1.50

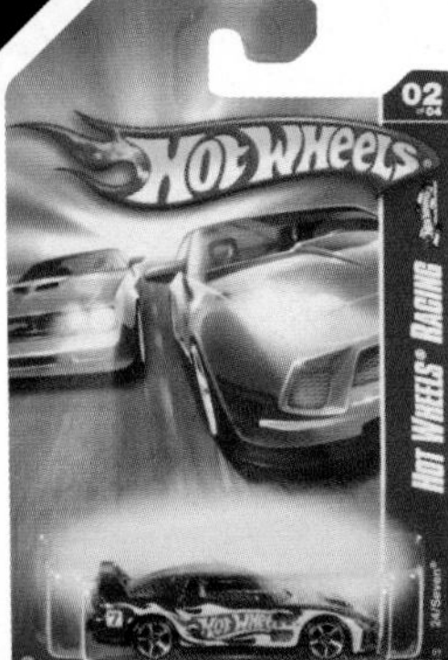

Hot Wheels Racing 2 of 4

2007 078

❏ 24/Seven/M Dark Blue/OH5SP $1.50

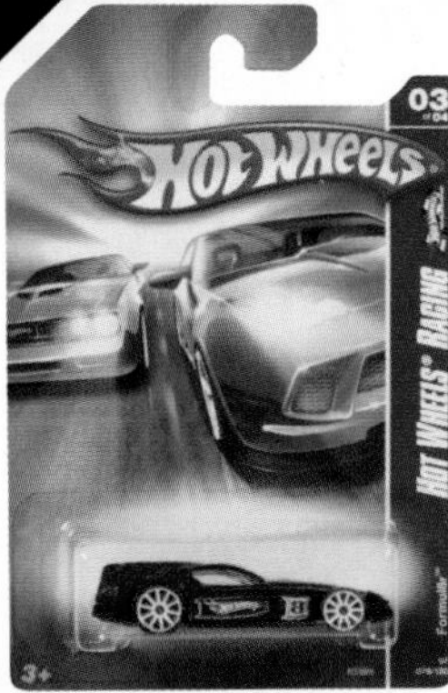

HOT WHEELS RACING 3 OF 4

❑ Formul8r/M Dark Blue/White10SP $1.50

HOT WHEELS RACING 4 OF 4

❑ Datsun 240Z/M Dark Blue/Y5 .... $1.50

RAGTOPS & ROADSTERS 1 OF 4

❑ Tantrum/M Dark Red/3SP $1.50

2007

2007

Ragtops & Roadsters 2 of 4 — 2007 082

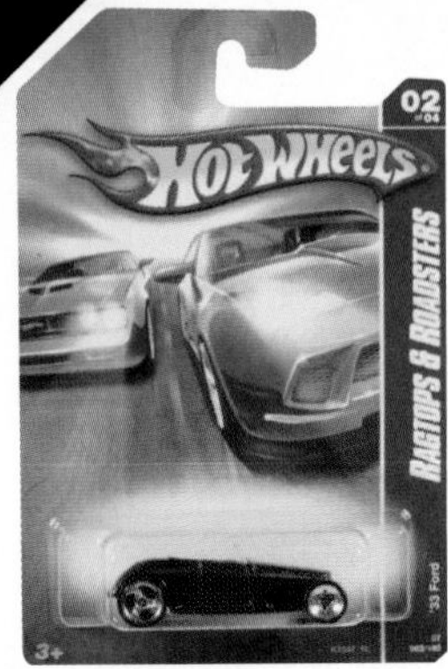

❑ '33 Ford/Black/SK5 front, 3SP rear $1.50
❑ **'33 Ford/Black/SK5 front, 5SP rear $1.50**

Ragtops & Roadsters 3 of 4 — 2007 083

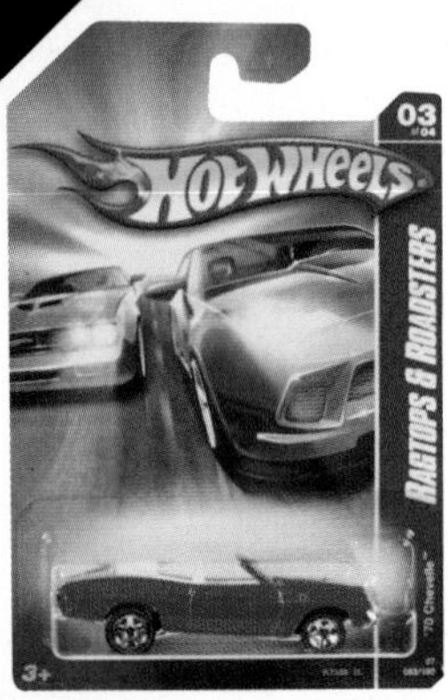

❑ '70 Chevelle (Convertible)/M Orange/RL5SP $3.00

Ragtops & Roadsters 4 of 4 — 2007 084

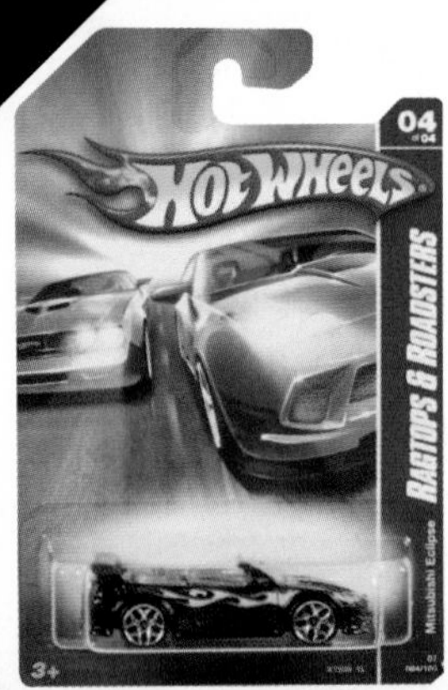

❑ Mitsubishi Eclipse/M Black/5SP $8.00
❑ **Mitsubishi Eclipse/M Black/Y5 .... $1.50**

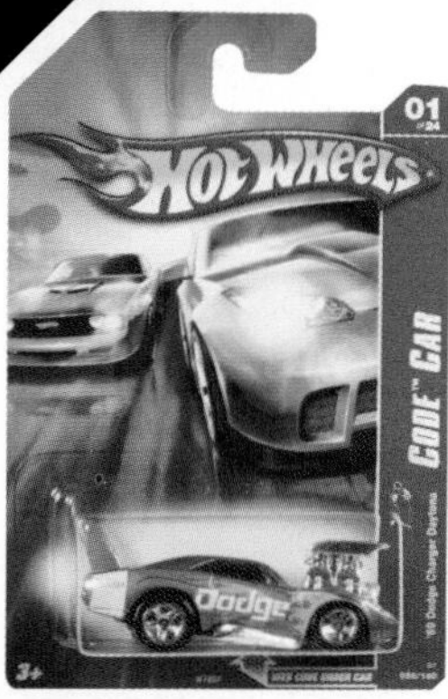

CODE CAR 1 OF 24

❑ Dodge Charger Daytona/M Blue/5SP $1.50

CODE CAR 1 OF 24

❑ Dodge Charger Daytona/M Green/5SP $1.50

CODE CAR 2 OF 24

❑ Cadillac Cien Concept/M Blue/PR5 .... $1.50

CODE CAR 3 OF 24

2007 087

❑ Muscle Tone/M Gold/OH5SP $1.50

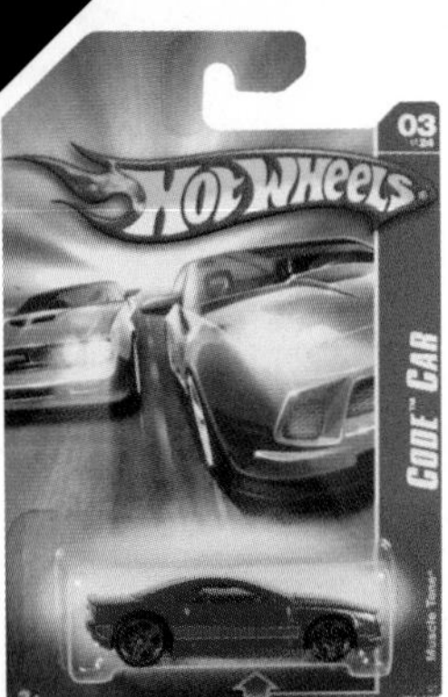

CODE CAR 3 OF 24

2007 087

❑ Muscle Tone/M Red/RedPR5 .... $1.50

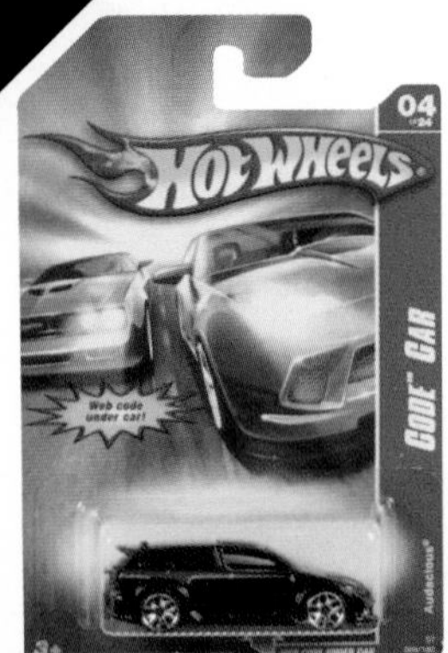

CODE CAR 4 OF 24

2007 088

❑ Audacious/Black/Y5 .... $1.50

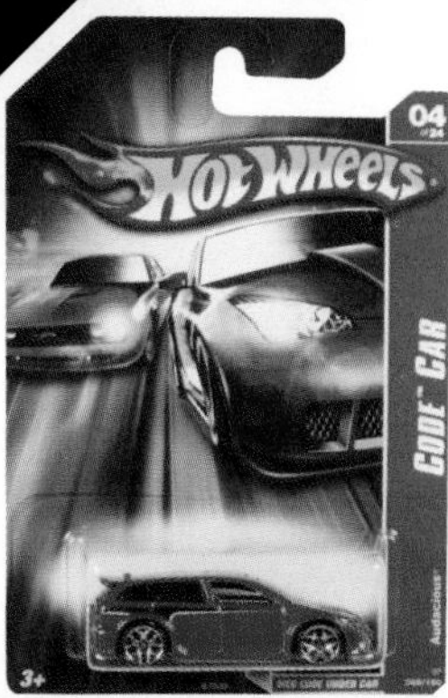

CODE CAR 4 OF 24

2007 088

- ❑ Audacious/M Dark Red/GoldPR5 .... $8.00
- ❑ **Audacious/M Dark Red/GoldY5 .... $1.50**

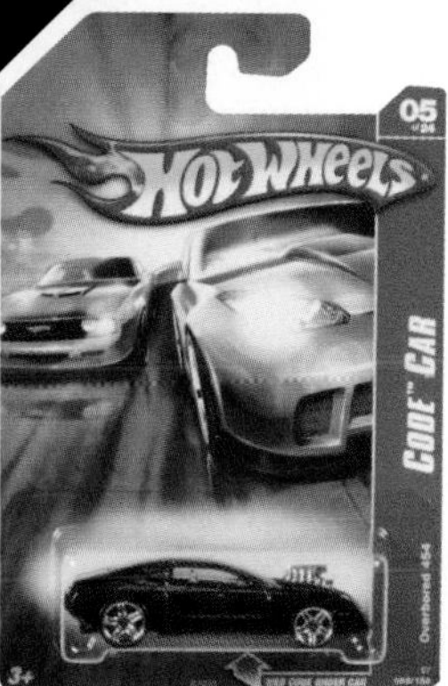

CODE CAR 5 OF 24

2007 089

- ❑ Overbored 454/Black/PR5.. $1.50

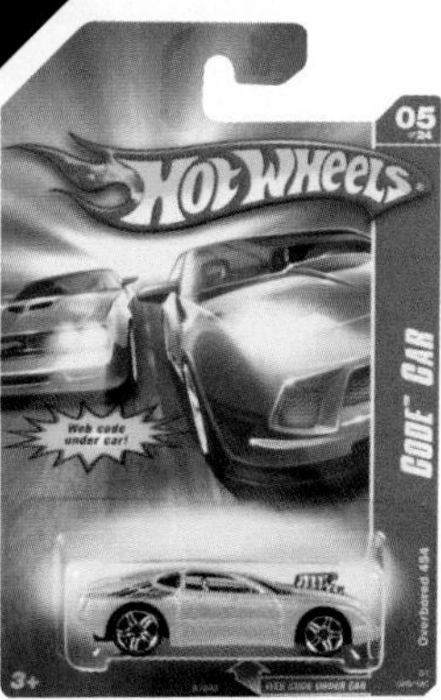

CODE CAR 5 OF 24

2007 089

- ❑ Overbored 454/M Silver/PR5 .... $1.50

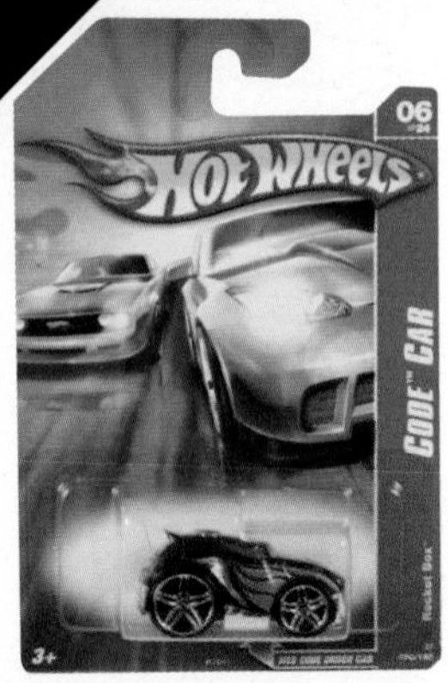

CODE CAR 6 OF 24

2007 090

❑ Rocket Box/M Purple/PR5 .... $1.50

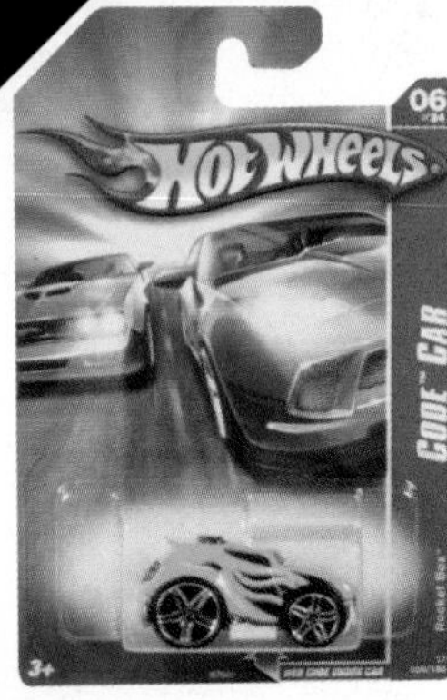

CODE CAR 6 OF 24

2007 090

❑ Rocket Box/Yellow/PR5.. $1.50

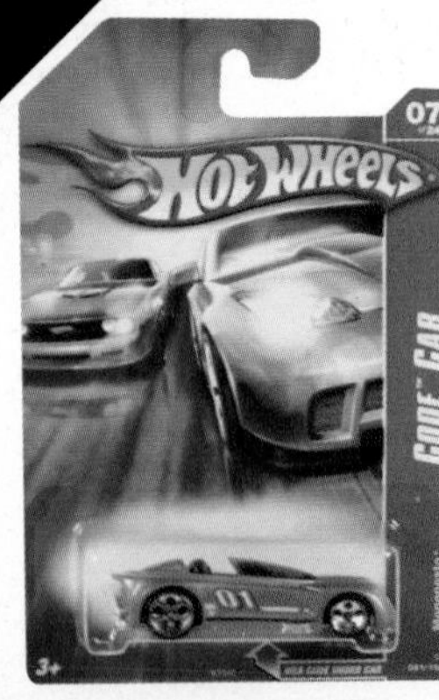

CODE CAR 7 OF 24

2007 091

❑ **Monoposto/M Dark Green/5DOT $1.50**

❑ Monoposto/M Dark Green/Y5 .... $3.00

CODE CAR 8 OF 24

❑ Aston Martin V8 Vantage/M Red/PR5 .... $1.50

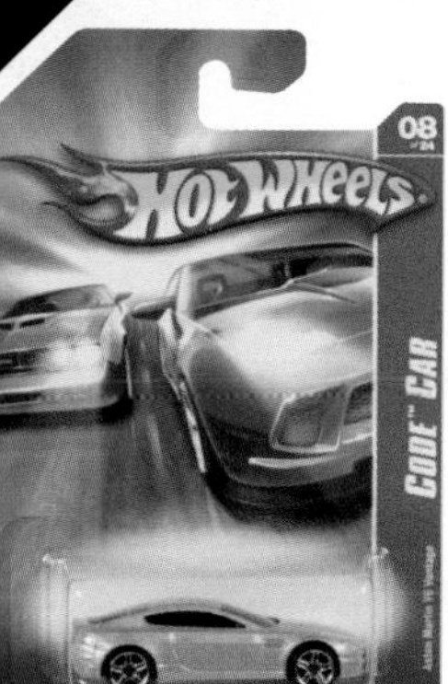

CODE CAR 8 OF 24

❑ Aston Martin V8 Vantage/M Silver/PR5 .... $1.50

CODE CAR 9 OF 24

❑ I Candy/Dark Blue/BluePR5 .... $1.50

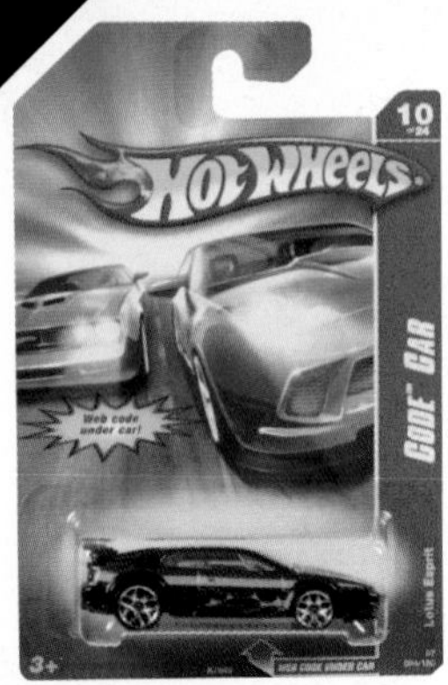

CODE CAR 10 OF 24

❑ Lotus Esprit/Black/Y5 .... $1.50

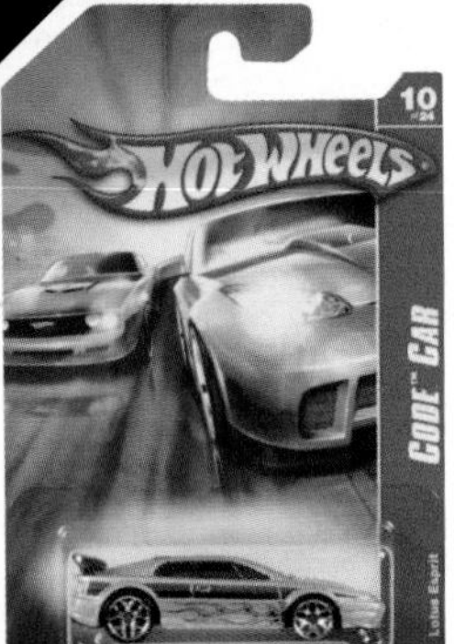

CODE CAR 10 OF 24

2007 094

❑ Lotus Esprit/M Silver/Y5 .... $1.50

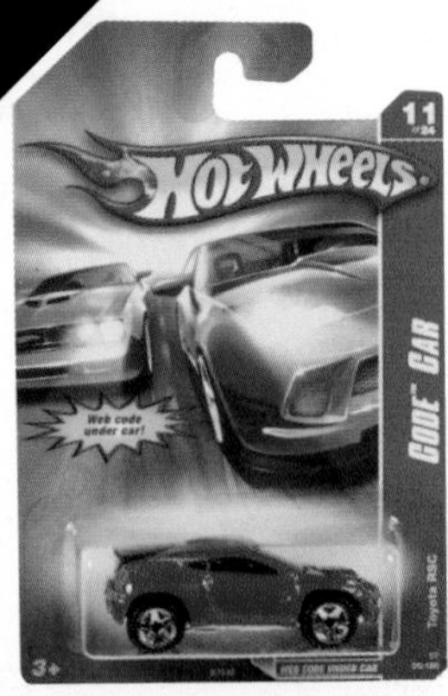

CODE CAR 11 OF 24

2007 095

❑ Toyota RSC/M Dark Orange/OR5SP $1.50

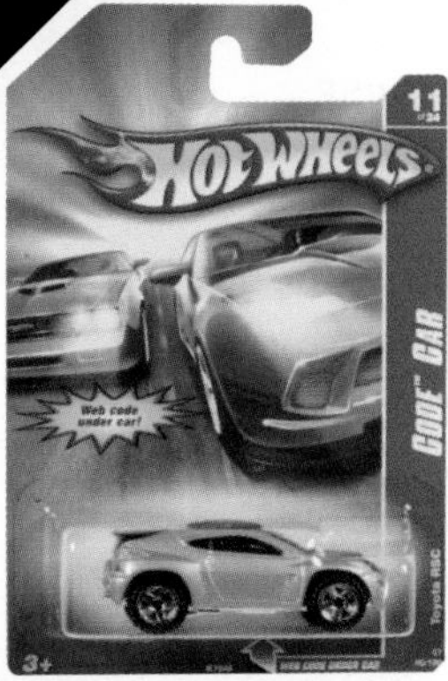

Code Car 11 of 24

2007 095

❑ Toyota RSC/Pearl Lt. Blue/OR5SP $1.50

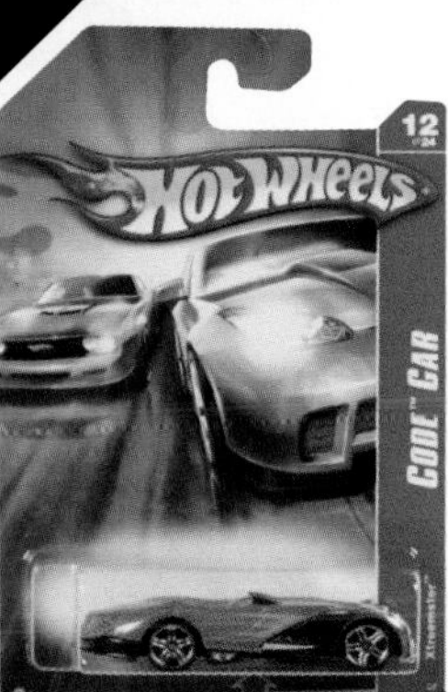

Code Car 12 of 24

❑ Xtreemster/M Gold/PR5 .... $1.50

Code Car 13 of 24

❑ Shelby Cobra 427 S/C/M Dark Blue/10SP $1.50

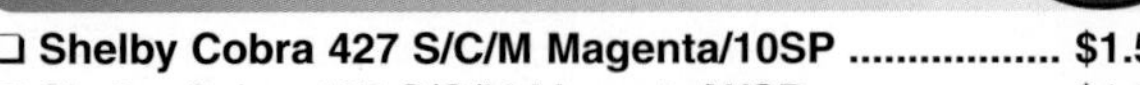

Code Car 13 of 24 2007 097

- ❑ **Shelby Cobra 427 S/C/M Magenta/10SP $1.50**
- ❑ Shelby Cobra 427 S/C/M Magenta/WSP $1.50

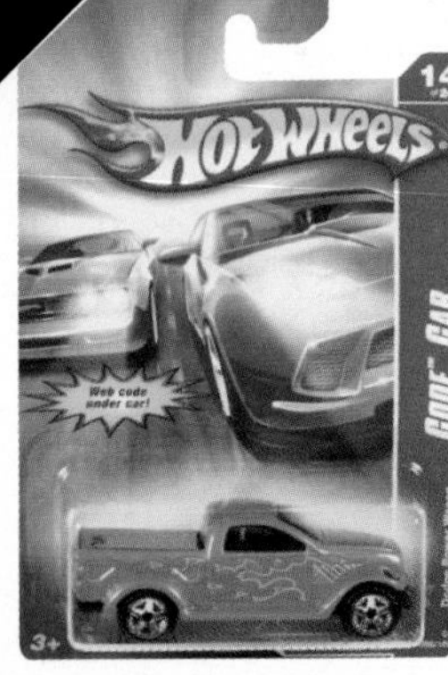

Code Car 14 of 24 2007 098

- ❑ Dodge Power Wagon/M Green/OR5SP $1.50

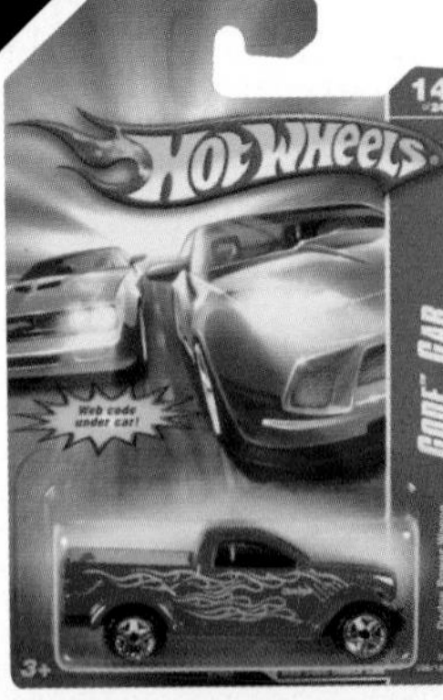

Code Car 14 of 24 2007 098

- ❑ Dodge Power Wagon/M Red/OR5SP $1.50

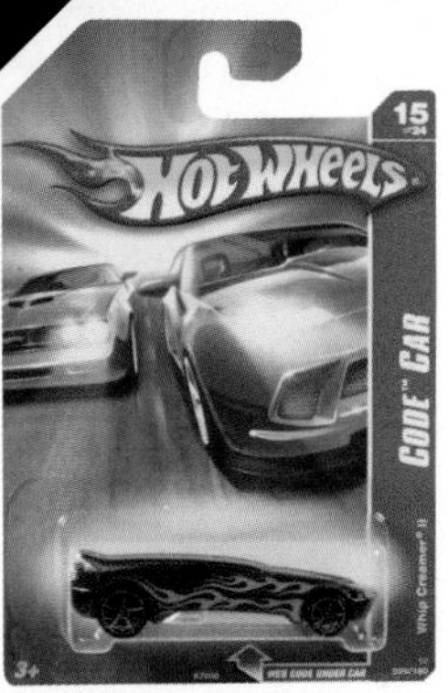

Code Car 15 of 24

2007 099

❑ Whip Creamer II/M Dark Purple/GreyOH5SP $1.50

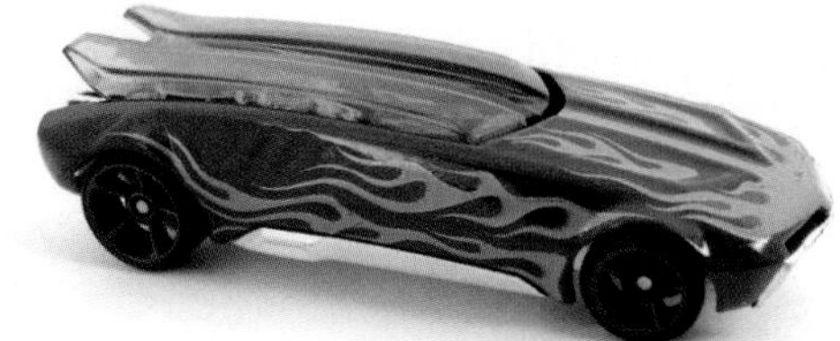

Code Car 15 of 24

2007 099

❑ Whip Creamer II/M Gold/Red5SP $1.50

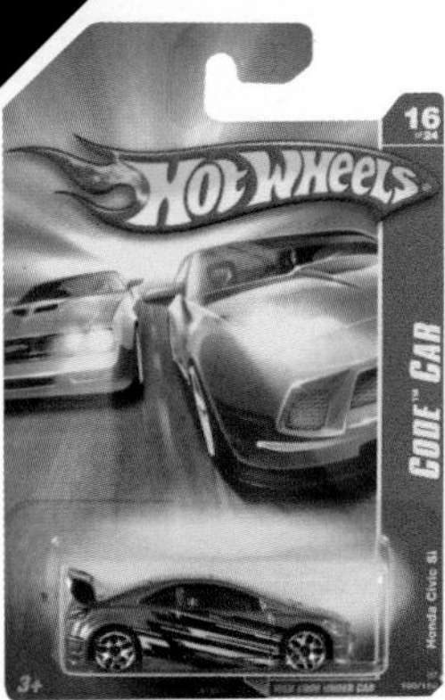

Code Car 16 of 24

2007 100

❑ Honda Civic Si/M Blue/Y5 .... $1.50

2007

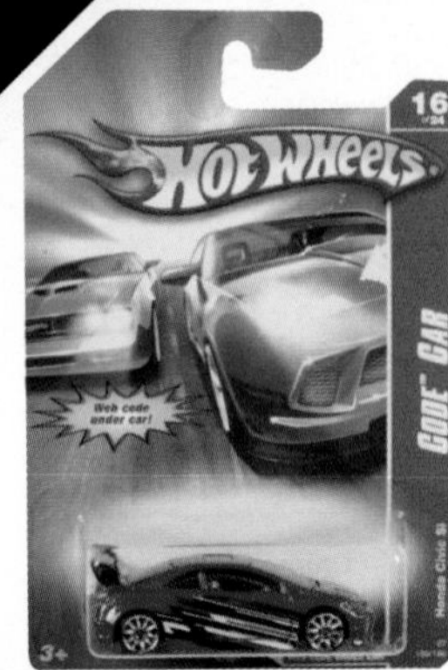

CODE CAR 16 OF 24 — 2007 100

❑ **Honda Civic Si/M Red/10SP $1.50**
❑ Honda Civic Si/M Red/OH5SP $1.50

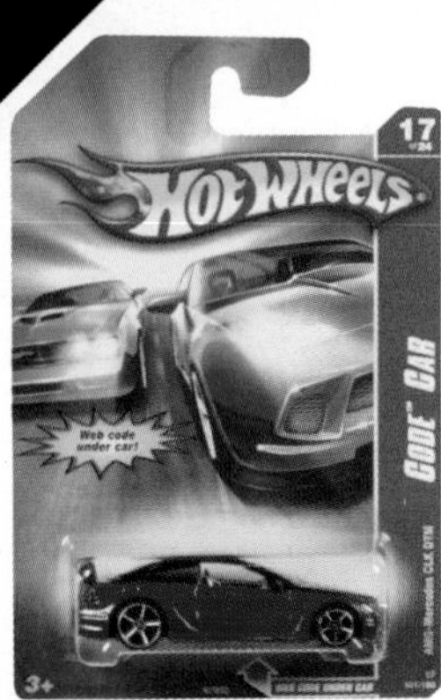

CODE CAR 17 OF 24 — 2007 101

❑ AMG-Mercedes CLK DTM/M Dark Red/OH5SP.......... $1.50

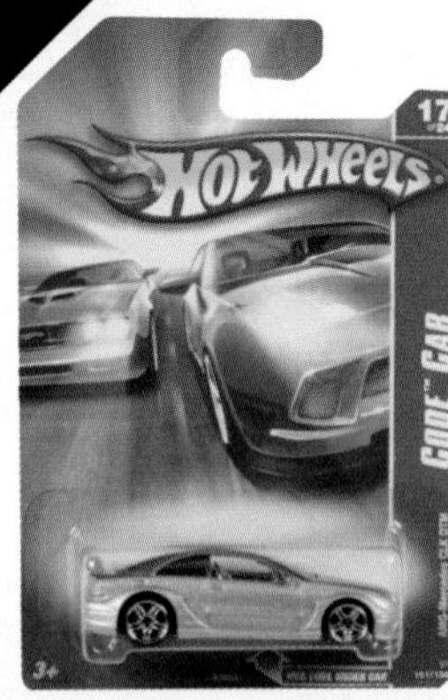

CODE CAR 17 OF 24 — 2007 101

❑ AMG-Mercedes CLK DTM/M Silver/PR5 .... $1.50

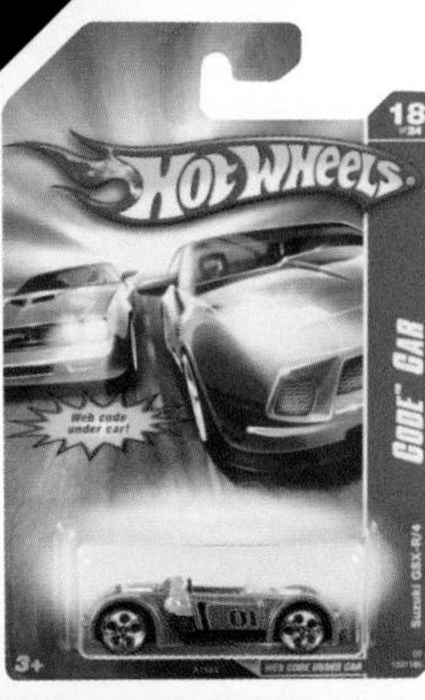

Code Car 18 of 24

- ❑ **Suzuki GSX-R/4/M Copper/5DOT $1.50**
- ❑ Suzuki GSX-R/4/M Copper/OrangeOH5SP $15.00

Code Car 19 of 24

- ❑ Dieselboy/M Blue/OH5SP $1.50

Code Car 19 of 24

- ❑ Dieselboy/M Copper/OH5SP.. $1.50

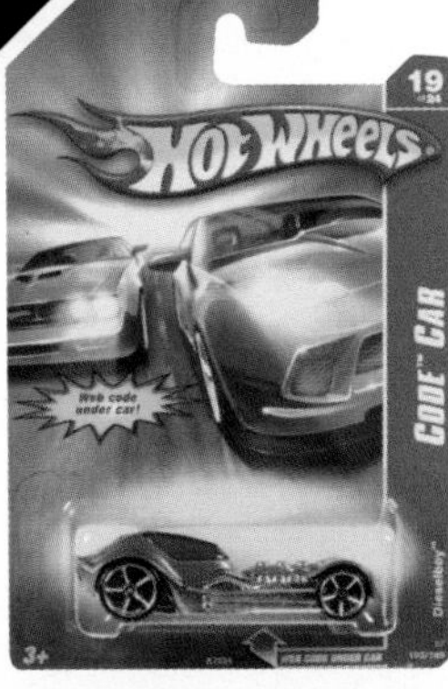

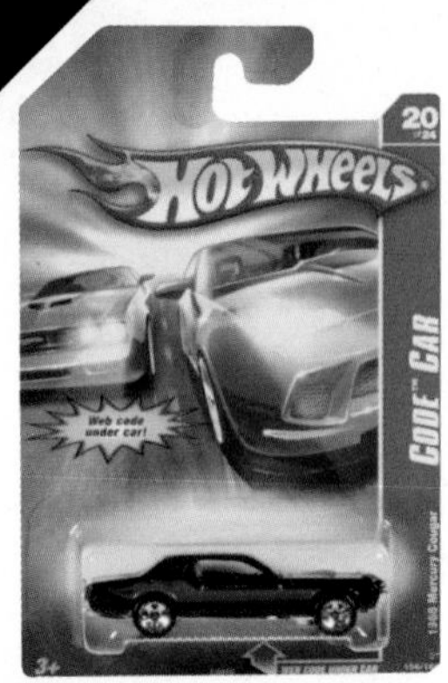

Code Car 20 of 24 — 2007 104

❑ '68 Cougar/Black/5SP $1.50

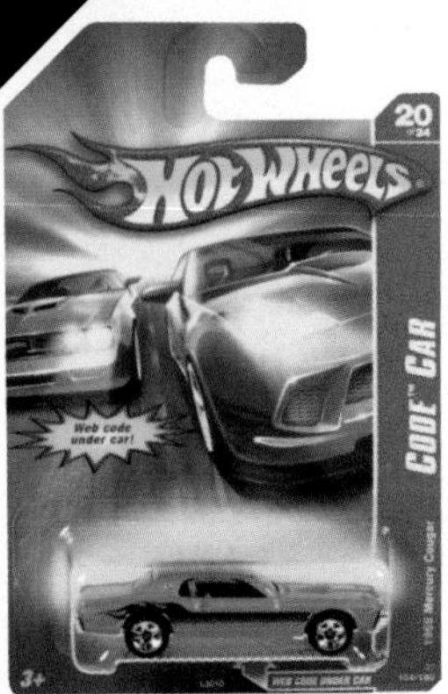

Code Car 20 of 24 — 2007 104

❑ '68 Cougar/M Green/5SP $1.50

Code Car 21 of 24 — 2007 105

❑ Motoblade/M Green/OH5SP $1.50

CODE CAR 21 OF 24

❑ Motoblade/M Red/OH5SP $1.50

CODE CAR 22 OF 24

❑ Custom Cougar/M Dark Orange/OrangePR5 .... $1.50

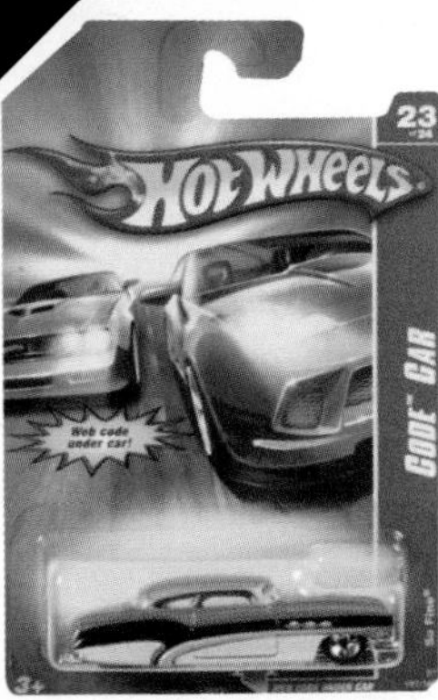

CODE CAR 23 OF 24

❑ So Fine/M Gold/5SP $1.50
❑ So Fine/M Gold/Y5 .... $3.00

2007

Code Car 23 of 24

2007 107

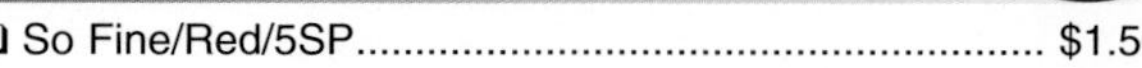

❑ So Fine/Red/5SP $1.50

Code Car 24 of 24

2007 108

❑ Mitsubishi Eclipse Concept/M Blue/Gold10SP $1.50

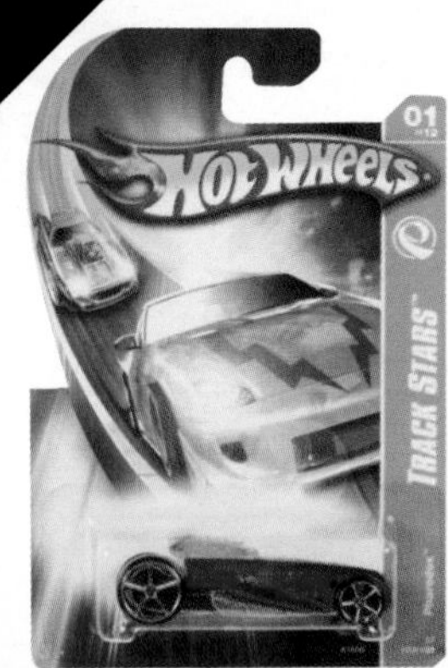

Track Stars 1 of 12

2007 109

❑ Pharodox/Clear Red/GoldOH5SP $1.50

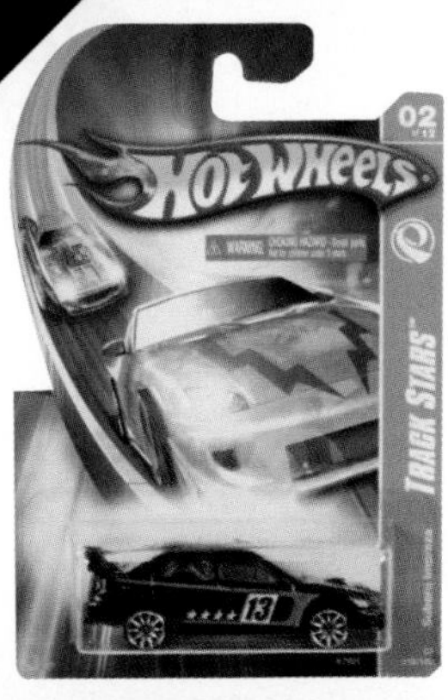

Track Stars 2 of 12

- ❑ **Subaru Impreza/Black/10SP $1.50**
- ❑ Subaru Impreza/Black/PR5 .... $8.00

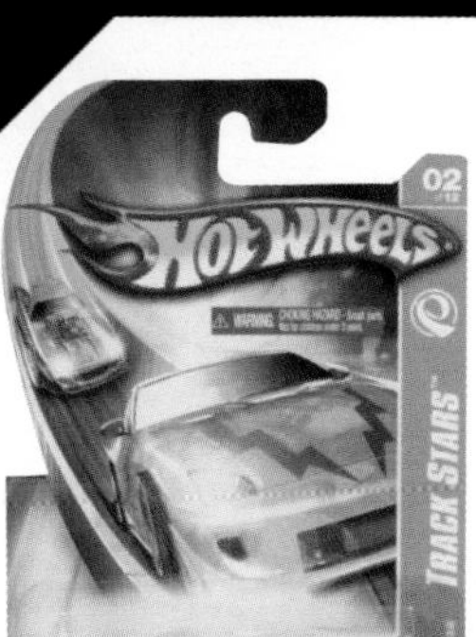

Track Stars 2 of 12

- ❑ **Subaru Impreza/White/10SP $1.50**
- ❑ Subaru Impreza/White/PR5 .... $8.00

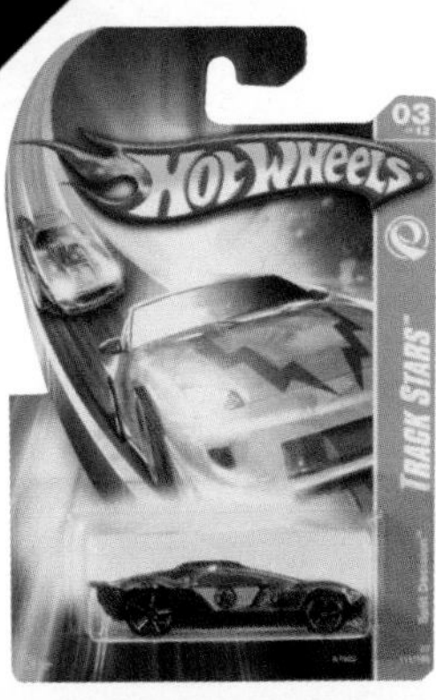

Track Stars 3 of 12

- ❑ Split Decision/Flat Black/BlueOH5SP $1.50

2007

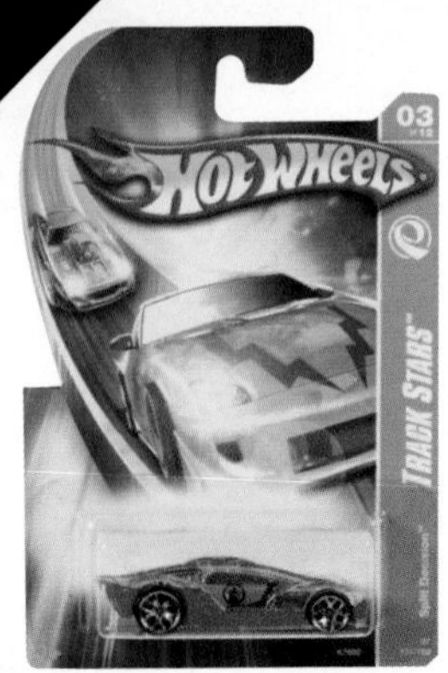

Track Stars 3 of 12

❑ Split Decision/Red/GoldY5 .... $1.50

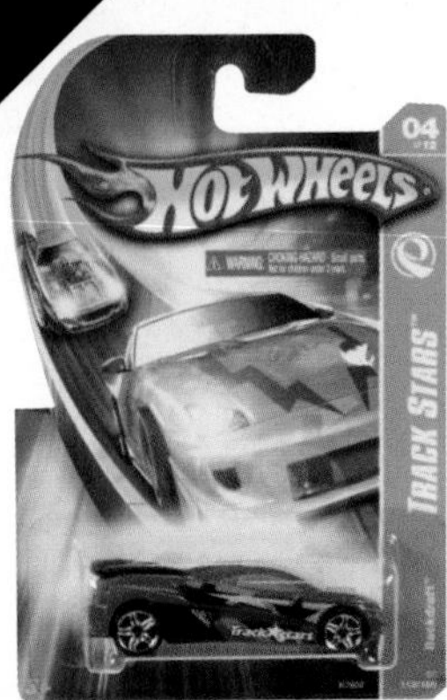

Track Stars 4 of 12

2007 112

❑ Backdraft/Magenta/PR5 .... $1.50

Track Stars

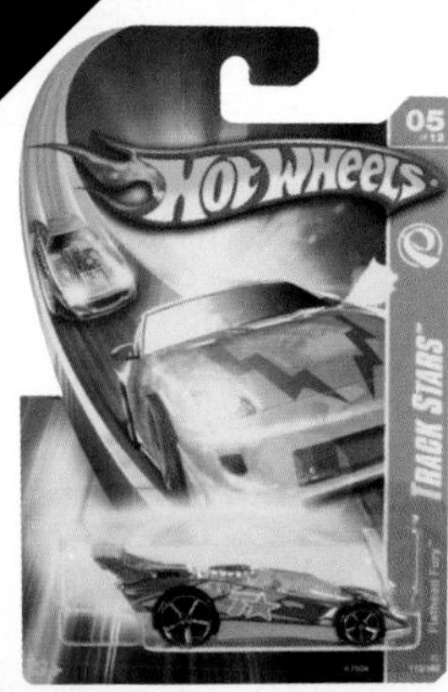

Track Stars 5 of 12

❑ Flathead Fury/Blue/GoldOH5SP $1.50

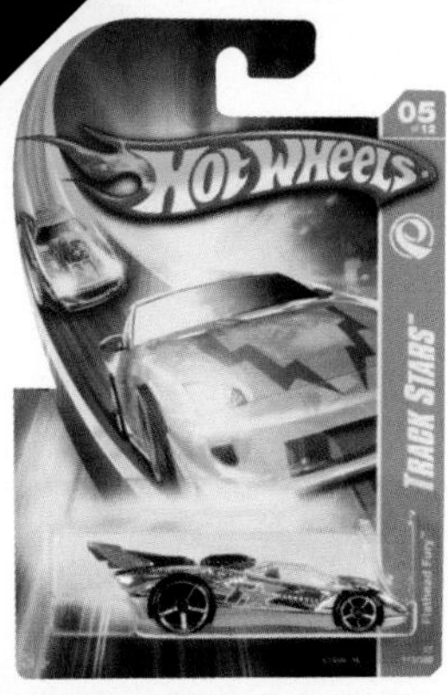

Track Stars 5 of 12

2007 113

- ❑ **Flathead Fury/Chrome/OH5SP $1.50**
- ❑ Flathead Fury/Chrome/PR5 .... $8.00

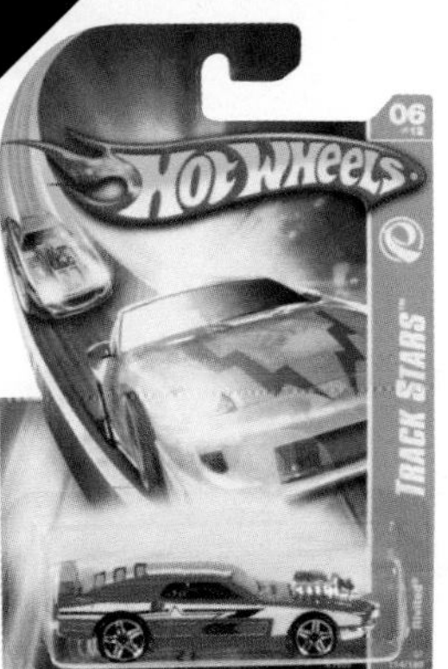

Track Stars 6 of 12

2007 114

- ❑ Rivited/Dark Orange/PR5 .... $1.50

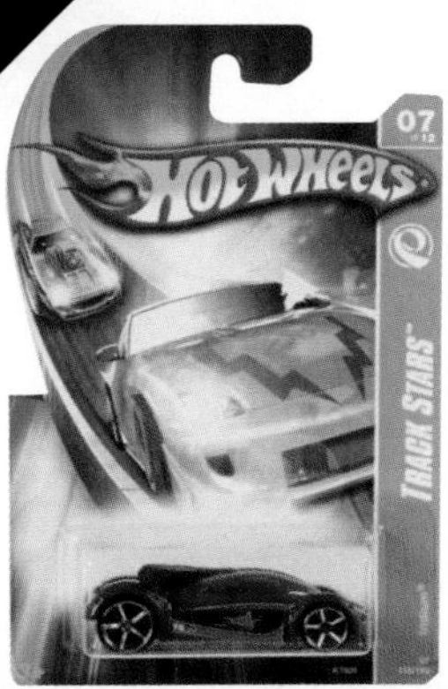

Track Stars 7 of 12

2007 115

- ❑ Iridium/Dark Red/OH5SP $1.50

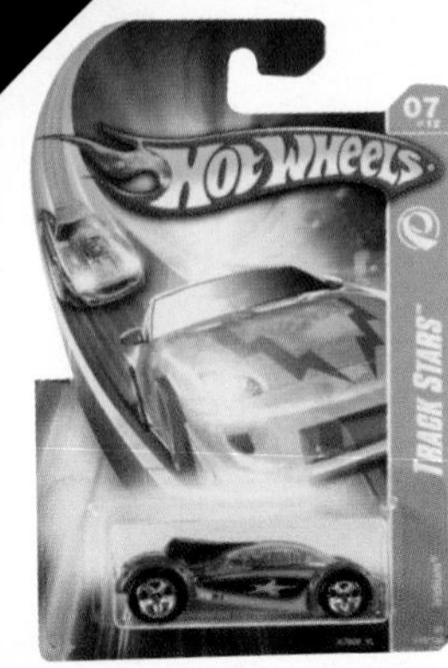

Track Stars 7 of 12

2007 115

❑ Iridium/M Blue/5SP $1.50
❑ **Iridium/M Blue/OH5SP $1.50**
❑ Iridium/M Blue/PR5 .... $1.50

Track Stars 8 of 12

2007 116

❑ Bassline/Black/5SP $1.50
❑ **Bassline/Black/OH5SP $1.50**

Track Stars 8 of 12

2007 116

❑ Bassline/Blue/OH5SP $1.50

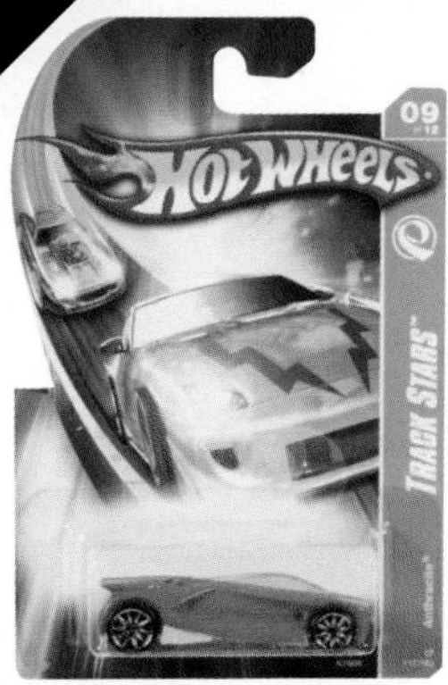

Track Stars 9 of 12

❑ Anthracite/Orange/Gold10SP $1.50

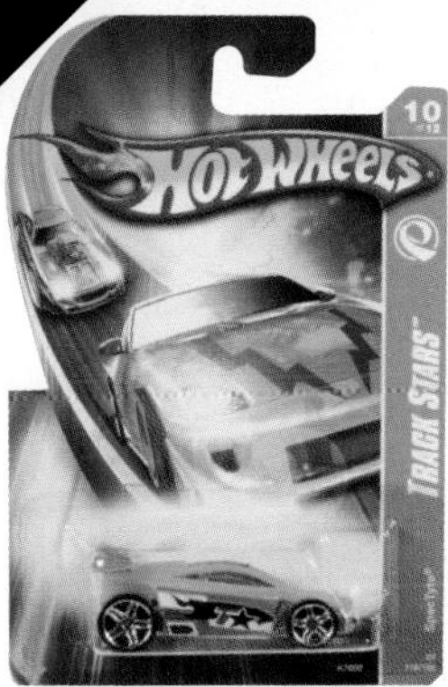

Track Stars 10 of 12

❑ Spectyte/Green/PR5 .... $1.50

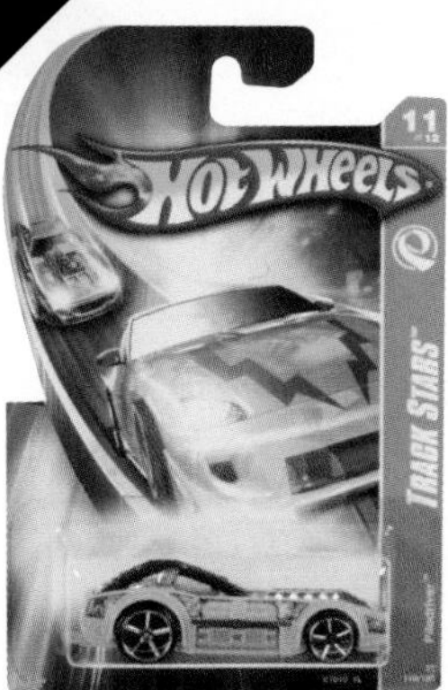

Track Stars 11 of 12

❑ Piledriver/Beige/OH5SP $1.50

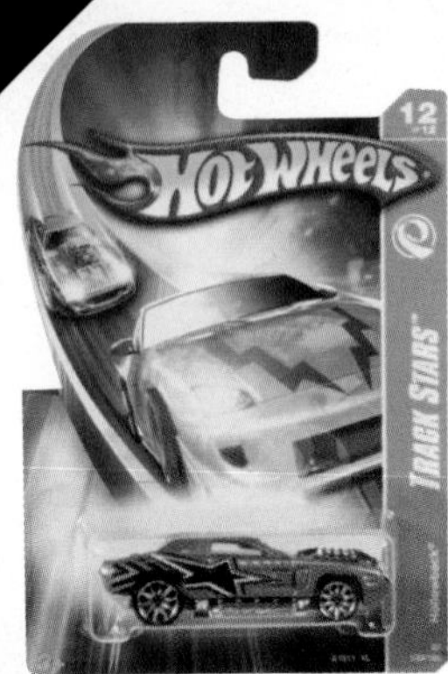

Track Stars 12 of 12

❑ Hollowback/M Grey/10SP $1.50

Treasure Hunts 1 of 12

2007 121

❑ '69 Pontiac GTO/Dark Blue & Yellow/5SP $10.00

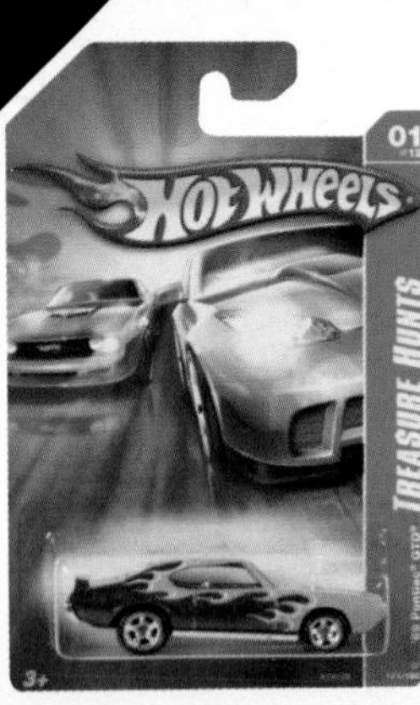

"Super" Treasure Hunts 1 of 12

2007 121

❑ '69 Pontiac GTO/M Blue & Yellow/RR5SP $40.00

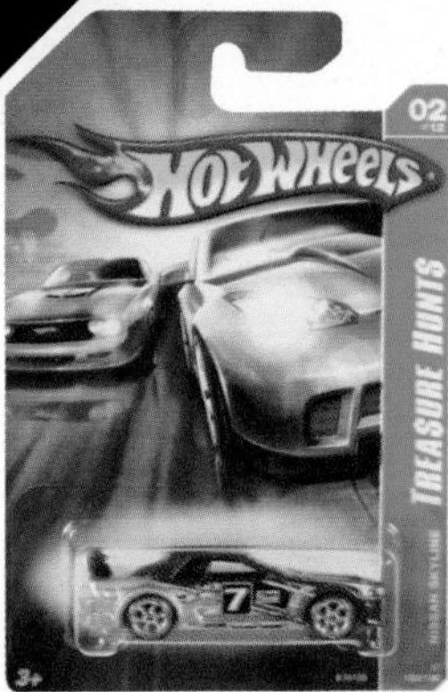

"SUPER" TREASURE HUNTS 2 OF 12

❑ Nissan Skyline/Copper/6SPBLING $30.00

TREASURE HUNTS 2 OF 12

2007 122

❑ Nissan Skyline/M Dark Orange/PR5.......................... $10.00

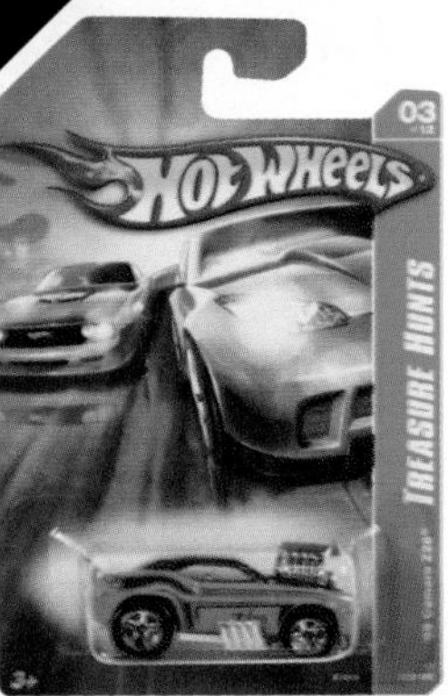

TREASURE HUNTS 3 OF 12

2007 123

❑ '69 Camaro Z28/Green/5SP $12.00

2007

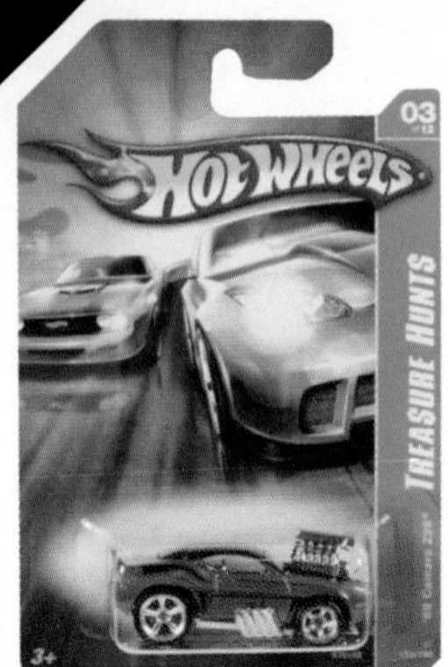

"SUPER" TREASURE HUNTS 3 OF 12

- ❑ '69 Camaro Z28/M Green/RR5SP $40.00

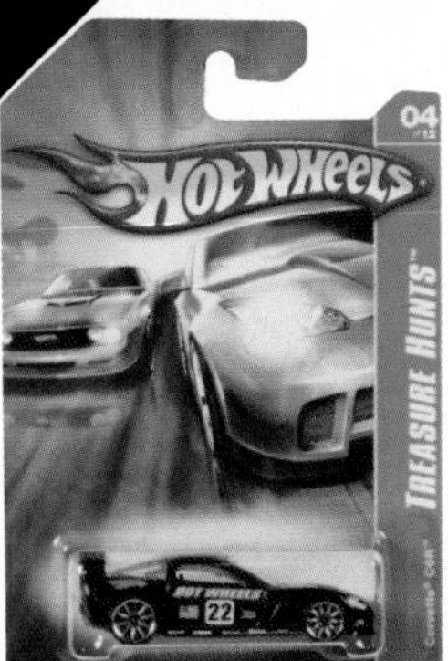

TREASURE HUNTS 4 OF 12

2007 124

- ❑ Corvette C6R/Black/Gold10SP $10.00

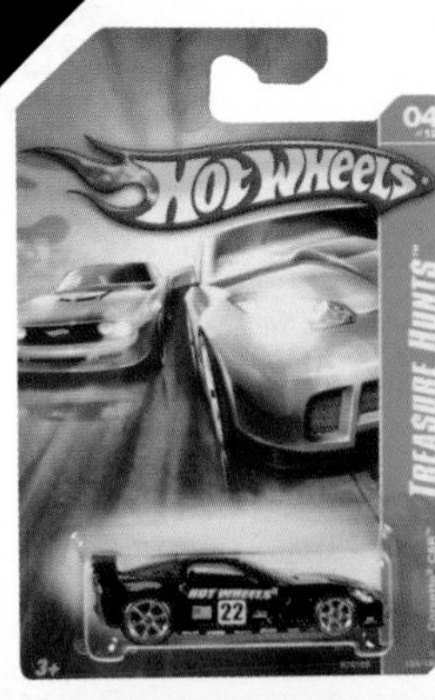

"SUPER" TREASURE HUNTS 4 OF 12

- ❑ Corvette C6R/Black/Gold6SPBLING......................... $30.00

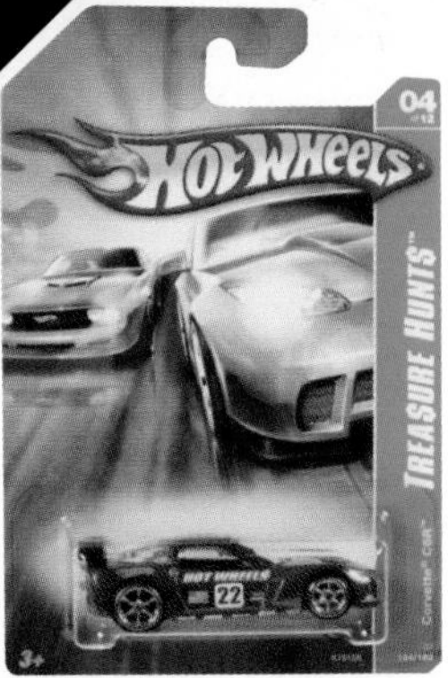

"SUPER" TREASURE HUNTS 4 OF 12

❑ Corvette C6R/Dark Grey/Gold6SPBLING (Toys-R-Us) $40.00

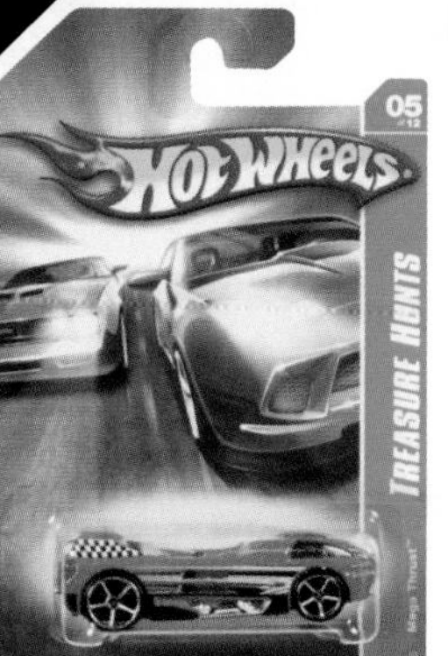

TREASURE HUNTS 5 OF 12

2007 125

❑ Mega Thrust/Orange/OH5SP $8.00

"SUPER" TREASURE HUNTS 5 OF 12

❑ Mega Thrust/Spectraflame Red/RR5SP $30.00

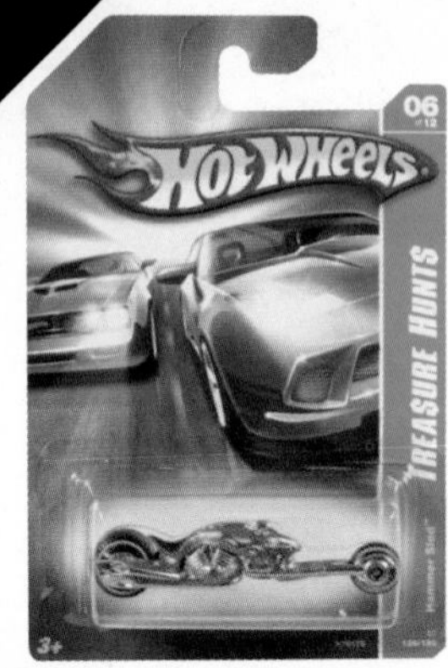

"Super" Treasure Hunts 6 of 12

❑ Hammer Sled/Spectraflame Antifreeze/YellowMC5 .. $30.00

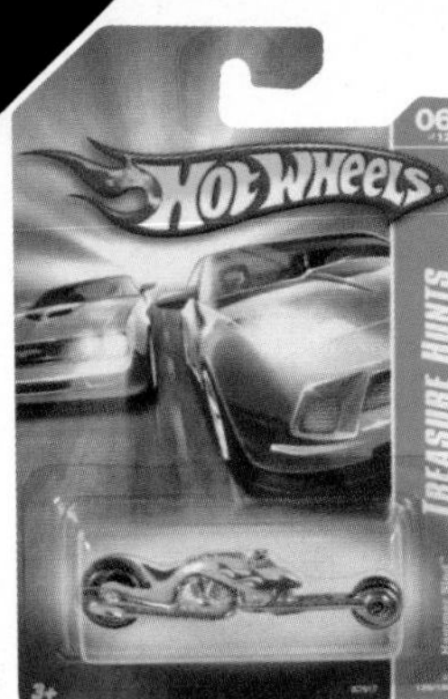

Treasure Hunts 6 of 12

❑ Hammer Sled/Yellow/MC5 .... $8.00

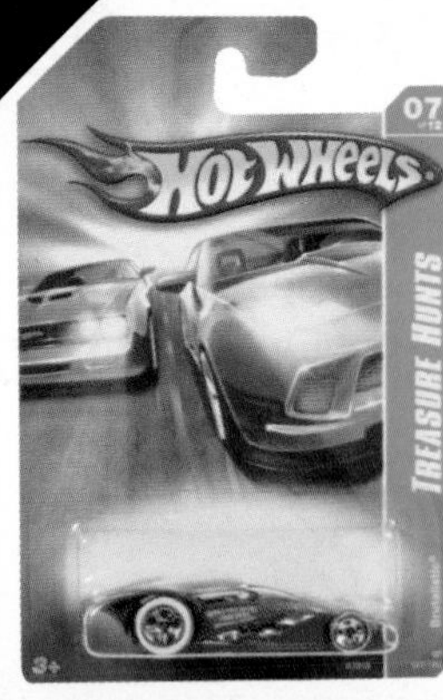

Treasure Hunts 7 of 12

❑ Brutalistic/Dark Olive Green/WW5SP $6.00

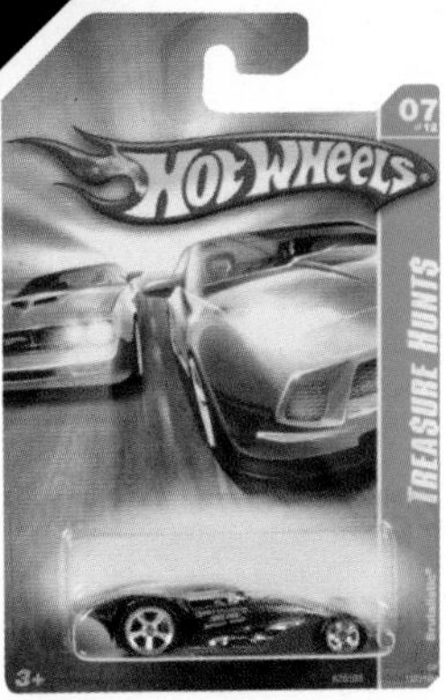

"SUPER" TREASURE HUNTS 7 OF 12

❑ Brutalistic/Spectraflame Olive/RR5SP $25.00

TREASURE HUNTS 8 OF 12

❑ Jaded/M Blue/5SP.. $6.00

"SUPER" TREASURE HUNTS 8 OF 12

❑ Jaded/Spectraflame Blue/RR5SP $25.00

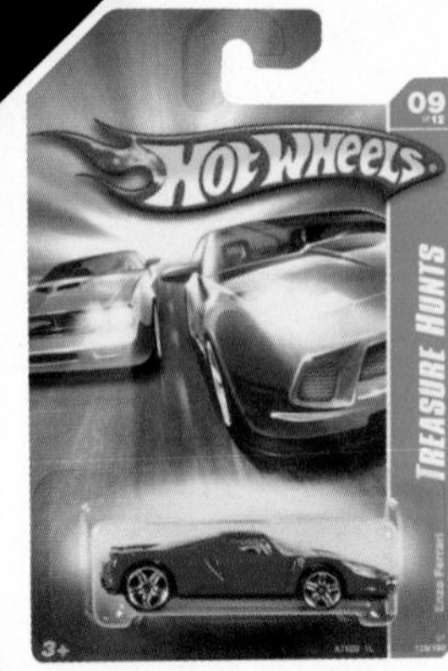

Treasure Hunts 9 of 12

- ❑ Enzo Ferrari/Red/PR5 black seats $10.00
- ❑ **Enzo Ferrari/Red/PR5 red seats.................................. $6.00**

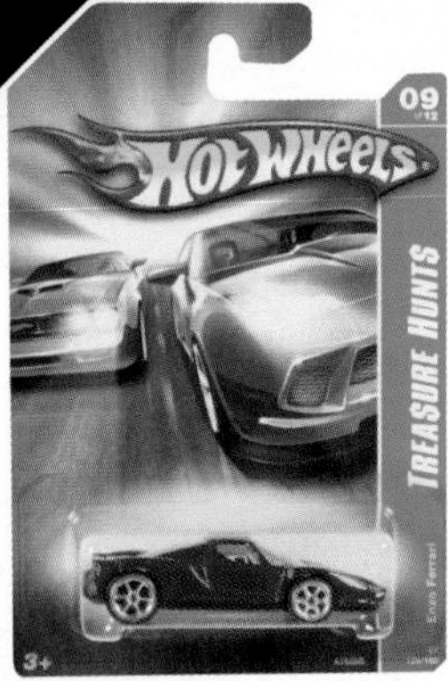

"Super" Treasure Hunts 9 of 12

- ❑ Enzo Ferrari/Spectraflame Red/6SPBLING $50.00

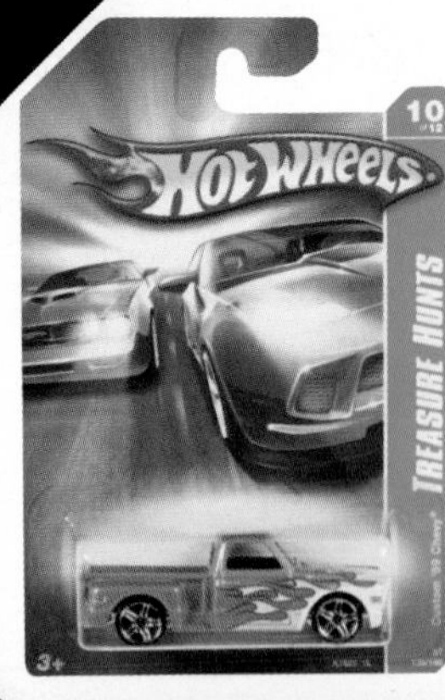

Treasure Hunts 10 of 12

- ❑ Custom '69 Chevy/M Gold/PR5 .... $8.00

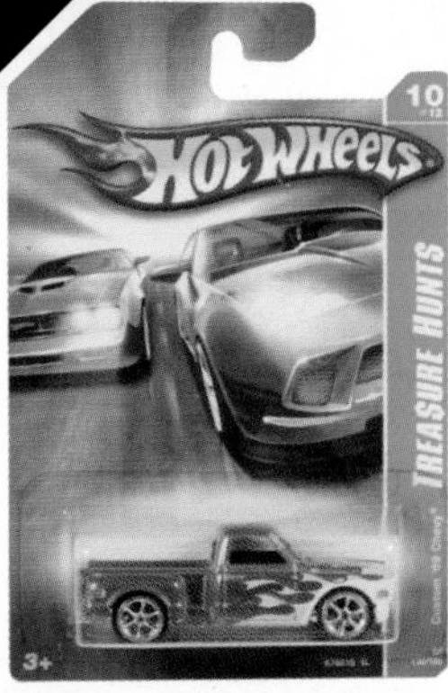

"Super" Treasure Hunts 10 of 12

❑ Custom '69 Chevy/Spectraflame Gold/6SPBLING $30.00

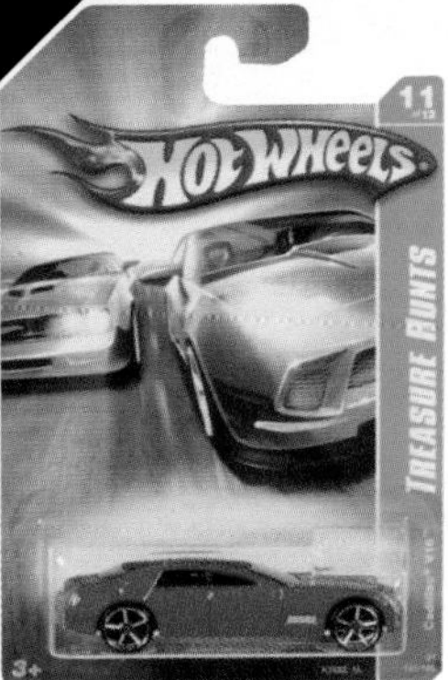

Treasure Hunts 11 of 12

❑ Cadillac V16/Pearl Pink/OH5SP $15.00

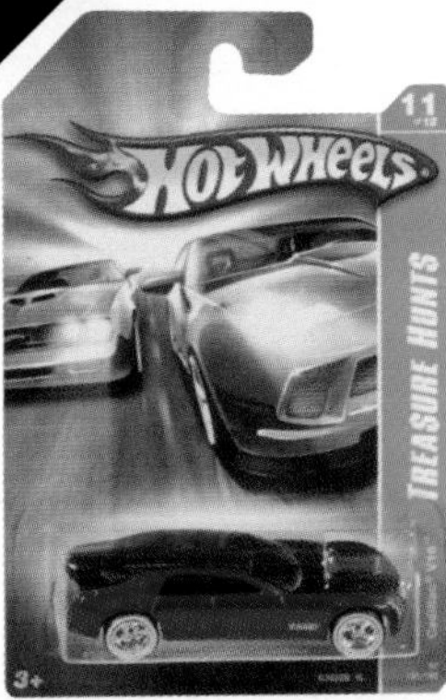

"Super" Treasure Hunts 11 of 12

❑ Cadillac V16/Spectraflame Pink/WWRR5SP $40.00

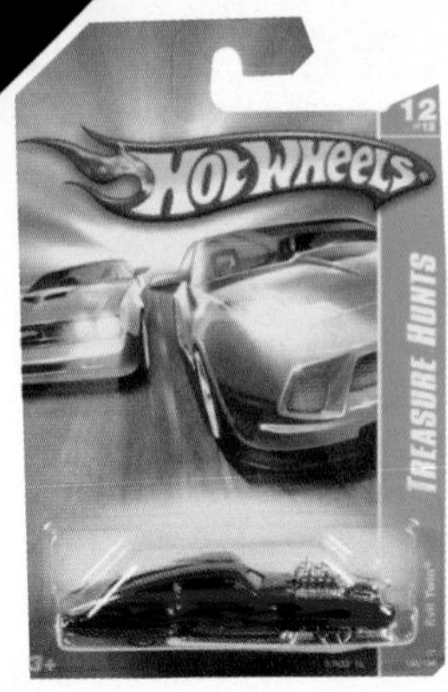

TREASURE HUNTS 12 OF 12

- ❑ Evil Twin/Red/OH5SP $8.00

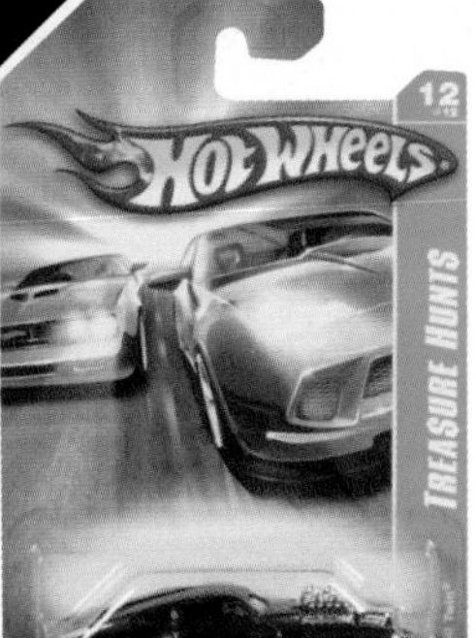

"SUPER" TREASURE HUNTS 12 OF 12

- ❑ Evil Twin/Spectraflame Red/WWRR6SP................... $30.00

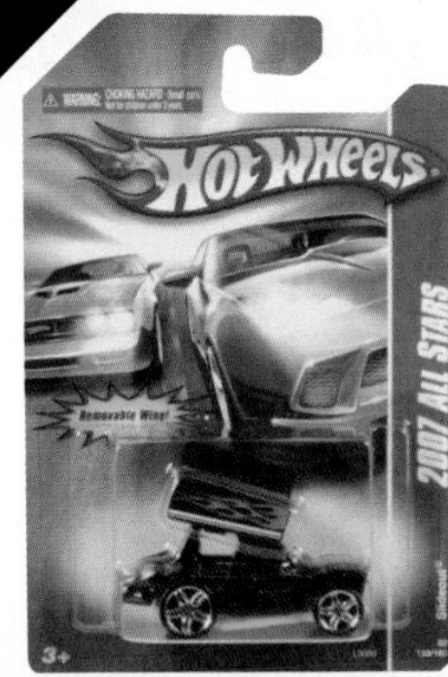

2007 ALL STARS

2007 133

- ❑ Slideout/Black/PR5's (K-Mart)..................................... $3.00

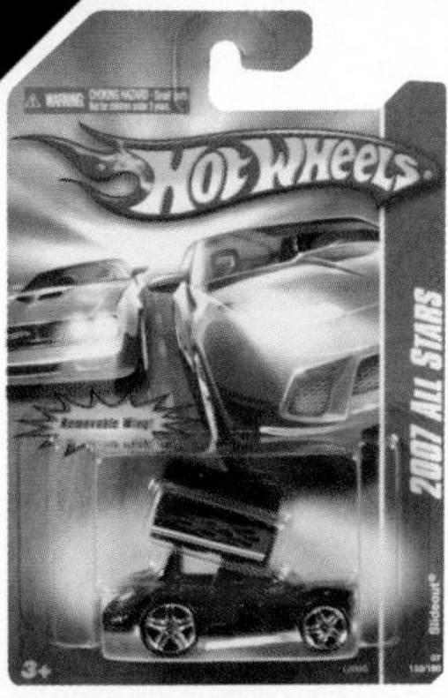

2007 All Stars

2007 133

❑ Slideout/M Dark Red/PR5 .... $1.50

2007 All Stars

2007 133

❑ Slideout/White/PR5 .... $1.50

2007 All Stars

2007 134

❑ Ford GT-40/M Dark Grey/5SP $1.50

2007 All Stars

❑ Ford GT-40/M Red/5SP $1.50

2007 All Stars

❑ Go Kart/Antifreeze Green/5DOT (Wal-Mart) $5.00

2007 All Stars

2007 135

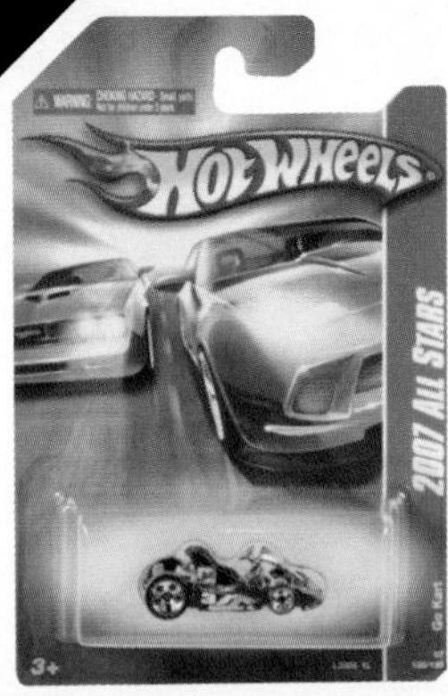

❑ **Go Kart/M Blue/5DOT $3.00**
❑ Go Kart/M Blue/5SP $3.00

2007 All Stars

❑ Deuce Roadster/Flat Black/Gold5SP $1.50

2007 All Stars

❑ Deuce Roadster/Flat Brown/Gold5SP.......................... $1.50

2007 All Stars

❑ Deuce Roadster/Olive Green/Gold5SP........................ $1.50

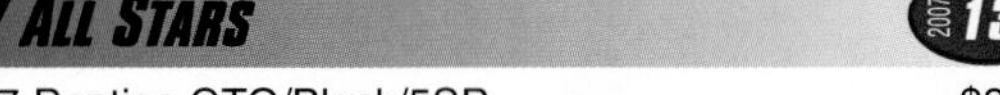

2007 All Stars

2007 137

❑ 1967 Pontiac GTO/Black/5SP $3.00

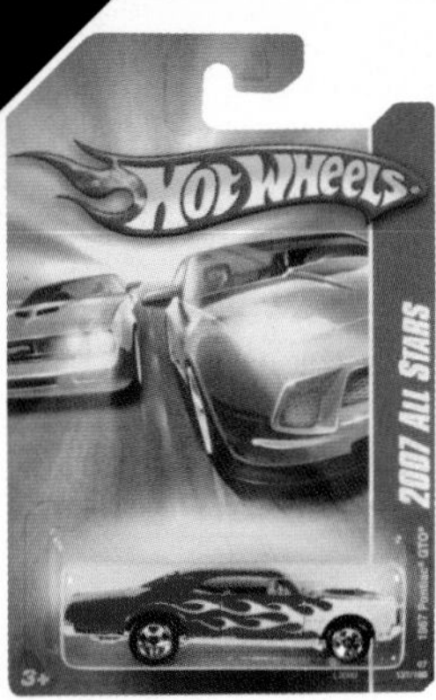

2007 All Stars

2007 137

❑ 1967 Pontiac GTO/M Red/5SP $3.00

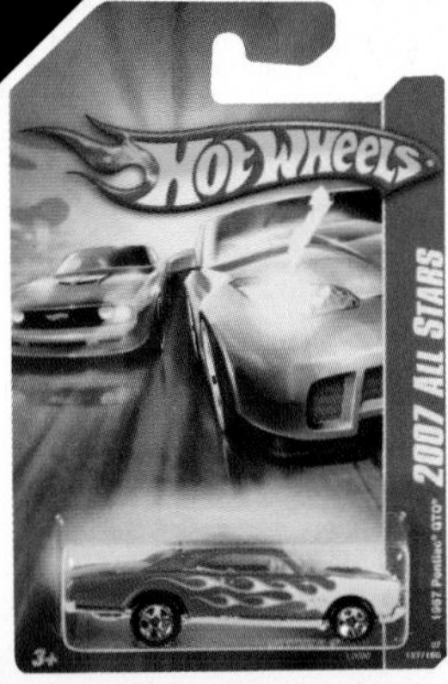

2007 All Stars

2007 137

❑ 1967 Pontiac GTO/M Teal/5SP $3.00

2007 All Stars

❑ Blast Lane/M Dark Blue/MC3 .... $3.00

2007 All Stars

❑ Blast Lane/M Dark Purple/MC3.................................... $3.00

2007 All Stars

❑ Blast Lane/M Lt. Blue/MC3 (K-Mart) $6.00

2007 All Stars

❑ Ferrari 333 SP/Flat Black/5SP $1.50

2007 All Stars

❑ Ferrari 333 SP/Red/White5SP $1.50

2007 All Stars

❑ Ferrari 333 SP/Yellow/White5SP.................................. $1.50

2007 All Stars

❑ 1964 Buick Riviera/M Gold/10SP $1.50

2007 All Stars

❑ 1964 Buick Riviera/M Grey/10SP (Wal-Mart) $3.00

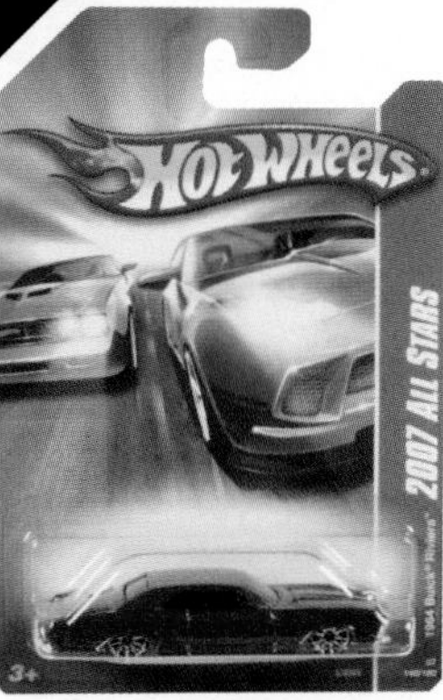

2007 All Stars

❑ 1964 Buick Riviera/M Purple/10SP $1.50

2007

2007 All Stars

❑ Shift Kicker/Flat Black\RedSK5 front Red5SP rear...... $1.50

2007 All Stars

❑ Shift Kicker/Flat Grey/BlackSK5 front, Black5SP rear $1.50

2007 All Stars

❑ Shift Kicker/M Red/SK5 front, 5SP rear (Wal-Mart) $3.00

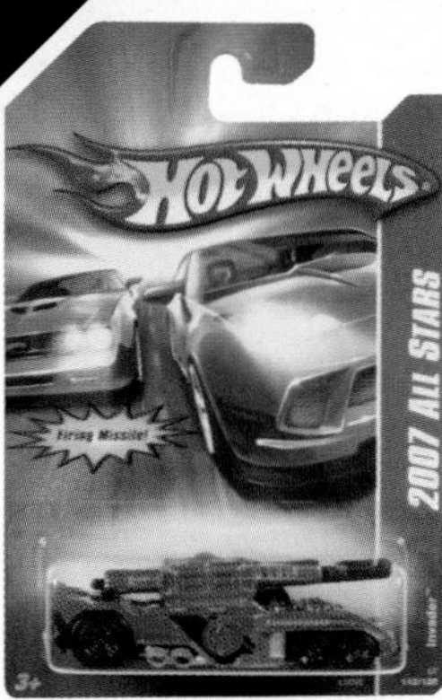

2007 All Stars

❑ Invader/M Grey/Black5SP $1.50

2007 All Stars

❑ Invader/Olive Green/Black5SP $1.50

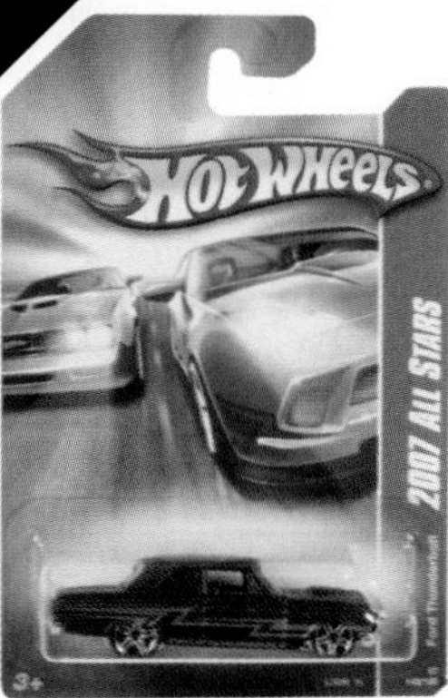

2007 All Stars

❑ Ford Thunderbolt/Flat Black/5SP $3.00
❑ **Ford Thunderbolt/Flat Black/PR5.............................. $1.50**

2007

2007

2007 All Stars

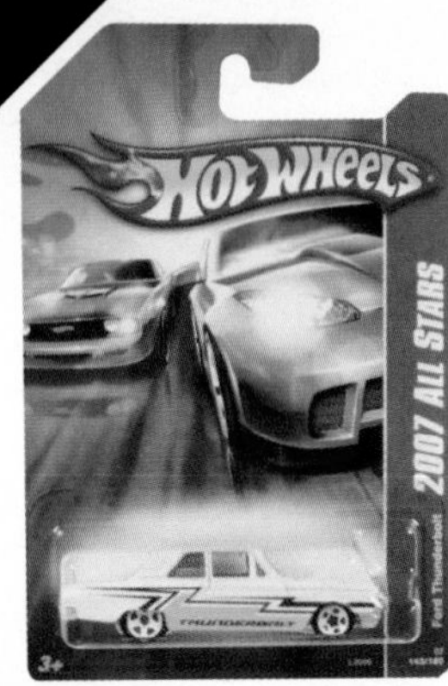

- ❑ **Ford Thunderbolt/Pearl White/White 5SP silver base $1.50**
- ❑ Ford Thunderbolt/Pearl White/White 5SP white base .. $10.00

2007 All Stars

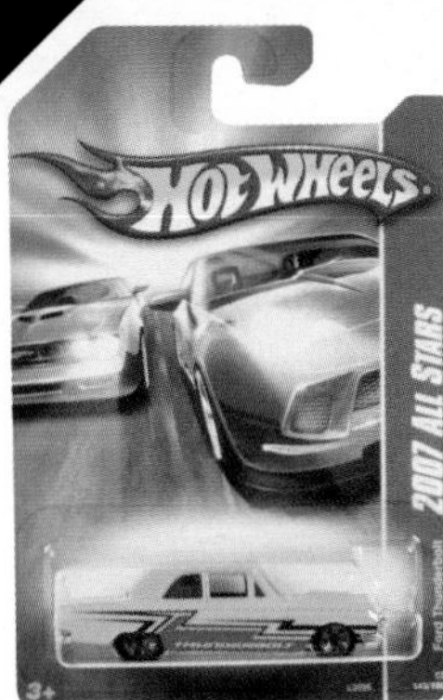

- ❑ Ford Thunderbolt/Yellow/Red5SP black base............ $12.00
- ❑ **Ford Thunderbolt/Yellow/Red5SP chrome base...... $1.50**
- ❑ Ford Thunderbolt/Yellow/Red5SP grey base $8.00

2007 All Stars

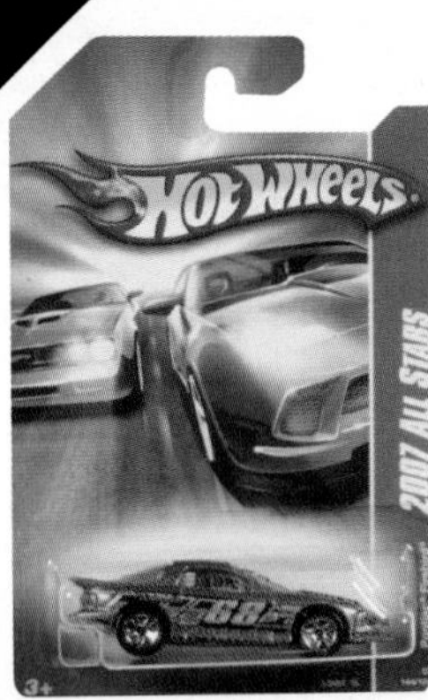

- ❑ Pontiac Firebird/M Dark Grey/5DOT $5.00
- ❑ **Pontiac Firebird/M Dark Grey/5SP $1.50**

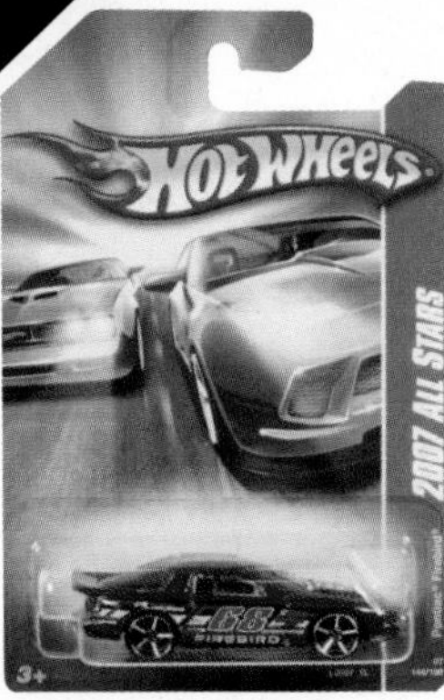

2007 All Stars

❑ Pontiac Firebird/M Dark Red/OH5SP $1.50

2007 All Stars

❑ **Pontiac Firebird/M Lt. Blue/OH5SP $1.50**
❑ Pontiac Firebird/M Lt. Blue/Y5 .... $1.50

2007 All Stars

❑ Mo' Scoot/Grey/Black SCR $1.50

2007 All Stars

- ❑ Porsche 911 GT3 Cup/Black/10SP (Wal-Mart) $8.00
- ❑ **Porsche 911 GT3 Cup/Black/PR5 (Wal-Mart) $1.50**

2007 All Stars

- ❑ Porsche 911 GT3 Cup/M Dark Red/PR5 .... $1.50

2007 All Stars

- ❑ Whatta Drag/Black/SK5.. $1.50

2007 All Stars

❑ Whatta Drag/Yellow/5SP $1.50

2007 All Stars

❑ Ferrari F50/Red/PR5 .... $1.50

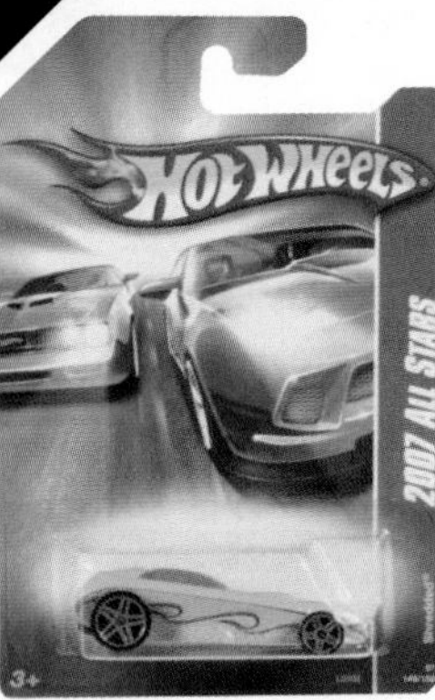

2007 All Stars

❑ Shredded/Yellow & M Silver/OrangePR5 .... $1.50

2007 All Stars

❑ '63 Corvette/Dark Blue/10SP $1.50

2007 All Stars

❑ '63 Corvette/Pearl White/10SP $1.50

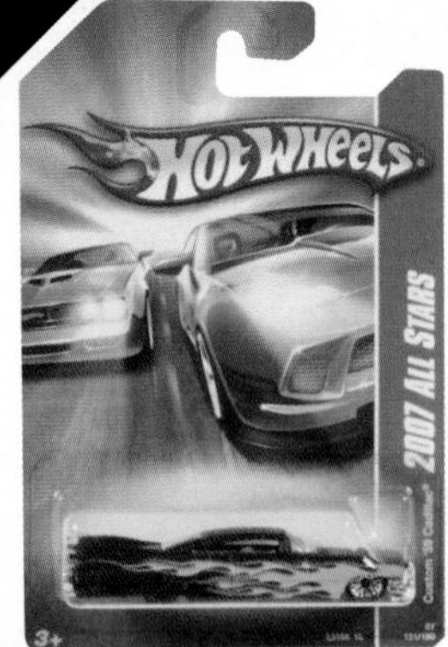

2007 All Stars

❑ Custom '59 Cadillac/Flat Black/WSP (K-Mart) $5.00

2007 All Stars

2007 151

- ❑ Custom '59 Cadillac/M Dark Blue/WSP $3.00

2007 All Stars

2007 152

- ❑ Nissan Z/M Gold/GoldOH5SP Malaysia base.............. $1.50
- ❑ Nissan Z/M Gold/GoldOH5SP Thailand base $1.50
- **❑ Nissan Z/M Gold/GoldPR5 .... $1.50**

2007 All Stars

2007 152

- ❑ Nissan Z/M Silver/PR5 .... $1.50

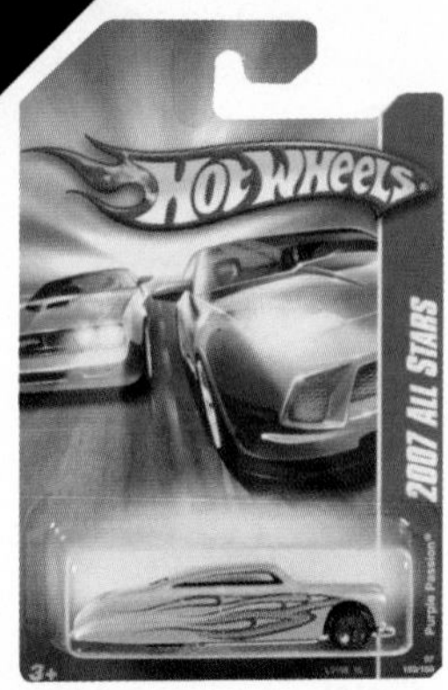

2007 All Stars

2007 153

❑ Purple Passion/M Silver/Red5SP $1.50

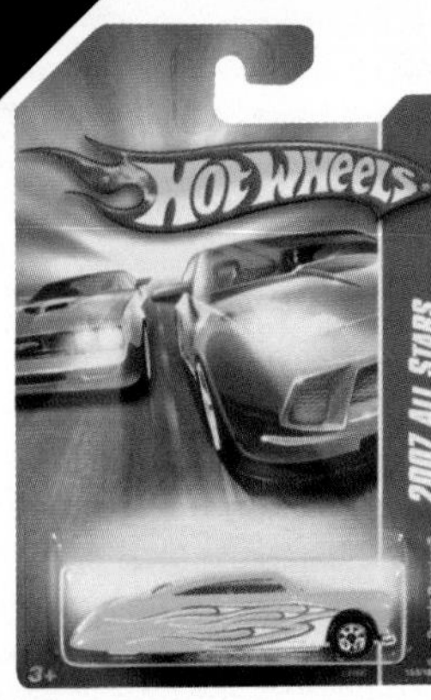

2007 All Stars

2007 153

❑ Purple Passion/Pearl Yellow/7SP $5.00
❑ Purple Passion/Pearl Yellow/PR5 .... $3.00

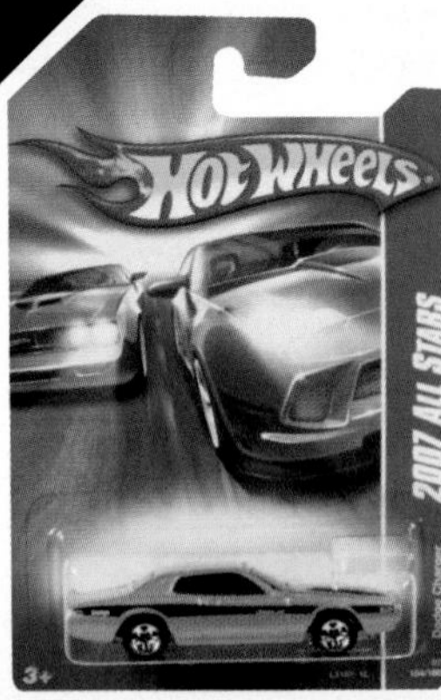

2007 All Stars

2007 154

❑ Dodge Charger/M Champagne/5SP $3.00

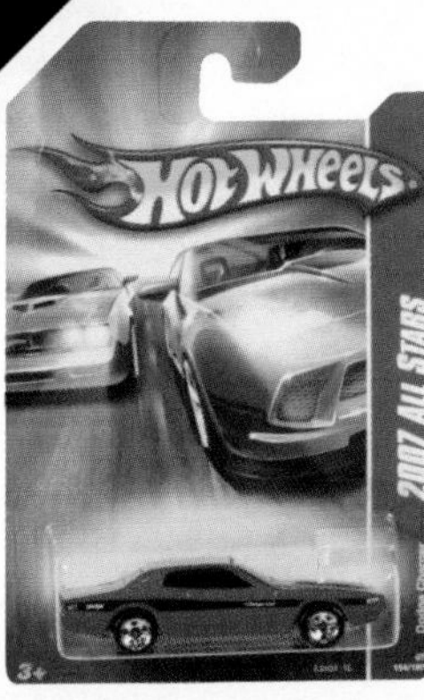

2007 All Stars

2007 154

❑ Dodge Charger/Red/5SP $1.50

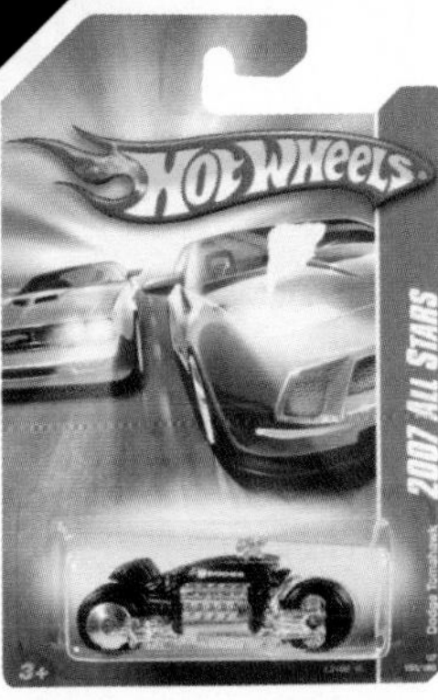

2007 All Stars

2007 155

❑ Dodge Tomahawk/Black/TMHK.................................... $1.50

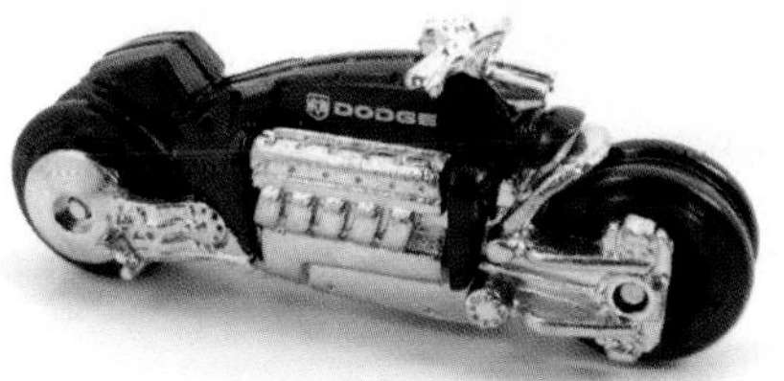

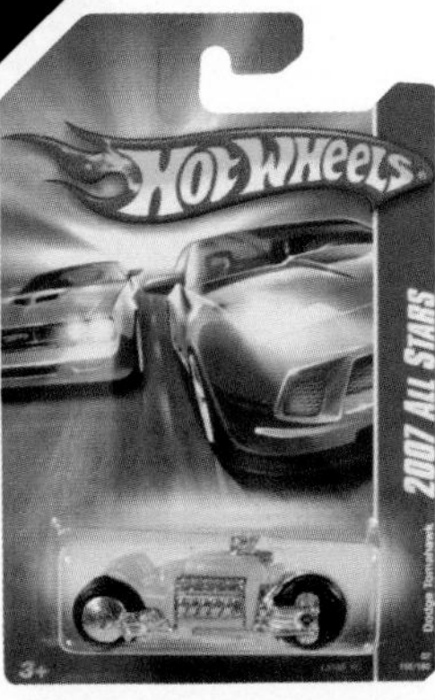

2007 All Stars

2007 155

❑ Dodge Tomahawk/Yellow/TMHK $1.50

2007

2007 All Stars

❑ Dodge Sidewinder/M Dark Teal/5SP $1.50

2007 All Stars

❑ Dodge Sidewinder/M Lt. Blue/5SP $1.50

Mystery

❑ 1970 Plymouth Barracuda/Black/PR5 black windows $1.50

* Mystery Cars are priced as loose, out of package, vehicles.

MYSTERY

❑ 1970 Plymouth Barracuda/Black/PR5 clear windows.. $5.00

* Mystery Cars are priced as loose, out of package, vehicles.

MYSTERY

❑ 1970 Plymouth Barracuda/M Dark Red/PR5 .... $1.50

* Mystery Cars are priced as loose, out of package, vehicles.

MYSTERY

❑ What-4-2/Black/Blue10SP $5.00
❑ What-4-2/Black/BluePR5 .... $1.50

* Mystery Cars are priced as loose, out of package, vehicles.

2007

MYSTERY

❑ What-4-2/Pearl White/OH5SP $1.50

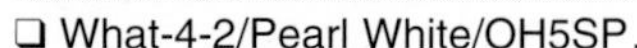

* Mystery Cars are priced as loose, out of package, vehicles.

MYSTERY

❑ Corvette C6/M Red/PR5 .... $1.50

* Mystery Cars are priced as loose, out of package, vehicles.

MYSTERY

❑ Corvette C6/Yellow/PR5 .... $1.50

* Mystery Cars are priced as loose, out of package, vehicles.

Mystery

❑ Symbolic/Neon Lt. Green/5SP $1.50

* Mystery Cars are priced as loose, out of package, vehicles.

Mystery

❑ Power Rage/Chrome/BlueOH5SP $1.50

* Mystery Cars are priced as loose, out of package, vehicles.

Mystery

❑ Power Rage/Gold Chrome/RedCM6 .... $8.00
❑ Power Rage/Gold Chrome/RedOH5SP $1.50

* Mystery Cars are priced as loose, out of package, vehicles.

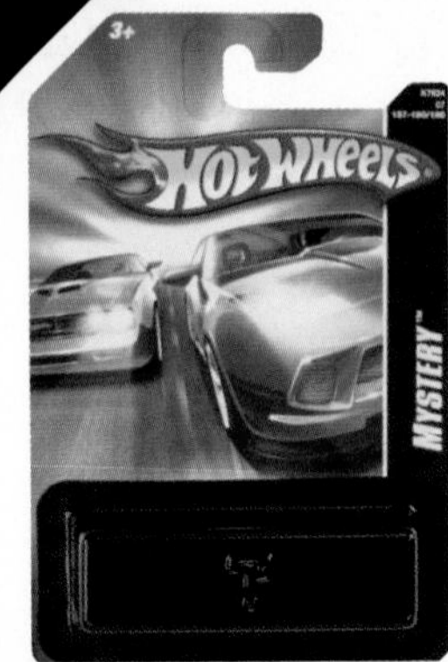

Mystery

❑ **Batmobile (Animated)/Black/PR5 black motor $1.50**
❑ Batmobile (Animated)/Black/PR5 chrome motor.......... $3.00

* Mystery Cars are priced as loose, out of package, vehicles.

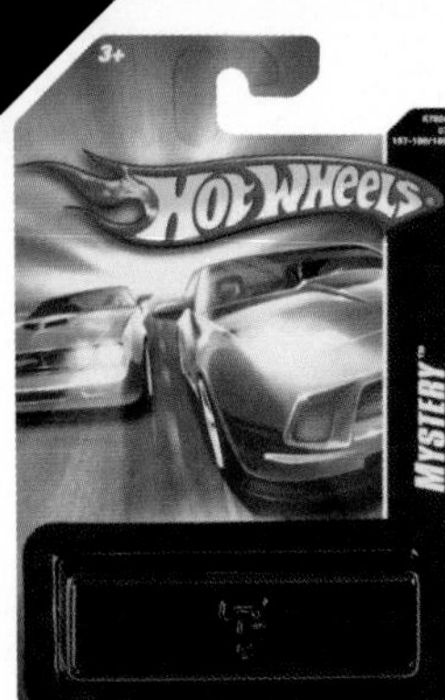

Mystery

❑ Side Draft/Grey/PR5 .... $1.50

* Mystery Cars are priced as loose, out of package, vehicles.

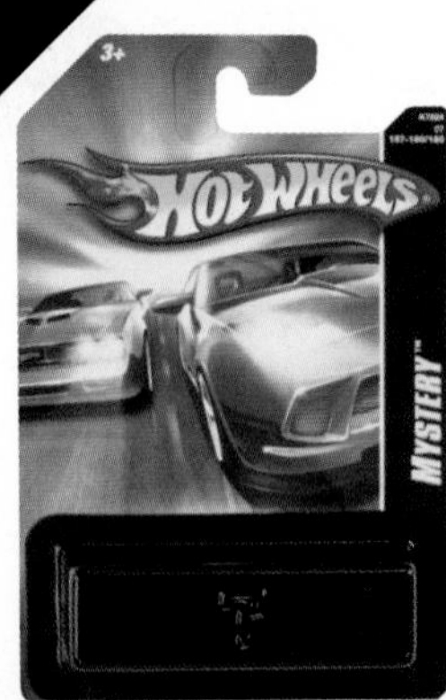

Mystery

❑ Sand Stinger/M Dark Orange/OR5SP front, 5SP rear $1.50

* Mystery Cars are priced as loose, out of package, vehicles.

MYSTERY

❑ 1965 Pontiac Bonneville/Flat Black/10SP $3.00

* Mystery Cars are priced as loose, out of package, vehicles.

MYSTERY

❑ 1965 Pontiac Bonneville/Red/10SP $3.00

* Mystery Cars are priced as loose, out of package, vehicles.

MYSTERY

❑ Maserati MC12/M Dark Blue/10SP $1.50

* Mystery Cars are priced as loose, out of package, vehicles.

2007

Mystery

❑ Volkswagon Beetle/M Green/10SP $3.00

* Mystery Cars are priced as loose, out of package, vehicles.

Mystery

❑ Volkswagon Beetle/M Magenta/10SP $3.00

* Mystery Cars are priced as loose, out of package, vehicles.

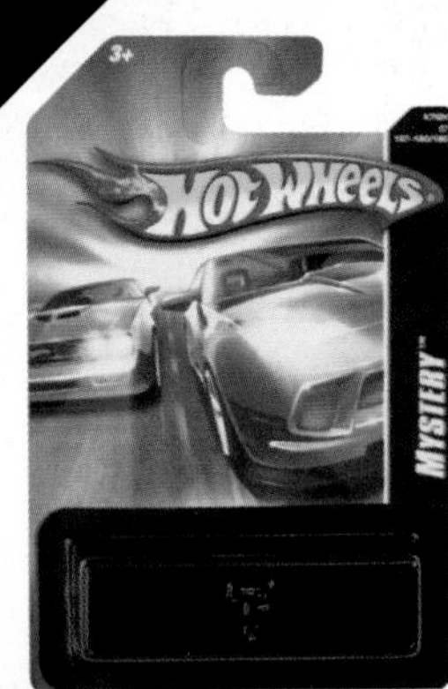

Mystery

❑ Dodge M80/M Silver/RedPR5 .... $1.50

* Mystery Cars are priced as loose, out of package, vehicles.

MYSTERY

❑ F-Racer/White/GoldPR5 .... $1.50

* Mystery Cars are priced as loose, out of package, vehicles.

MYSTERY

❑ Bugatti Veyron/M Yellow/Gold10SP $1.50

* Mystery Cars are priced as loose, out of package, vehicles.

MYSTERY

❑ Bugatti Veyron/Pearl White/10SP $1.50

* Mystery Cars are priced as loose, out of package, vehicles.

MYSTERY

❑ Battle Spec/Chrome/OH5SP $1.50

* Mystery Cars are priced as loose, out of package, vehicles.

MYSTERY

❑ Corvette Stingray/M Orange/5SP $1.50

* Mystery Cars are priced as loose, out of package, vehicles.

MYSTERY

❑ Steel Flame/Flat Black/OH5SP $1.50

* Mystery Cars are priced as loose, out of package, vehicles.

MYSTERY

- ❑ Riley & Scott Mk III/M Lt. Blue/10SP $5.00
- ❑ **Riley & Scott Mk III/M Lt. Blue/WSP $1.50**

* Mystery Cars are priced as loose, out of package, vehicles.

MYSTERY

- ❑ Track T/Flat Grey/5SP black interior $1.50
- ❑ **Track T/Flat Grey/5SP tan interior $5.00**

* Mystery Cars are priced as loose, out of package, vehicles.

MYSTERY

- ❑ **Track T/White/3SP $5.00**
- ❑ Track T/White/SB $1.50

* Mystery Cars are priced as loose, out of package, vehicles.

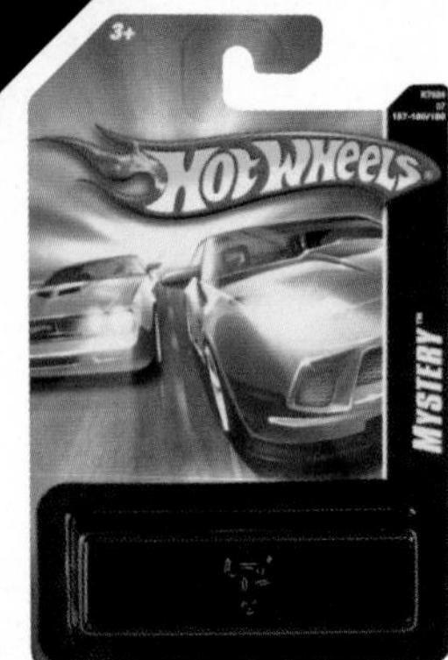

MYSTERY

❑ Rapid Transit/Orange/WhitePR5 .... $1.50

* Mystery Cars are priced as loose, out of package, vehicles.

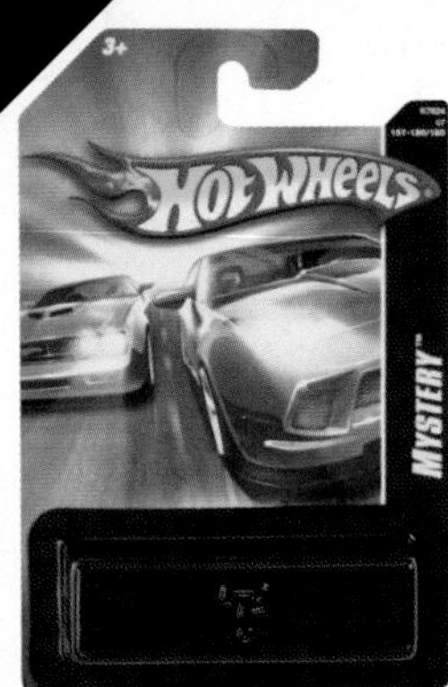

MYSTERY

❑ Rapid Transit/Red/WhitePR5 .... $1.50

* Mystery Cars are priced as loose, out of package, vehicles.

MYSTERY

❑ Road Rocket/Gold Chrome/GoldY5 .... $1.50

* Mystery Cars are priced as loose, out of package, vehicles.

MYSTERY

❑ Fish'd & Chip'd/M Brown/10SP $1.50

* Mystery Cars are priced as loose, out of package, vehicles.

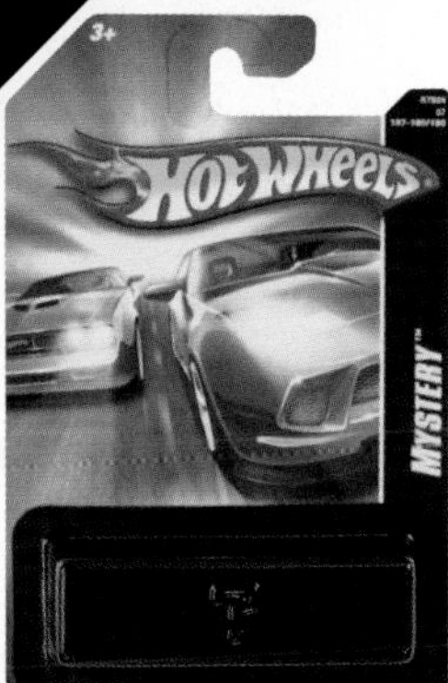

MYSTERY

❑ Chaparral 2D/Blue/PR5.. $1.50

* Mystery Cars are priced as loose, out of package, vehicles.

MYSTERY

❑ Super Comp Dragster/Black/Gold5SP $1.50

* Mystery Cars are priced as loose, out of package, vehicles.

2008 HOT WHEELS PRICE GUIDE

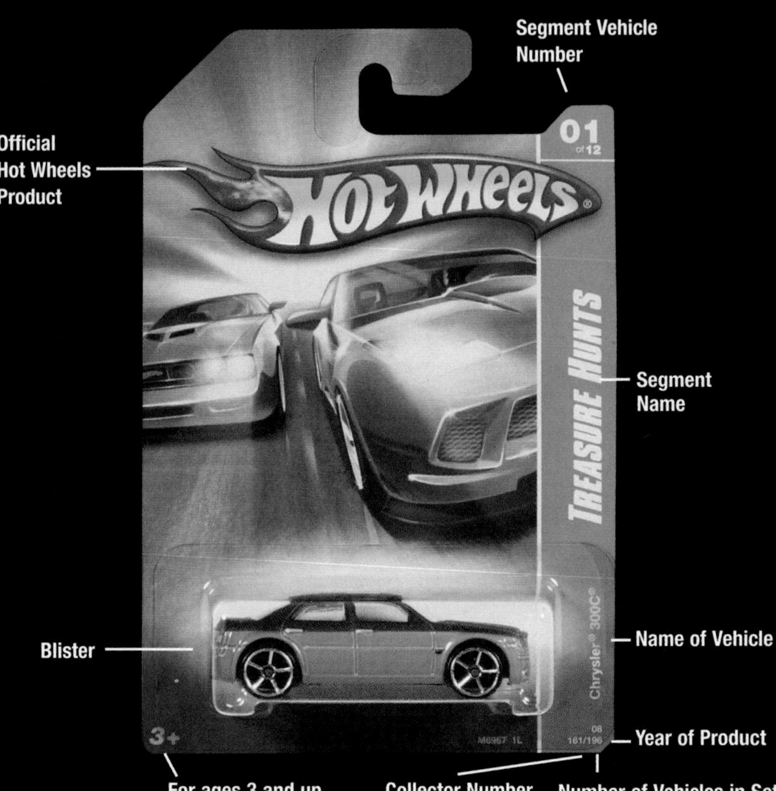

IMPORTANT NOTE: Unpriced cards were not live at the time of print. Some of the cars were also delayed due to production issues. You can find the full list later in the book.

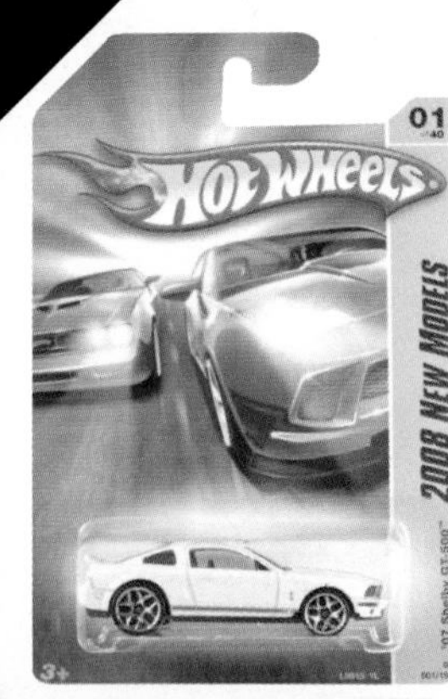

2008 New Models 1 of 40

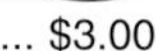

❑ '07 Shelby GT-500/Pearl White/Y5 .... $3.00

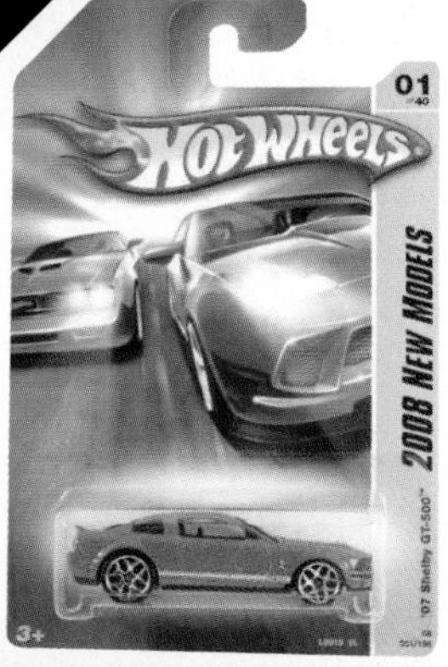

2008 New Models 1 of 40

❑ '07 Shelby GT-500/Red/Y5 .... $3.00

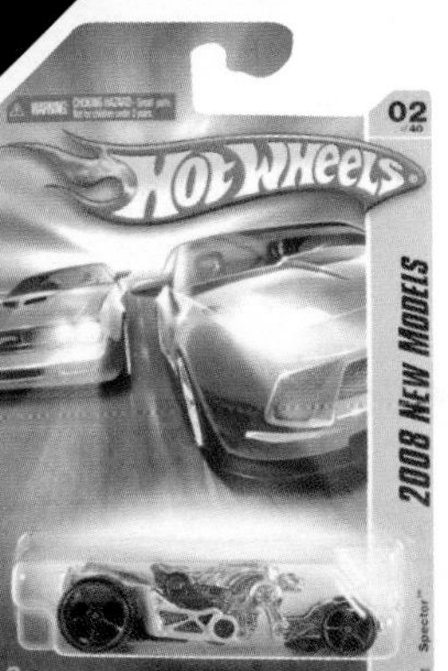

2008 New Models 2 of 40

❑ Spector/Satin Silver/RedOH5SP $1.50

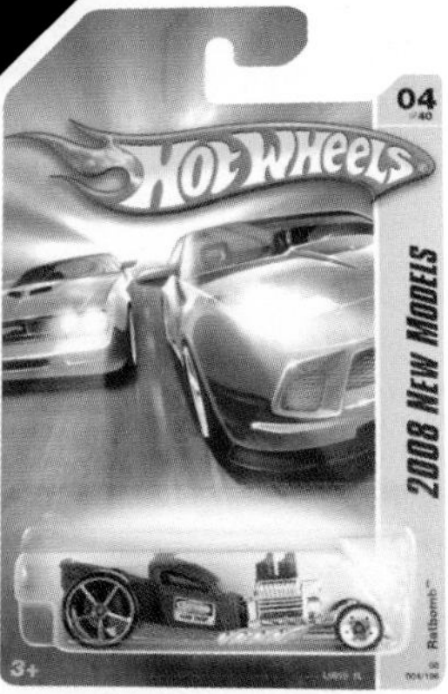

2008 New Models 4 of 40

❑ Ratbomb/Satin Purple/SK5 front, OH5SP rear $1.50

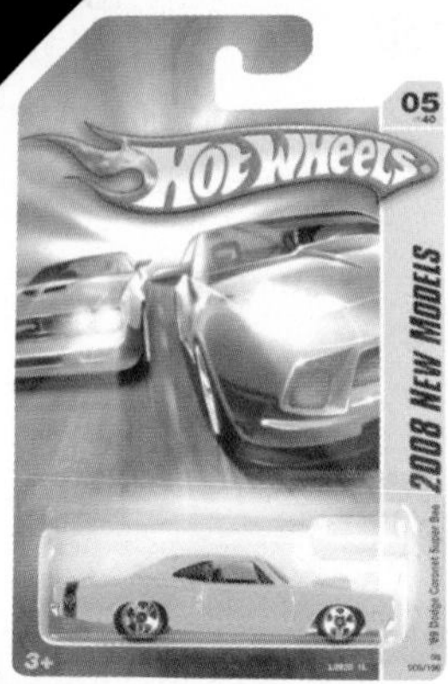

2008 New Models 5 of 40

❑ **'69 Dodge Coronet Super Bee/Pearl Yellow/5SP $1.50**
❑ '69 Dodge Coronet Super Bee/Pearl Yellow/5SP w/o side stripe $5.00

2008 New Models 6 of 40

❑ Dragtor/M Green/SK5 front, OH5SP rear $3.00

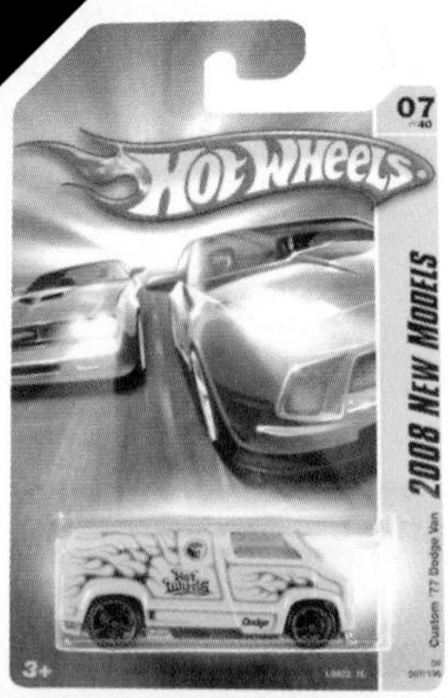

2008 New Models 7 of 40

❑ Custom '77 Dodge Van/Pearl Yellow/RedOH5SP........ $1.50

2008

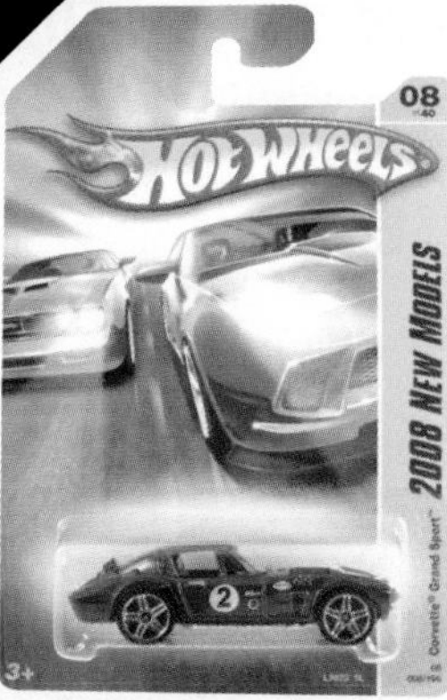

2008 New Models 8 of 40

2008 008

- ❑ **Corvette Grand Sport/Dark Blue/PR5 .... $1.50**
- ❑ Corvette Grand Sport/Dark Blue/PR5 silver vents $3.00

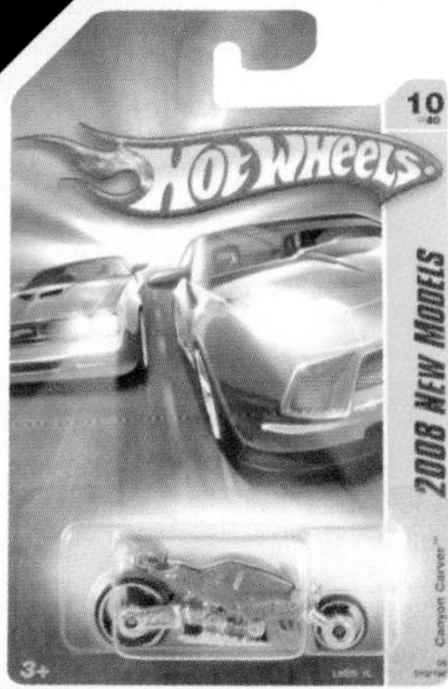

2008 New Models 10 of 40

2008 010

- ❑ **Canyon Carver/M Orange/MC3................................. $1.50**
- ❑ Canyon Carver/M Blue/MC3 .... $3.00

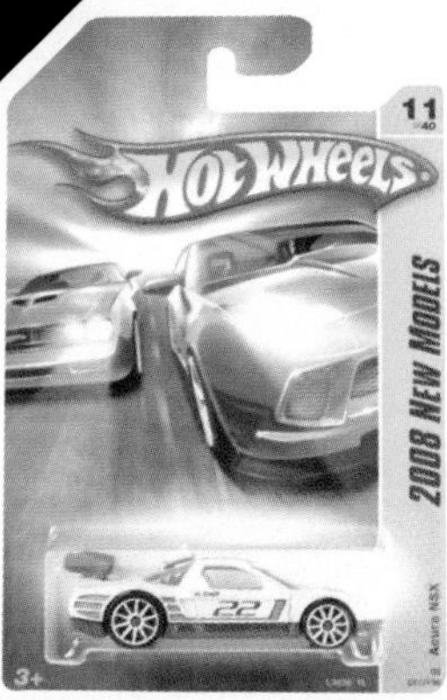

2008 New Models 11 of 40

2008 011

- ❑ Acura NSX/Pearl White/White10SP $1.50

2008 New Models 13 of 40

- ❑ **Custom '62 Chevy/M Dark Magenta/GoldOH5SP.... $1.50**
- ❑ Custom '62 Chevy/M Dark Magenta/GoldOH5SP w/o surfboard $25.00
- ❑ Custom '62 Chevy/M Purple/GoldOH5SP.................... $3.00

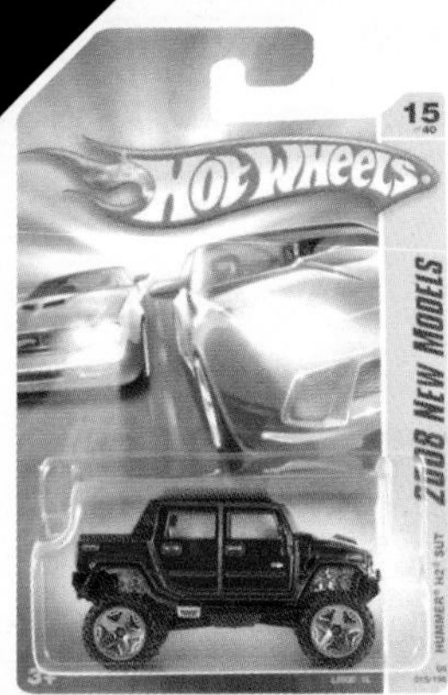

2008 New Models 15 of 40

- ❑ Hummer H2 SUT/Dark Blue/OR5SP........................... $1.50

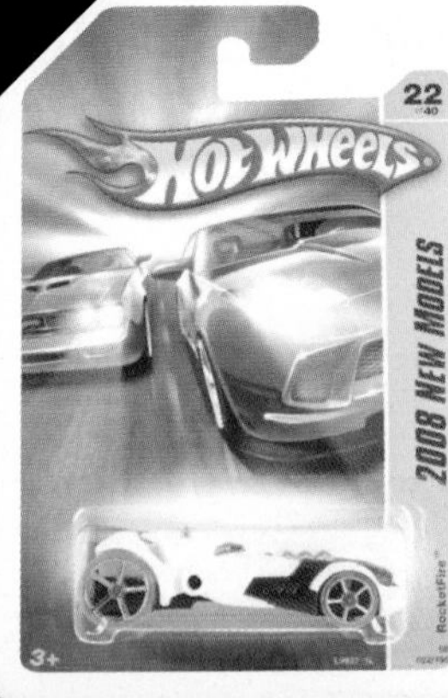

2008 New Models 22 of 40

- ❑ **RocketFire/White & Flat Black/ClearOrangeOH5SP $1.50**
- ❑ RocketFire/White & Black/ClearOrangeOH5SP $8.00

2008 All Stars

- ❑ CUL8R/Flat Black/GoldOH5SP $1.50

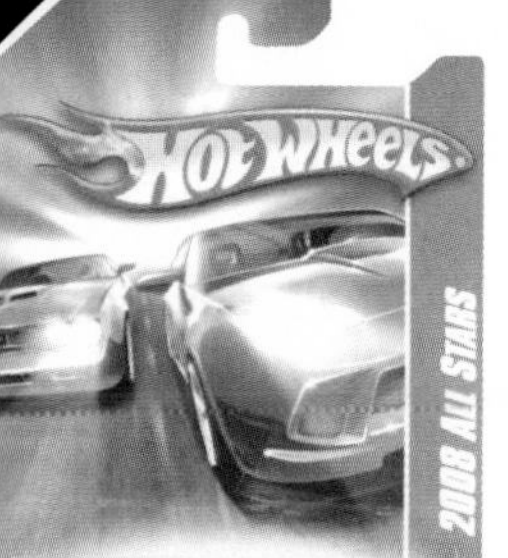

2008 All Stars

- ❑ La Troca/Flat Brown/5SP $1.50

2008 All Stars

- ❑ Sand Stinger/Dark Green/5SP front, OR5SP rear $1.50

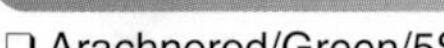

2008 All Stars

- ❑ Arachnorod/Green/5SP $1.50

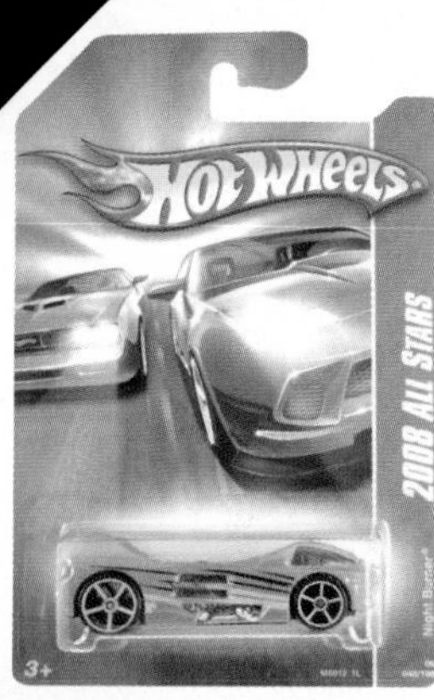

2008 All Stars

2008 046

- ❑ Night Burner/Aqua Blue/Yellow5SP $4.00
- ❑ **Night Burner/Aqua Blue/YellowOH5SP $1.50**

2008

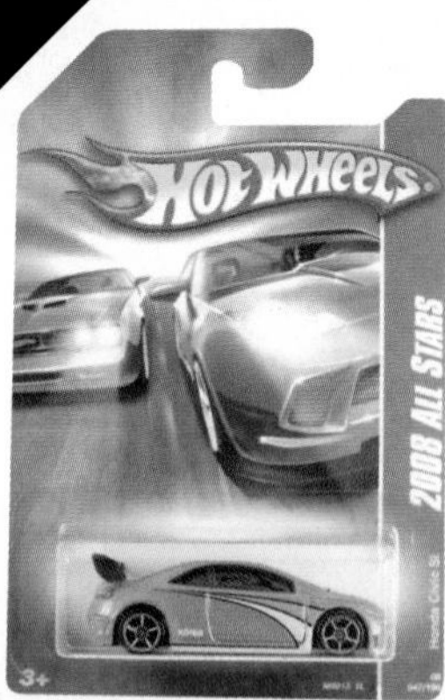

2008 All Stars

- ❑ Honda Civic Si/Gold/GoldOH5SP $1.50

2008 All Stars

❑ Aston Martin V8 Vantage/Black/PR5 .... $1.50

2008 All Stars

❑ Swoop Coupe/Dark BurgundySK5 front, 5DOT rear .. $1.50

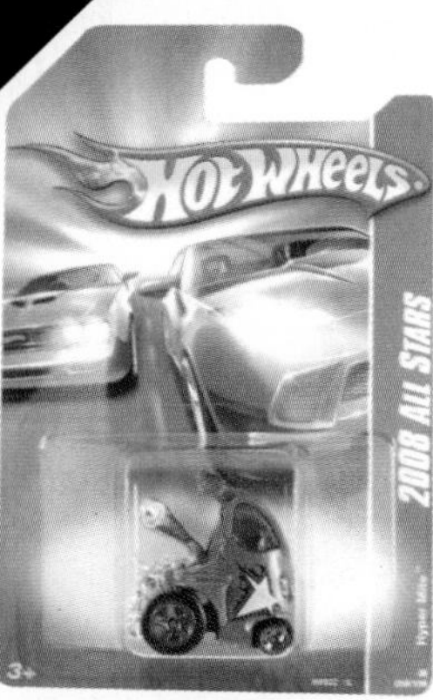

2008 All Stars

❑ Hyper Mite/Pearl Purple/Red5SP $1.50

2008 All Stars

❑ Roll Cage/Grey/OR5SP $1.50

2008 All Stars

❑ '65 Chevy Impala/Magenta/OrangeWSP $1.50

Web Trading Cars 2 of 24

❑ MX48 Turbo/Blue/3SP $1.50

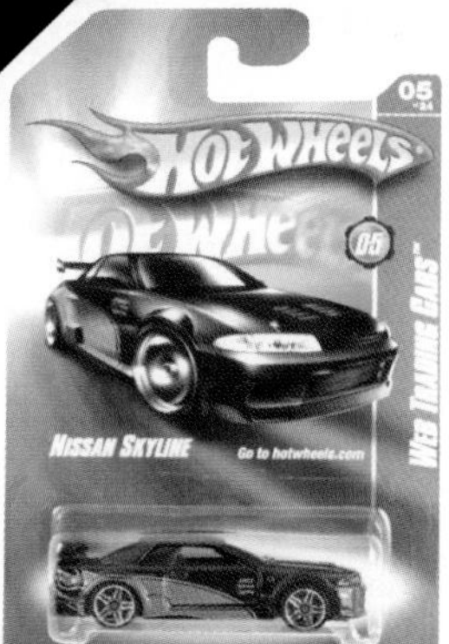

WEB TRADING CARS 5 OF 24

❑ Nissan Skyline/Black/PR5 .... $1.50

WEB TRADING CARS 8 OF 24

❑ **Mega-Duty/M Copper/5DOT $2.00**
❑ Mega-Duty/M Copper/OR5SP $3.00

WEB TRADING CARS 10 OF 24

❑ Pony-Up/Blue/OH5SP $1.50

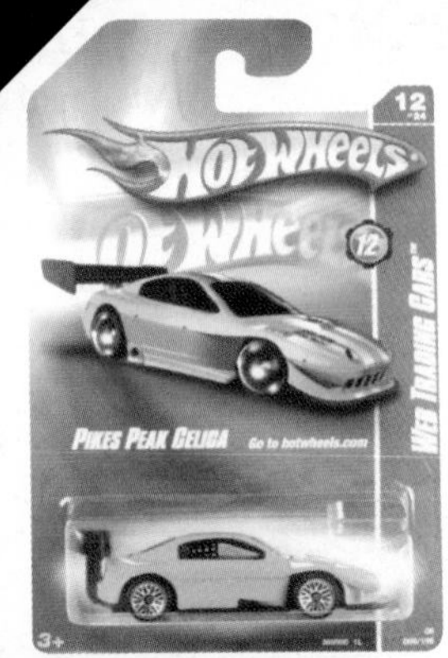

❑ Pikes Peak Celica/Lt. Green/WSP $1.50

Web Trading Cars 13 of 24

2008 089

❑ At-A-Tude/Burgundy/PR5 .... $1.50

Web Trading Cars 14 of 24

❑ 1/4 Mile Coupe/Flat Black & Red/5SP $1.50

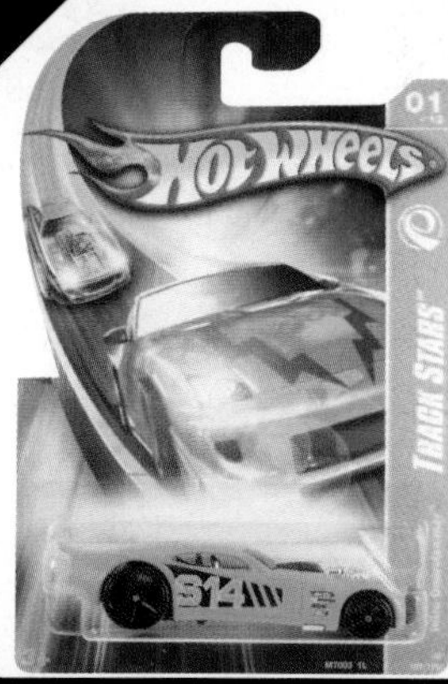

TRACK STARS 1 OF 12

2008 101

❑ **Nitro Doorslammer/Lt. Green/BlackOH5SP black base $1.50**

❑ Nitro Doorslammer/Lt. Green/BlackOH5SP grey base $3.00

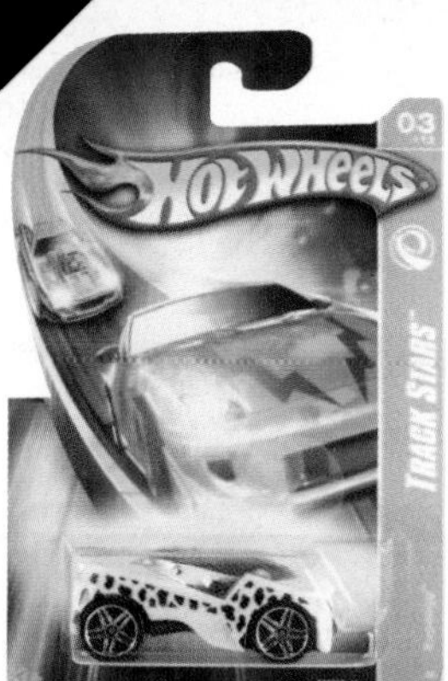

TRACK STARS 3 OF 12

2008 103

❑ Supdogg/White/GoldPR5 .... $1.50

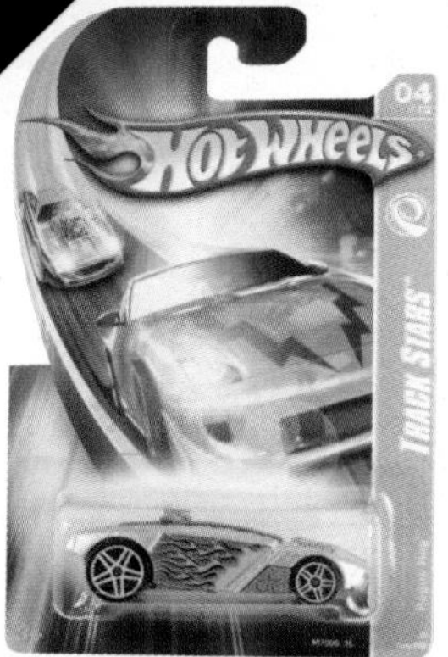

TRACK STARS 4 OF 12

2008 104

❑ Rogue Hog/Silver/WhitePR5 .... $1.50

Track Stars 6 of 12

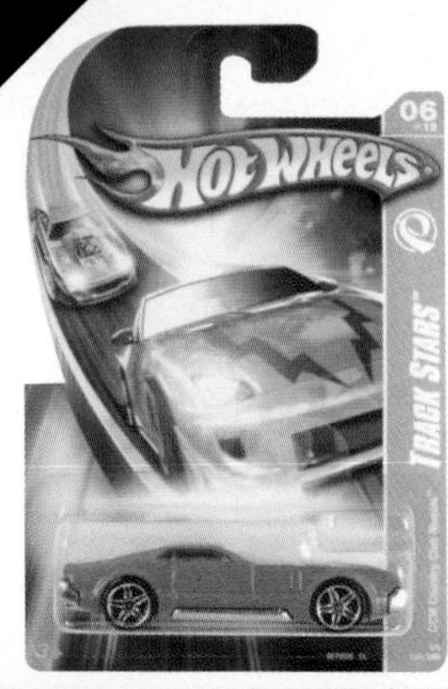

❑ CCM Country Club Muscle/Red/PR5 .... $1.50

Team: Exotics 1 of 4

2008 113

❑ Lotus Esprit/Pearl Dark Yellow/PR5 .... $1.50

Team: Exotics 2 of 4

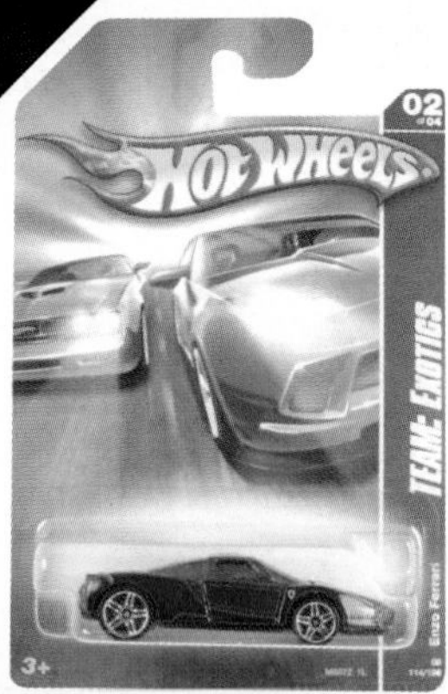

❑ Enzo Ferrari/Dark Blue/PR5 .... $2.00

2008

Team: Exotics 3 of 4 — 2008 115

❑ Porsche Carrera GT/Black/PR5 .... $1.50

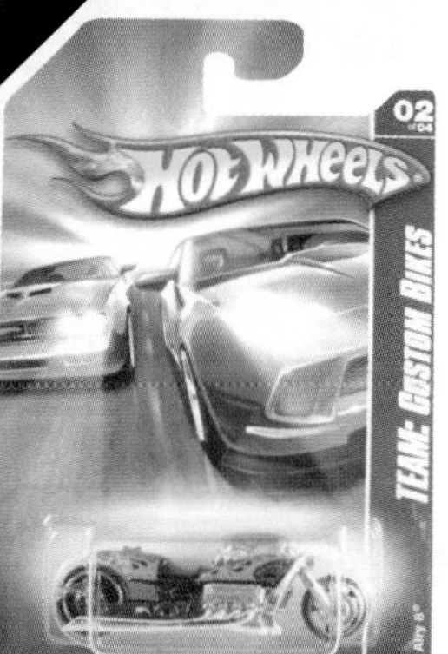

Team: Custom Bikes 2 of 4 — 2008 150

❑ Airy 8/Purple/MC5 .... $1.50

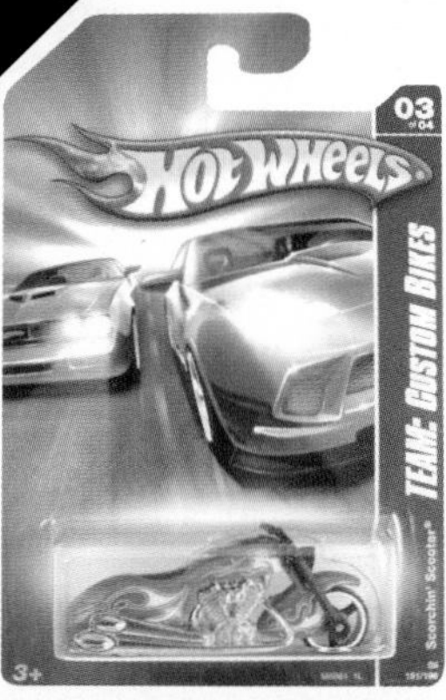

Team: Custom Bikes 3 of 4 — 2008 151

❑ Scorchin' Scooter/Blue/WhiteMC3 .... $1.50

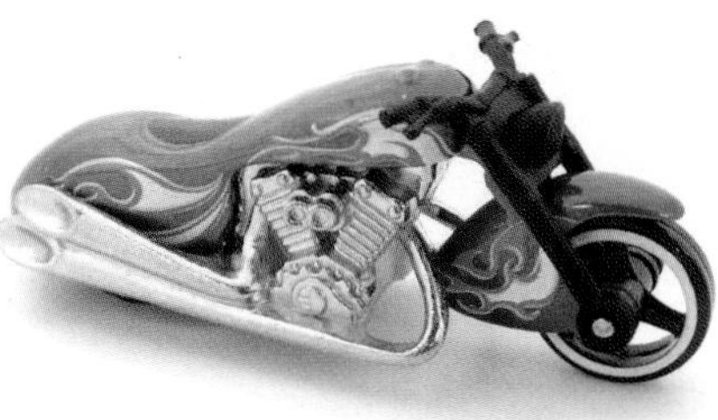

TEAM: CUSTOM BIKES 4 OF 4

❑ Hammer Sled/Teal/MC3 .... $1.50

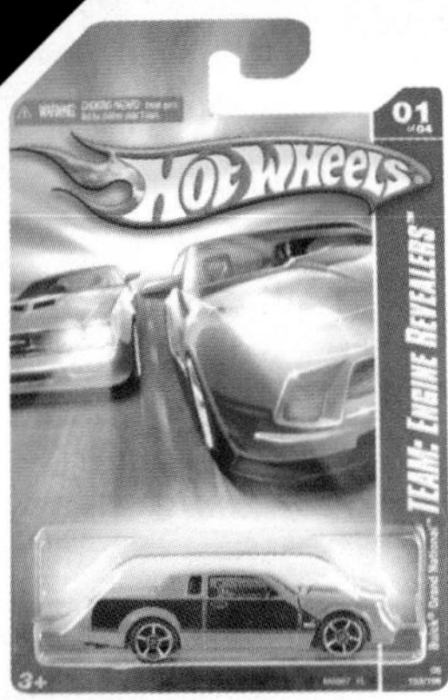

TEAM: ENGINE REVEALERS 1 OF 4

2008 153

❑ Buick Grand National/Gold/OH5SP $1.50

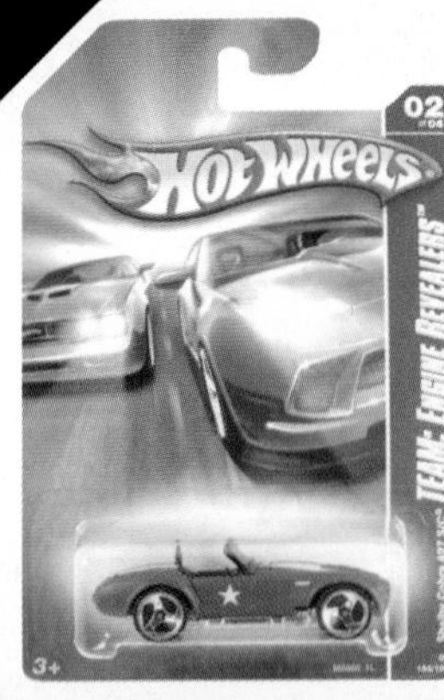

TEAM: ENGINE REVEALERS 2 OF 4

❑ **Shelby Cobra 427 S/C/Dark Green/3SP.................... $3.00**

❑ Shelby Cobra 427 S/C/Dark Green/small3SP front, 3SP rear $25.00

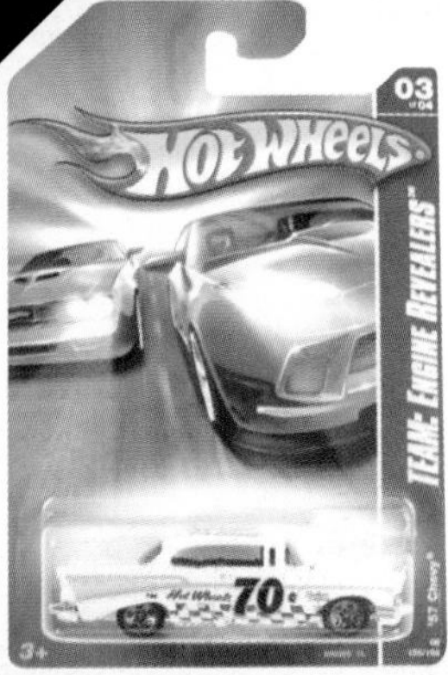

Team: Engine Revealers 3 of 4

2008 155

❑ '57 Chevy/Pearl White/Red5SP $1.50

Team: Engine Revealers 4 of 4

2008 156

❑ Sooo Fast/Purple/5SP.. $1.50

Team: Drag Racing 1 of 4

2008 157

❑ Mustang Funny Car/Black/5SP $4.00

 TEAM: DRAG RACING 2 OF 4 

- ❑ Jaded/Flat Olive Green/5SP $1.50

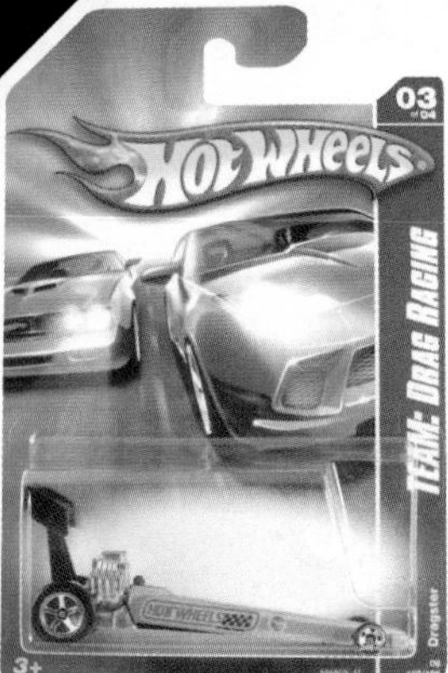

TEAM: DRAG RACING 3 OF 4 

- ❑ Dragster/Grey/5SP $1.50

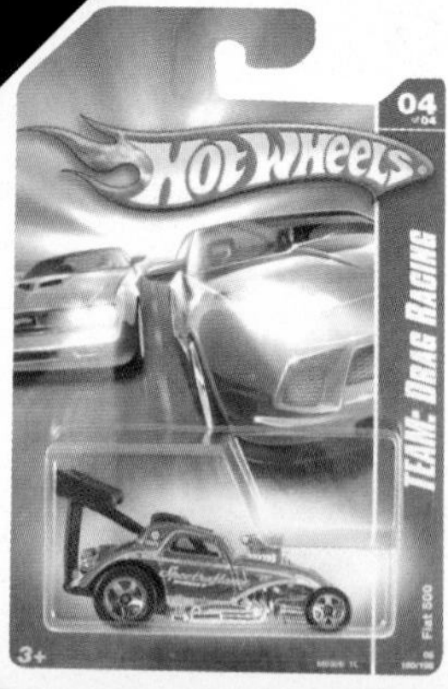

TEAM: DRAG RACING 4 OF 4 

- ❑ Fiat 500/Red/Gold5SP $1.50

2008

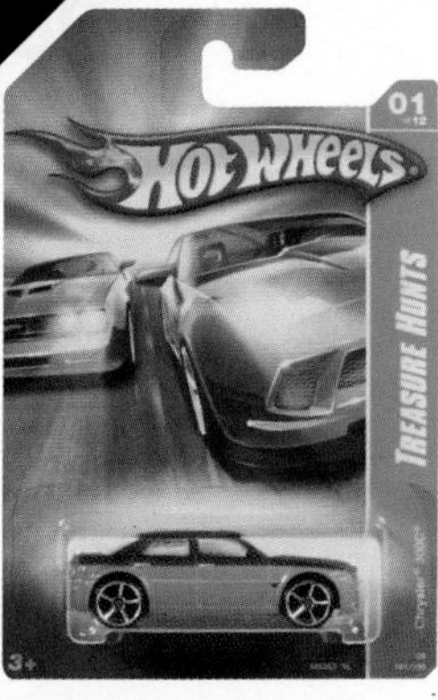

Treasure Hunt 3 of 12

2008 161

❑ **Chrysler 300C HEMI/Black & Spectraflame Green/RR5SP $50.00**
❑ Chrysler 300C HEMI/Flat Black & M Green/OH5SP $25.00

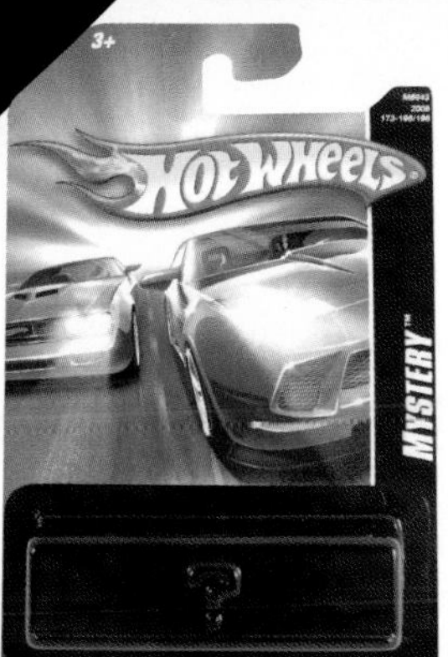

Mystery

2008 173

❑ '69 Corvette/Black/GoldOH5SP $1.50

Mystery

2008 175

❑ '66 Chevy Nova/M Burgandy/PR5 .... $2.00

* Image not available at time of printing.

MYSTERY

❑ Cloak And Dagger/Clear Blue/PR5 .... $1.50

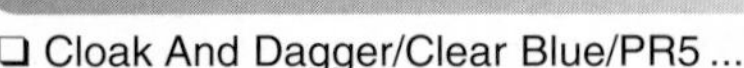

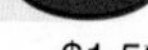

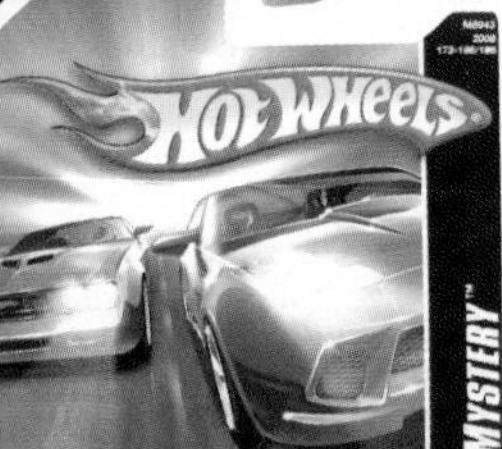

MYSTERY

❑ Ballistik/Red/Y5 .... $1.50

MYSTERY

❑ Hooligan/Flat Black/RL5SP $1.50

2008

Mystery

2008 184

❑ Monoposto/Blue/PR5 .... $1.50

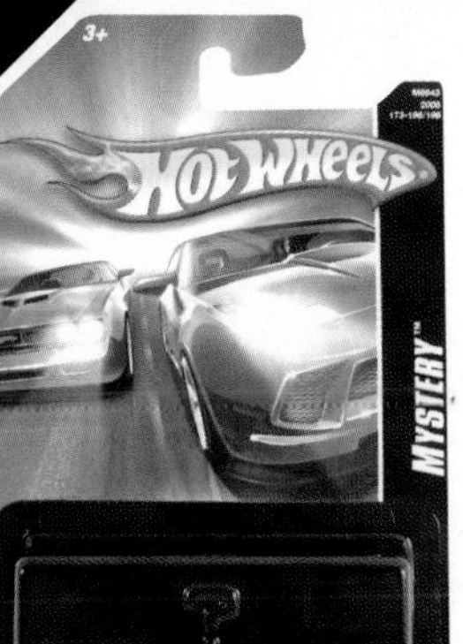

Mystery

2008 185

❑ Lancia Stratos/Silver/White5SP $1.50

Mystery

2008 188

❑ GT-03/Grey/PR5 .... $2.00

2008

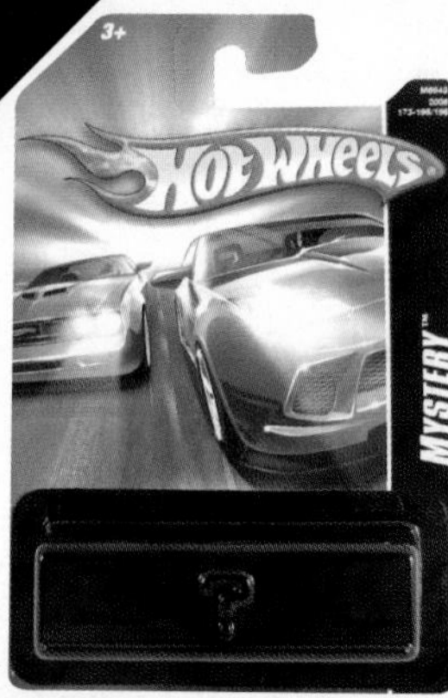

❑ Saltflat Racer/Blue/Magenta/PR5 .... $1.50

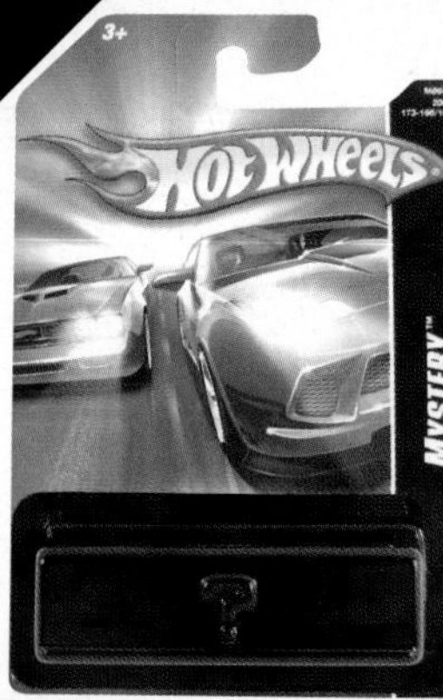

MYSTERY

❑ '57 T-Bird/Orange/5SP $1.50

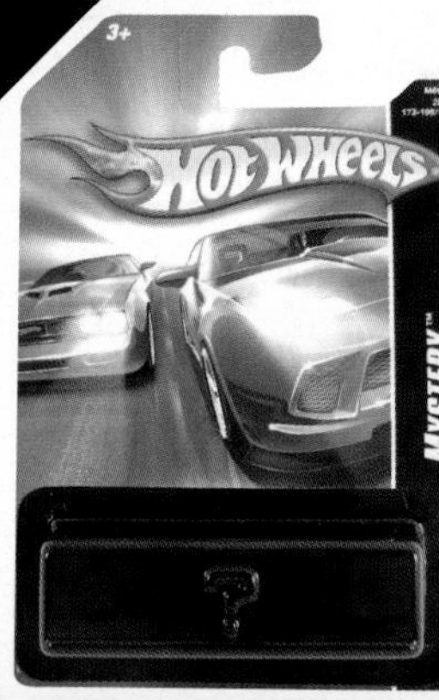

MYSTERY

❑ '58 Corvette/M Blue/5SP $2.00

COMPLETE 2008 HOT WHEELS CHECKLIST & PRICE GUIDE

PRICE RANGES ARE FOR MINT IN PACKAGE.

2008 Hot Wheels New Models

	Price Range LO	HI
❑ 001 '07 Shelby GT-500/Pearl White/Y5	1.50	3.00
❑ 001 '07 Shelby GT-500/Red/Y5	1.50	3.00
❑ 002 Spector/Satin Silver/RedOH5SP	.75	1.50
❑ 003 Audi R8		
❑ 004 Rat Bomb/Satin Purple/SK5 front, OH5SP rear	.75	1.50
❑ 005 '69 Dodge Coronet Super Bee/Pearl Yellow/5SP	.75	1.50
❑ 005 '69 Dodge Coronet Super Bee/Pearl Yellow/5SP w/o side stripe	2.50	5.00
❑ 006 Dragtor/M Green/SK5 front, OH5SP rear	1.50	3.00
❑ 007 Custom '77 Dodge Van/Pearl Yellow/RedOH5SP	.75	1.50
❑ 008 Corvette Grand Sport/Dark Blue/PR5	.75	1.50
❑ 008 Corvette Grand Sport/Dark Blue/PR5 silver vents	1.50	3.00
❑ 009 Corvette		
❑ 010 Canyon Carver/M Blue/MC3	1.50	3.00
❑ 010 Canyon Carver/M Orange/MC3	.75	1.50
❑ 011 Acura NSX/Pearl White/White10SP	.75	1.50
❑ 012 Prototype H-24		
❑ 013 Custom '62 Chevy/M Dark Magenta/GoldOH5SP	.75	1.50
❑ 013 Custom '62 Chevy/M Dark Magenta/GoldOH5SP w/o surfboard	12.50	25.00
❑ 013 Custom '62 Chevy/M Purple/GoldOH5SP	1.50	3.00
❑ 014 Fast Fish		
❑ 015 Hummer H2 SUT/Dark Blue/OR5SP	.75	1.50
❑ 016 '08 Dodge Challenger SRT8		
❑ 017 '69 Chevelle SS 396		
❑ 018 Croc Rod		
❑ 019 '69 Ford Torino Talladega		
❑ 020 Bad Mudder 2		
❑ 021 Custom Ford Bronco		
❑ 022 RocketFire/White & Flat Black/ClearOrangeOH5SP	.75	1.50
❑ 022 RocketFire/White & Gloss Black/ClearOrangeOH5SP	4.00	8.00
❑ 023 2008 Lancer Evolution		
❑ 024 Duel Fueler		
❑ 025 Pass'n Gasser		
❑ 026 2008 Tesla Roadster		
❑ 027 '65 Mustang Fastback		
❑ 028 Impavido 1		
❑ 029 '70 Pontiac GTO		
❑ 030 Amazoom		
❑ 031 '08 Ford Focus		
❑ 032 Locked N' Loaded		
❑ 033 Ferrari FXX		
❑ 034 Madfast		
❑ 035 Unknown (TBD)		
❑ 036 Carbonator		
❑ 037 Camaro Convertible Concept		
❑ 038 Ferrari 288 GTO		
❑ 039 '65 Volkswagen Fastback		
❑ 040 Twin Mill III		

2008 Hot Wheels All Stars

	LO	HI
❑ 041 CUL8R/Flat Black/GoldOH5SP	.75	1.50
❑ 042 La Troca/Flat Brown/5SP	.75	1.50
❑ 043 Sand Stinger/Dark Green/5SP front, OR5SP rear	.75	1.50
❑ 044 Arachnorod/Green/5SP	.75	1.50

* Unpriced cars were not live at the time of print.

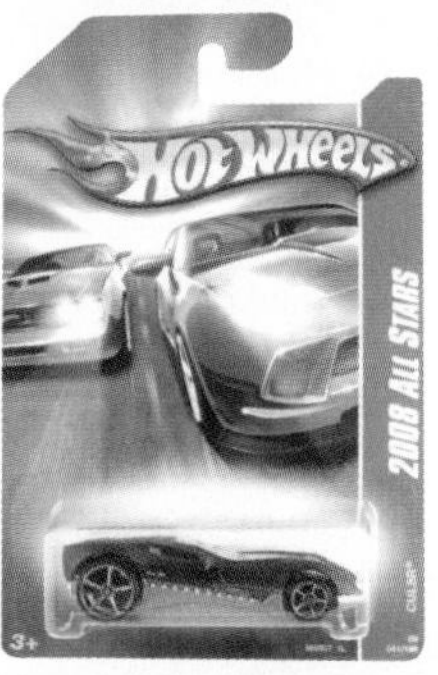

PRICE GUIDE

❑ 045	'63 Corvette		
❑ 046	Night Burner/Aqua Blue/Yellow5SP	2.00	4.00
❑ 046	Night Burner/Aqua Blue/YellowOH5SP	.75	1.50
❑ 047	Honda Civic Si/Gold/GoldOH5SP	.75	1.50
❑ 048	Unknown (TBD)		
❑ 049	'32 Ford Sedan Delivery		
❑ 050	Aston Martin V8 Vantage/Black/PR5	.75	1.50
❑ 051	Swoop Coupe/Dark BurgundySK5 front, 5DOT rear	.75	1.50
❑ 052	HW450F		
❑ 053	Screamin' Hauler		
❑ 054	Mad Propz		
❑ 055	Ford Stake Bed		
❑ 056	Hyper Mite/Pearl Purple/Red5SP	.75	1.50
❑ 057	Roll Cage/Grey/OR5SP	.75	1.50
❑ 058	'65 Chevy Impala/Magenta/OrangeWSP	.75	1.50
❑ 059	Split Decision		
❑ 060	'71 Plymouth GTX		
❑ 061	'41 Willys Coupe		
❑ 062	Go Kart		
❑ 063	Covelight		
❑ 064	Buzz Bomb		
❑ 065	'07 Cadillac Escalade		
❑ 066	'Tooned Enzo Ferrari		
❑ 067	Track T		
❑ 068	Ferrari 360 Modena		
❑ 069	'40 Ford Convertible		
❑ 070	'65 Pontiac GTO		
❑ 071	Toyota Off-Road Truck		
❑ 072	Saleen S7		
❑ 073	Sling Shot		
❑ 074	Super Tuned		
❑ 075	Sweet 16 II		
❑ 076	'62 Chevy		

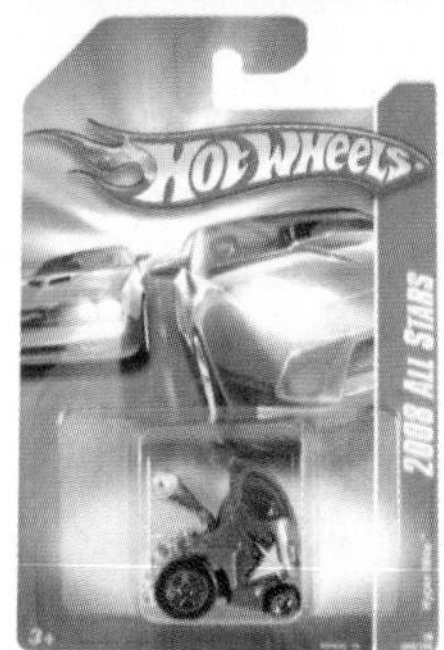

2008 Hot Wheels Web Trading Cars

❑ 077	Chevy Camaro Concept		
❑ 078	MX48 Turbo/Blue/3SP	.75	1.50
❑ 079	So Fine/Red/5SP	1.50	3.00
❑ 080	Meyers Manx		
❑ 081	Nissan Skyline/Black/PR5	.75	1.50
❑ 082	Whip Creamer II		
❑ 083	Austin-Healey		
❑ 084	Mega-Duty/M Copper/5DOT	1.00	2.00
❑ 084	Mega-Duty/M Copper/OR5SP	1.50	3.00
❑ 085	Cadillac V-16		
❑ 086	Pony-Up/Blue/OH5SP	.75	1.50
❑ 087	Dodge Concept Car		
❑ 088	Pikes Peak Celica/Lt. Green/WSP	.75	1.50
❑ 089	At-A-Tude/Burgundy/PR5	.75	1.50
❑ 090	1-Mile Coupe/Flat Black & Red/5SP	.75	1.50
❑ 091	'70 Chevelle SS		
❑ 092	Greased Lightnin'		
❑ 093	'70 HEMI Challenger		
❑ 094	Maelstrom		
❑ 095	Ford GT-40		
❑ 096	Splittin' Image		
❑ 097	'69 Camaro Z28		
❑ 098	AMG-Mercedes CLK DTM		
❑ 099	What-4-2		
❑ 100	Brutalistic		

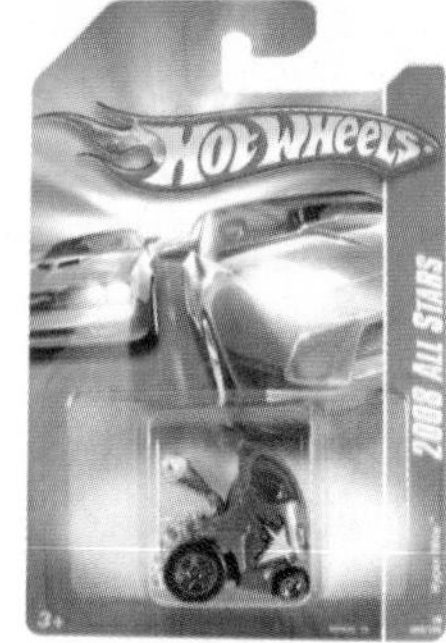

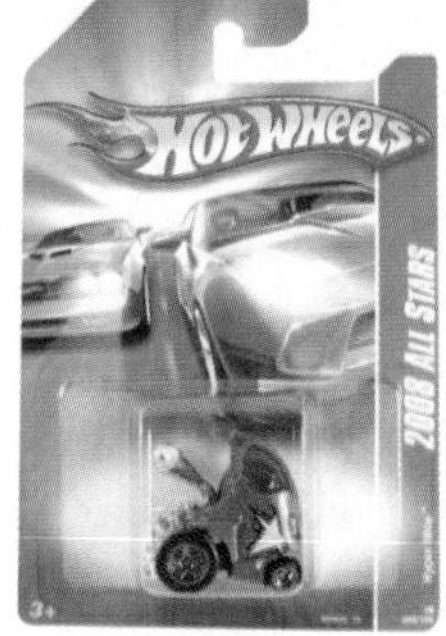

2008 Hot Wheels Track Stars

❑ 101	Nitro Doorslammer/Lt. Green/BlackOH5SP black base	.75	1.50
❑ 101	Nitro Doorslammer/Lt. Green/BlackOH5SP grey base	1.50	3.00
❑ 102	RD-02		
❑ 103	Sup Dogg/Pearl White/GoldOH5SP		
❑ 103	Sup Dogg/Pearl White/GoldPR5	.75	1.50
❑ 104	Rogue Hog/Silver/WhitePR5	.75	1.50

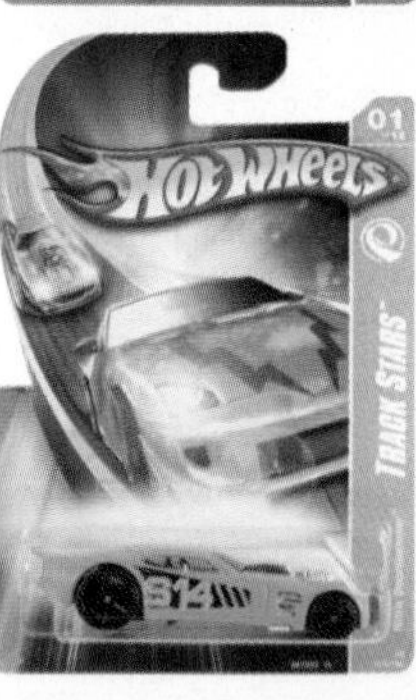

* Unpriced cars were not live at the time of print.

❑ 105	Motoblade/M Red/OH5SP	.75	1.50
❑ 106	CCM Country Club Muscle/Red/PR5	.75	1.50
❑ 107	Vulture		
❑ 108	Battle Spec		
❑ 109	Chrysler Firepower Concept		
❑ 110	Lancer Evolution 7		
❑ 111	Accelium		
❑ 112	Trak-Tune		

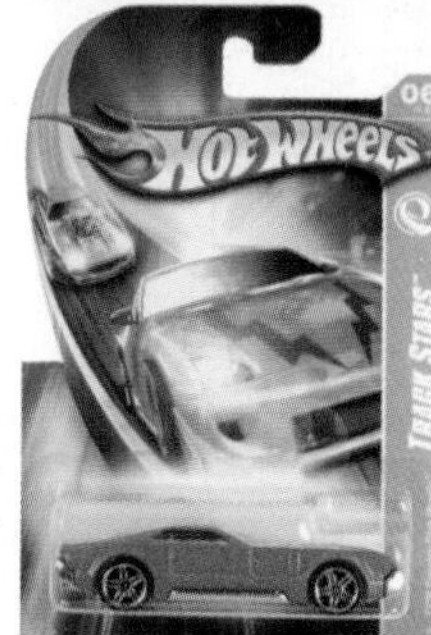

2008 Hot Wheels Team: Exotics

❑ 113	Lotus Esprit/Pearl Dark Yellow/PR5	.75	1.50
❑ 114	Enzo Ferrari/Dark Blue/PR5	1.00	2.00
❑ 115	Porsche Carrera GT/Black/PR5	.75	1.50
❑ 116	Zotic		

2008 Hot Wheels Team: Surf's Up

❑ 117 HUMMER H3T
❑ 118 '40s Woodie
❑ 119 Switchback
❑ 120 Surf Crate

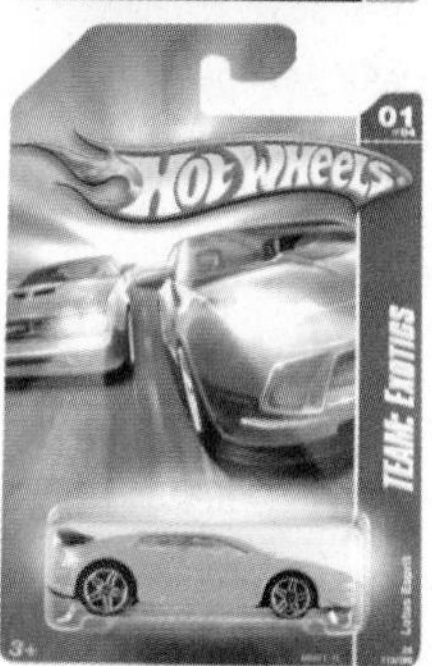

2008 Hot Wheels Team: Jet Rides

❑ 121 Jet Threat 4.0
❑ 122 Shadow Jet
❑ 123 Firestorm
❑ 124 Jet Threat 3.0

2008 Hot Wheels Team: Rat Rods

❑ 125 T-Bucket
❑ 126 Dieselboy
❑ 127 Rat-ified
❑ 128 Way 2 Fast

2008 Hot Wheels Team: Volkswagen

❑ 129	Volkswagen Beetle		
❑ 130	Volkswagen New Beetle Cup		
❑ 131	Baja Beetle		
❑ 132	Volkswagen Golf GTI/Pearl White/Y5	.75	1.50

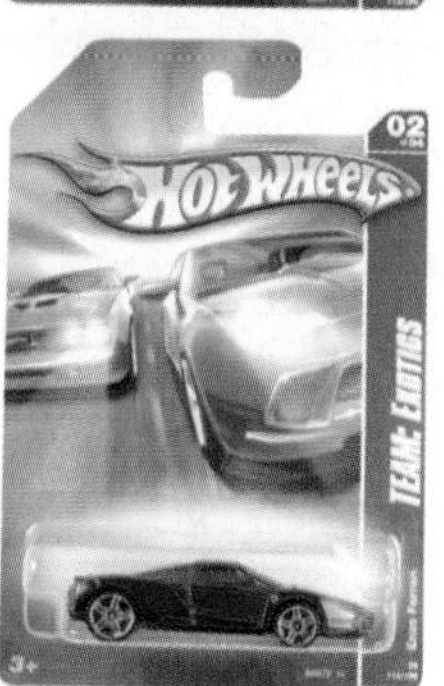

2008 Hot Wheels Team: Muscle Mania

❑ 133 '69 Pontiac GTO
❑ 134 '68 Plymouth Hemi 'Cuda
❑ 135 '69 Dodge Charger
❑ 136 '68 Nova

2008 Hot Wheels Team: Hot Trucks

❑ 137 Boom Box
❑ 138 Dodge Ram 1500
❑ 139 Nissan Titan
❑ 140 Custom '69 Chevy

2008 Hot Wheels Team: Ford Racing

❑ 141 Ford GTX1
❑ 142 Ford F-150
❑ 143 Mustang Cobra
❑ 144 Deuce Roadster

2008 Hot Wheels Team: Hot Wheels Racing

❑ 145 Chaparral 2D
❑ 146 Dodge Charger

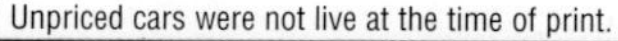
* Unpriced cars were not live at the time of print.

PRICE GUIDE

❑ 147	Double Vision		
❑ 148	Nissan Silvia S15		

2008 Hot Wheels Team: Custom Bikes

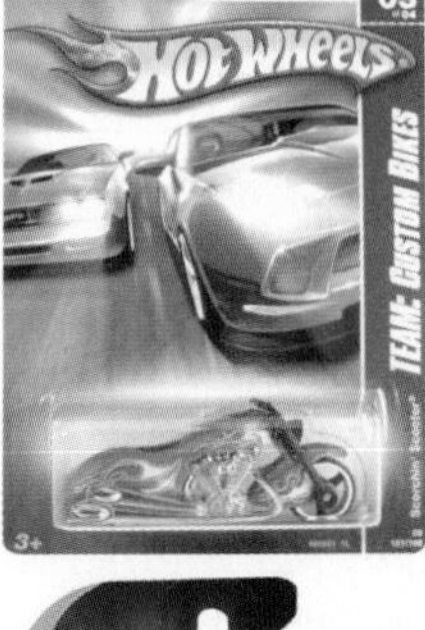

❑ 149	Pit Cruiser		
❑ 150	Airy 8/Purple/MC5	.75	1.50
❑ 151	Scorchin' Scooter/Blue/WhiteMC3	.75	1.50
❑ 152	Hammer Sled/Teal/MC3	.75	1.50

2008 Hot Wheels Team: Engine Revealers

❑ 153	Buick Grand National/Gold/OH5SP	.75	1.50
❑ 154	Shelby Cobra 427 SC/Dark Green/3SP	1.50	3.00
❑ 154	Shelby Cobra 427 SC/Dark Green/small3SP front, 3SP rear	12.50	25.00
❑ 155	'57 Chevy/Pearl White/Red5SP	.75	1.50
❑ 156	Sooo Fast/Purple/5SP	.75	1.50

2008 Hot Wheels Team: Drag Racing

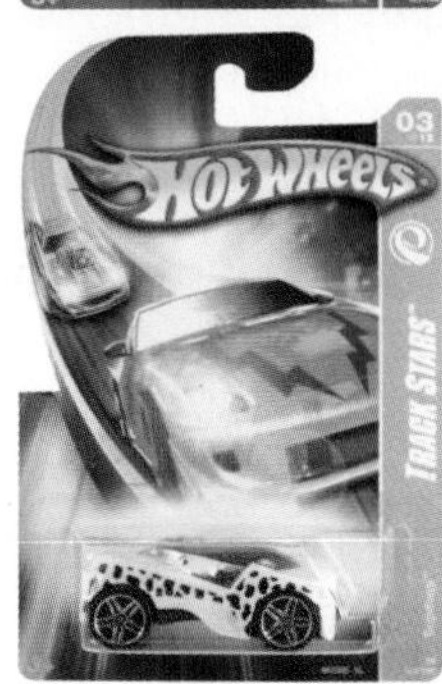

❑ 157	Mustang Funny Car/Black/5SP	2.00	4.00
❑ 158	Jaded/Flat Olive Green/5SP	.75	1.50
❑ 159	Dragster/Grey/5SP	.75	1.50
❑ 160	Fiat 500/Red/Gold5SP	.75	1.50

2008 Hot Wheels Treasure Hunts

❑ 161	Chrysler 300C HEMI/Black & Spectraflame Green/RR5SP	25.00	50.00
❑ 161	Chrysler 300C HEMI/Flat Black & M Green/OH5SP	12.50	25.00
❑ 162	'70 Plymouth Road Runner		
❑ 163	Rockster		
❑ 164	2005 Ford Mustang GT		
❑ 165	Hot Bird		
❑ 166	Qombee		
❑ 167	Dodge Challenger Funny Car		
❑ 168	'06 Dodge Viper		
❑ 169	16 Angels		
❑ 170	'64 Buick Riviera		
❑ 171	Drift King		
❑ 172	'69 Chevy Camaro		

2008 Hot Wheels Mystery

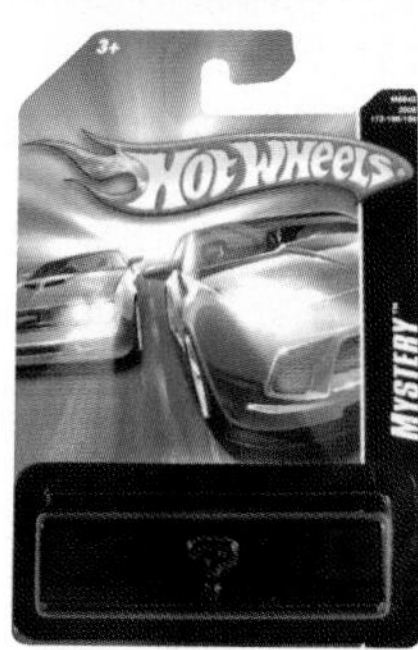

❑ 173	'69 Corvette/Black/GoldOH5SP	.75	1.50
❑ 174	Bon Voyage		
❑ 175	'66 Chevy Nova/M Burgandy/PR5	1.00	2.00
❑ 176	Cloak and Dagger/Clear Blue/PR5	.75	1.50
❑ 177	Jester		
❑ 178	Altered State		
❑ 179	Ballistik/Red/Y5	.75	1.50
❑ 180	'70 Mustang Mach 1		
❑ 181	Ford Shelby GR-1 Concept		
❑ 182	Hooligan/Flat Black/RL5SP	.75	1.50
❑ 183	Shoe Box		
❑ 184	Monoposto/Blue/PR5	.75	1.50
❑ 185	Lancia Stratos/Silver/White5SP	.75	1.50
❑ 186	Super Tsunami		
❑ 187	Lane Splitter		
❑ 188	GT-03/Grey/PR5	1.00	2.00
❑ 189	Callaway C-7	1.00	2.00
❑ 190	Scion XB		
❑ 191	Corvette C6R		
❑ 192	Saltflat Racer/Blue/MagentaPR5		
❑ 193	Ford Mustang GT Concept		
❑ 194	'57 T-Bird/Orange/5SP	.75	1.50
❑ 195	'58 Corvette/M Blue/5SP	1.00	2.00
❑ 196	Technetium		

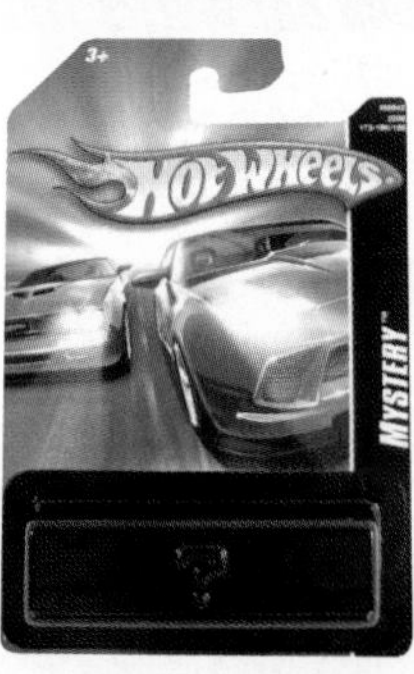

* Unpriced cars were not live at the time of print.

PRICE GUIDE

you're not just collecting cars,
you're collecting Dreams

DieCast X

it's our passion too.

$14.00 for one year (4 issues)

DieCast X magazine—the passion, products & personalities

EACH ISSUE IS PACKED WITH:

- Expert, detailed evaluations of the newest and most compelling models
- Latest industry news and insider info
- Stunning photography of scale models and their full-size counterparts
- Profiles of designers and legends in both full-scale and diecast
- The most popular motorsports products and personalities
- Star cars and celebrity collectors
- The hot trends in customizing and show cars
- The latest releases in all scales, categories and price ranges from manufacturers large and small

ER NOW AT

astxmagazine.com/specialoffer – enter code: A8BBCK

OR CALL TOLL FREE 866.298.5652

BECKETT'S TOP 10 ALL TIME HOT LIST

The following Hot Wheels cars are based on popularity and Mint in Package value except where noted.

1 **1969 Rear Loader Beach Bomb**
Spectraflame Pink (loose only)
PRICE RANGE: $70,000 to $75,000

2 **1968 Custom Camaro**
White Enamel (loose only)
PRICE RANGE: $3000 to $4000

3 **1971 Classic Cord**
Spectraflame Pink
PRICE RANGE: $2500 to $3000

4 **1971 Olds 442**
Spectraflame Purple
PRICE RANGE: $6000 to $10000

5 **1975 Super Van**
Chrome w/ 'Toy Fair 75' on sides (loose only)
PRICE RANGE: $4000 to $5000

6 **1974 Heavy Chevy**
Lt. Green
PRICE RANGE: $1000 to $1500

7 **1990 Funny Car**
Collector Card #271
PRICE RANGE: $2300 to $2500

8 **1976 Staff Car (Olds 442)**
Olive Green (In 6-pack)
PRICE RANGE: $600 to $800

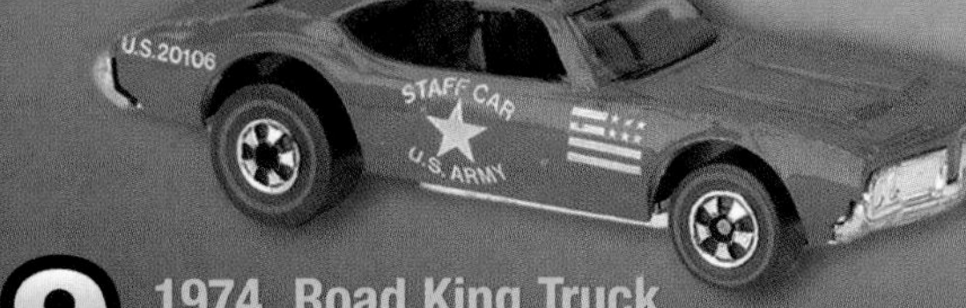

9 **1974 Road King Truck**
Yellow (loose only)
PRICE RANGE: $800 to $1000

10 **1995 '67 Camaro**
Treasure Hunt - Pearl White
PRICE RANGE: $400 to $450

ATTENTION READERS: **What are your top 10 favorites? Tell us about them. Send your responses to hotwheels@beckett.com**

*Top 10 selection is based on secon
values collected from dealers and c